# MCQs IN COMPUTER SCIENCE

AF518474

# MCQs IN COMPUTER SCIENCE

*By*

**Dr. B. L. SHIVAKUMAR**

*Professor*

*Sri Ramakrishna Engineering College*

*Coimbatore, Tamil Nadu*

UNIVERSITY SCIENCE PRESS

(An Imprint of Laxmi Publications Pvt. Ltd.)

An ISO 9001:2008 Company

BENGALURU • CHENNAI • COCHIN • GUWAHATI • HYDERABAD
JALANDHAR • KOLKATA • LUCKNOW • MUMBAI • RANCHI • NEW DELHI
BOSTON (USA) • ACCRA (GHANA) • NAIROBI (KENYA)

**MCQs IN COMPUTER SCIENCE**

© by Laxmi Publications (P) Ltd.
All rights reserved including those of translation into other languages. In accordance with the Copyright (Amendment) Act, 2012, no part of this publication may be reproduced, stored in a retrieval system, or transmitted in any form or by any means, electronic, mechanical, photocopying, recording or otherwise. Any such act or scanning, uploading, and or electronic sharing of any part of this book without the permission of the publisher constitutes unlawful piracy and theft of the copyright holder's intellectual property. If you would like to use material from the book (other than for review purposes), prior written permission must be obtained from the publishers.

Printed and bound in India
*Typeset at* Kalyani Computer Services, Delhi
First Edition : 2015
*ISBN* 978-93-83828-23-4

**Limits of Liability/Disclaimer of Warranty:** The publisher and the author make no representation or warranties with respect to the accuracy or completeness of the contents of this work and specifically disclaim all warranties. The advice, strategies, and activities contained herein may not be suitable for every situation. In performing activities adult supervision must be sought. Likewise, common sense and care are essential to the conduct of any and all activities, whether described in this book or otherwise. Neither the publisher nor the author shall be liable or assumes any responsibility for any injuries or damages arising herefrom. The fact that an organization or Website if referred to in this work as a citation and/or a potential source of further information does not mean that the author or the publisher endorses the information the organization or Website may provide or recommendations it may make. Further, readers must be aware that the Internet Websites listed in this work may have changed or disappeared between when this work was written and when it is read.

All trademarks, logos or any other mark such as Vibgyor, USP, Amanda, Golden Bells, Firewall Media, Mercury, Trinity, Laxmi appearing in this work are trademarks and intellectual property owned by or licensed to Laxmi Publications, its subsidiaries or affiliates. Notwithstanding this disclaimer, all other names and marks mentioned in this work are the trade names, trademarks or service marks of their respective owners.

**Branches**

| | | |
|---|---|---|
| Bengaluru | 080-26 75 69 30 | |
| Chennai | 044-24 34 47 26, | 24 35 95 07 |
| Cochin | 0484-237 70 04, | 405 13 03 |
| Guwahati | 0361-254 36 69, | 251 38 81 |
| Hyderabad | 040-27 55 53 83, | 27 55 53 93 |
| Jalandhar | 0181-222 12 72 | |
| Kolkata | 033-22 27 43 84 | |
| Lucknow | 0522-220 99 16 | |
| Mumbai | 022-24 91 54 15, | 24 92 78 69 |
| Ranchi | 0651-220 44 64 | |

PUBLISHED IN INDIA BY

UNIVERSITY SCIENCE PRESS
(An Imprint of Laxmi Publications Pvt.Ltd.)

An ISO 9001:2008 Company
113, GOLDEN HOUSE, DARYAGANJ,
NEW DELHI - 110002, INDIA
Telephone : 91-11-4353 2500, 4353 2501
Fax : 91-11-2325 2572, 4353 2528
www.laxmipublications.com info@laxmipublications.com

C— 10103/015/04
Printed at:
Printed at Repro Knowledgecast Limited, Thane

# PREFACE

In present days many Universities adopt objective type questions particularly multiple choice questions (MCQs) to test the skill of the student. Leading IT industries too conduct objective type test at the time of their requirement. To meet this scenario, this book has been compiled. It contains more than 1650 questions that are selected from twelve different subjects which are included in the curriculum of many universities.

Every effort has been made to make this book more interesting by giving practical examples. Algorithms of some subjects have been implemented with practical examples. Explanations are given at the end of each subject for some of the problems. This book will be highly useful for the students pursuing MCA, M.Sc. Computer Science, Information Technology and other undergraduate courses such as BE, B.Sc Computer Science, BCA etc.

This book is divided into twelve different chapters. The first chapter deals with Computer Organisation and architecture. An attempt has been made to explain most of the important topics on this subject. The second chapter deals with C programming. Different concepts have been explained with sample programs.

The third chapter contains question on Data Structures and Algorithm. Topics such as Stack, Queue, Linked List, Graph have been discussed with suitable problems. The fourth chapter is about Software Engineering. Every effort has been taken to cover important topics in software engineering. The fifth chapter has questions related to operating system, where most of the algorithms have been discussed with problems. The next chapter is about OOPS and C++. Sample programs are included to explain different concepts.

Questions from Computer Graphics and Multimedia are included in chapter seven followed by Microprocessor and ALP in chapter eight. In chapter nine questions related to Computer Network are included. Effort has been made to include questions both from OSI and TCP/IP model.

Data Mining, Data Warehouse and Digital Image Processing are the current research topics. Questions from these subjects have been included in chapters ten and eleven respectively. Chapter twelve contains questions related to J2EE.

Every effort has been made to make the book simple and error free.

**—Author**

# ACKNOWLEDGEMENTS

First of all, I would like to thank almighty God, for giving me energy and strength for writing this book.

I would like to thank Dr. S. Santhosh Baboo, Professor, Department of MCA, DG Vaishnav College, Chennai for his continuous support and encouragement.

I am indebted to my colleague Mr K.Velmurugan, for sparing time and helping me. I am also thankful to my other colleagues Mrs N. Sumathi and Mrs Maria Pericella for their valuable suggestions. I also thank Mr J. Prabhu, Software Engineer, PRICOL industries, Coimbatore for his valuable contribution.

I am indebted to my teachers from whom I have received a lot. I would like to thank Dr. S. Arockiasamy, Asst. Dean, Department of Information Systems, University of Oman and my friend Mr M. Murali Manohar, IBM, Australia, for their encouragement.

Special thanks to Prof. Rajib Mall, Indian Institute of Technology, Kharagpur who encouraged me to write a book.

I would like to thank my beloved parents for their support and blessing. I want to acknowledge the support and understanding of my wife Mrs Jayalaxmi Shivakumar. I am indebted to my children Ms S. Indhu Lekha and Ms S. Anisha for their patience and allowing me remain busy with the project for long, without disturbing me.

Finally, I would like to thank the entire team of Laxmi Publications for their support and motivation.

**—Author**

# CONTENTS

CHAPTER 1

# COMPUTER ORGANISATION AND ARCHITECTURE

1. Why is digital electronic better than analog systems?
   (*a*) Easier to design
   (*b*) Information storage is easy
   (*c*) Accuracy and precision are greater
   (*d*) All the above.
2. The process of converting a familiar number or symbol to some coded form is called
   (*a*) encoding
   (*b*) decoding
   (*c*) multiplexing
   (*d*) demultiplexing.
3. Which of the following computers is smallest?
   (*a*) Minicomputer
   (*b*) Microcomputer
   (*c*) Mainframe
   (*d*) Supercomputer.
4. Which of the following computers is fastest?
   (*a*) Minicomputer
   (*b*) Microcomputer
   (*c*) Mainframe
   (*d*) Supercomputer.
5. The devices commonly used for making digital circuits are
   (*a*) switches
   (*b*) semiconductors
   (*c*) vacuum tubes
   (*d*) amplifiers.
6. The radix of binary system is
   (*a*) 2
   (*b*) 4
   (*c*) 8
   (*d*) 16.
7. The fourth generation computer uses
   (*a*) vacuum tube
   (*b*) transistor
   (*c*) integrated circuit
   (*d*) VLSI.
8. The term terabyte refers to
   (*a*) 1024 bytes
   (*b*) 1024 kilobytes
   (*c*) 1024 megabytes
   (*d*) 1024 gigabytes.

9. The Central Processing Unit (CPU) consists of
   (*a*) input, output and processing
   (*b*) control unit, primary storage, and secondary storage
   (*c*) control unit, arithmetic-logic unit and primary storage
   (*d*) control unit, interface, and primary storage.

10. The output quality of a printer is measured by
   (*a*) dots per inch (*b*) dots per sq inch
   (*c*) dots printed per unit time (*d*) all the above.

11. How are the instruction executed in the latest generation computers?
   (*a*) Parallelly only (*b*) Sequentially only
   (*c*) Both sequentially and parallelly (*d*) All the above.

12. Who designed the first electronics computer — ENIAC?
   (*a*) Van-Neumann (*b*) Joseph M. Jacquard
   (*c*) J. Presper Eckert and John W Mauchly
   (*d*) Bill Gates.

13. Who invented the high level language C?
   (*a*) Dennis M. Ritchie (*b*) Niklaus Writh
   (*c*) Bill Gates (*d*) Charles Babbage.

14. The software or hardware error is called as a bug. What is the alternative computer jargon for it?
   (*a*) Leech (*b*) Squid
   (*c*) Slug (*d*) Glitch.

15. Personal computers use a number of chips mounted on a main circuit board. What is the common name for such a board?
   (*a*) Daughter board (*b*) Motherboard
   (*c*) Father board (*d*) Sister board.

16. What is meant by a dedicated computer?
   (*a*) Which is used by one person only
   (*b*) Which is assigned to one and only one task
   (*c*) Which uses one kind of software
   (*d*) which is meant for application software.

17. Which of the following is not found in a personal computer?
   (*a*) Microprocessor (*b*) Disk controller
   (*c*) Serial interface (*d*) Modem.

18. A software that converts an entire program into machine language is called a/an
   (*a*) interpreter (*b*) simulator
   (*c*) compiler (*d*) commander.

**19.** The ALU of a computer responds to the commands coming from

(*a*) primary memory (*b*) control section

(*c*) associative memory (*d*) cache memory.

**20.** All modern computers operate on

(*a*) information (*b*) floppies

(*c*) data (*d*) hard disk.

**21.** Instructions and memory address are represented by

(*a*) alphanumeric code (*b*) binary code

(*c*) binary word (*d*) parity bit.

**22.** The most important advantage of a video disk is

(*a*) compactness (*b*) potential capacity

(*c*) durability (*d*) cost effectiveness.

**23.** As compared to floppy disk, the hard disks are

(*a*) large storage (*b*) more portable

(*c*) low price (*d*) slowly accessed.

**24.** Floppy disks made from flexible plastic material are also called

(*a*) hard disks (*b*) high-density disks

(*c*) diskettes (*d*) templates.

**25.** Which of the following statements regarding VDU is most suitable?

(*a*) It is an output device (*b*) It is an input device

(*c*) It is a processor (*d*) It is storage device.

**26.** A kind of serial dot-matrix printer that forms characters with magnetically-charged ink sprayed dots is called

(*a*) laser printer (*b*) ink-jet printer

(*c*) dye Sublimation printer (*d*) chain printer.

**27.** Which of the following printers is very commonly used for desktop publishing?

(*a*) Laser printer (*b*) Inkjet printer

(*c*) LCD printer (*d*) Dot matrix printer.

**28.** Choose printer that is widely used in demanding graphic arts and photographic applications.

(*a*) Laser printer (*b*) Ink-jet printer

(*c*) Dye Sublimation printer (*d*) Chain printer.

**29.** The register which contains the address of the next instruction pair to be fetched from memory is

(*a*) accumulator (*b*) program counter

(*c*) MBR (*d*) stack pointer.

**30.** The register that is used to receive a word from memory or contains a word to be stored in memory is

(*a*) accumulator (*b*) program counter

(*c*) MBR (*d*) stack pointer.

**31.** Which of the following is an independent I/O module with its own processor and its own instruction set?

(*a*) DMA controller (*b*) Data channels

(*c*) USART (*d*) PIC.

**32.** What happens when data is entered into a memory location?

(*a*) It will add to the content of the location

(*b*) It will change the address of the memory location

(*c*) It will erase the previous content

(*d*) It will not be fruitful if there is already some data at the location.

**33.** Division by zero belongs to which of the following class of interrupt?

(*a*) Program (*b*) Timer

(*c*) I/O (*d*) H/w failure.

**34.** Which of the following control lines causes data on the bus to be written into the address location?

(*a*) Memory read (*b*) Memory write

(*c*) I/O write (*d*) I/O read.

**35.** Which of the following memory devices does not support direct access?

(*a*) Magnetic Disk (*b*) CD

(*c*) DVD (*d*) Magnetic Tape.

**36.** Which of the following is responsible for allocating time on the bus in a centralized scheme?

(*a*) Bus controller (*b*) DMA controller

(*c*) Interrupt controller (*d*) Disk controller.

**37.** The rate at which data can be transferred into or out of a memory unit is known as

(*a*) access time (*b*) latency time

(*c*) transfer time (*d*) memory cycle time.

**38.** Choose the technique in which the updates are made only in the cache memory.

(*a*) Write back (*b*) Write through

(*c*) Write forward (*d*) None of the above.

**39.** Choose the memory which are made with cells that store data as charge on capacitors.

(*a*) ROM (*b*) PROM

(*c*) SRAM (*d*) DRAM.

**40.** Which of the following memories is volatile in nature?

(*a*) ROM (*b*) EPROM

(*c*) RAM (*d*) Flash memory.

**41.** Which of the following memories, this storage cells are erased using ultraviolet radiation before a write operation is performed?

(*a*) PROM (*b*) EPROM

(*c*) RAM (*d*) Flash memory.

**42.** In a movable-head system, the time it takes to position the head at the track is known as

(*a*) access time (*b*) transfer time

(*c*) seek time (*d*) latency time.

**43.** Data are transferred to and from the disk in

(*a*) track (*b*) sector

(*c*) cylinder (*d*) none of the above.

**44.** The peripheral device could be classified into which of the following categories?

(*a*) Human readable (*b*) Machine readable

(*c*) Communication (*d*) All the above.

**45.** Which of the following will convert data from electrical to other form of energy during output and *vice-versa* during input?

(*a*) Modem (*b*) Transducer

(*c*) Compiler (*d*) Interpreter.

**46.** Which of the following techniques does not require processor during exchange of data directly between I/O module and memory?

(*a*) Programmed I/O (*b*) Interrupt I/O

(*c*) DMA (*d*) None of the above.

**47.** Which of the following I/O devices can transfer large amount of data in less time?

(*a*) Keyboard (*b*) Mouse

(*c*) Floppy disk (*d*) Printer.

***48.** What is the range of signed decimal value that can be represented in 16 bits?

(*a*) –1024 to +1023 (*b*) –2048 to +2047

(*c*) –32768 to +32767 (*d*) –65536 to +65535.

**49.** During floating-point operation, when a positive exponent exceeds the maximum possible exponent value is known as

(*a*) exponent overflow (*b*) exponent underflow

(*c*) significand overflow (*d*) significand underflow.

**50.** The instruction that provide computational capabilities for processing numeric data is categorized as

(*a*) data storage (*b*) data processing instruction
(*c*) data movement (*d*) control.

***51.** What will be the value of *a* if $16_{10} = 100_a$?
(*a*) 2 (*b*) 4
(*c*) 8 (*d*) 16.

**52.** The method in which the decimal integer is converted to binary integer number by successive division by 2 and the decimal fraction is converted to binary fraction by successive multiplication by 2 is known as
(*a*) sum-of-weights method (*b*) double-dabble method
(*c*) single-dabble method (*d*) none of the above.

## The Next Two Questions (53–54) are Based on the Data 10100110

***53.** What will be the output when 3 bits arithmetic right shift is performed?
(*a*) 10110100 (*b*) 10100110
(*c*) 11110100 (*d*) 10111101.

***54.** What will be the output when 3 bits arithmetic right rotate is performed?
(*a*) 10110100 (*b*) 10100110
(*c*) 11110100 (*d*) 11010100.

***55.** What is the octal equivalent of $(1001101.1011)_2$?
(*a*) $(115.64)_8$ (*b*) $(115.54)_8$
(*c*) $(115.74)_8$ (*d*) $(115.44)_8$.

**56.** Which of the following is a stack-oriented operation that performs operation on the top element of the stack and replace top element with the result?
(*a*) PUSH (*b*) POP
(*c*) Unary (*d*) Binary operation.

***57.** A digital thermometer uses BCD to drive its digital display. How many BCD bits are required to drive a 2-digit thermometer display?
(*a*) 4 bit (*b*) 8 bit
(*c*) 12 bit (*d*) 16 bit.

***58.** Suppose a temperature of 98 degree Fahrenheit is to be displayed in a three digit thermometer, what bit is to be sent?
(*a*) 1100010 (*b*) 1001 1000
(*c*) 0000 1001 1000 (*d*) 0000 0000 1001 1000.

**59.** What will be the reverse polish notation for the infix expression a+(b*c)?
(*a*) ab*c+ (*b*) abc+*
(*c*) abc*+ (*d*) ab+c*.

***60.** What would be the final value in Stack if the following expression is executed? (A – B) × (C × D), where A = 8, B = 6, C = 2 and D = 3

(a) 8 (b) 12

(c) 6 (d) 14.

*61. How many flip-flops are required to divide a frequency by sixty-four?

(a) 4 (b) 5

(c) 6 (d) 7.

62. A binary code in which the least significant bits for code words $2^n$ through $2^{n+1} - 1$ are mirror images of those for 0 through $2^n - 1$ is called

(a) sequential code (b) self-complementing code

(c) cyclic codes (d) reflective codes.

*63. 57.6 – 27.8 in Excess-3 code is

(a) 0101 1110.1011 (b) 1101 1110.1011

(c) 0111 1110.1011 (d) 0101 1110.1101.

64. The number system with radix 16 is known as

(a) binary (b) decimal

(c) octal (d) hexadecimal.

*65. What will be the equivalent hexadecimal code for $(10111101100)_2$ ?

(a) $5AC_{16}$ (b) $5BC_{16}$

(c) $5DC_{16}$ (d) $5EC_{16}$.

*66. The binary equivalent of the octal number 777

(a) 101101101 (b) 111111001

(c) 110110110 (d) 111111111.

*67. Decimal number 16 is represented in BCD as

(a) 1111 1111 (b) 0001 0110

(c) 1010 0110 (d) 0001 0111.

### The Next Two Questions (68–69) are Based on Following Information

### A CD Player has a Capability of Converting 10-bit Signals from a CD into their Equivalent Analog Signals

*68. What is the number of analog value in decimal?

(a) 512 (b) 1024

(c) 2048 (d) 4096.

*69. What are the largest and smallest octal values that can be used in the CD system?

(a) AFF (b) 2FF

(c) 3FF (d) BFF.

70. Which of the following is a universal gate?

(a) AND (b) XOR

(c) OR (d) NOR.

***71.** What is the next number in the hexadecimal counting sequence 88C, 88D, 88E, 88F?

(*a*) 89F (*b*) 890

(*c*) 980 (*d*) 900.

## The Next Three (72–74) Questions are Based on the Decimal Number –49

***72.** What is the equivalent 8-bit number if the above decimal number is represented in sign-magnitude?

(*a*) 00110001 (*b*) 10110001

(*c*) 11001001 (*d*) 01001001.

***73.** What will be the one's compliment of the decimal number?

(*a*) 01111110 (*b*) 11001111

(*c*) 00110001 (*d*) 11001110.

***74.** What will be the two's compliment of the decimal number?

(*a*) 01111110 (*b*) 11001111

(*c*) 00110001 (*d*) None of the above.

**75.** Which of the following remarks about BCD is not true?

(*a*) BCD is also called as the natural binary code

(*b*) BCD is 8421 weighted code

(*c*) BCD is less efficient than pure binary

(*d*) BCD is non-sequential.

**76.** If negative numbers are stored in 2's complement form, the range of numbers that can be stored in 10 bits is

(*a*) –512 to +512 (*b*) –512 to +511

(*b*) –511 to +512 (*d*) –511 to +511.

***77.** Which of the following 4-bit numbers equals its 2's complement numbers?

(*a*) 1011 (*b*) 1000

(*c*) 1101 (*d*) 1001.

***78.** The 1's complement of 1010 is

(*a*) 1011 (*b*) 1111

(*c*) 0110 (*d*) 0101.

**79.** Which of the following statements does not hold good for Excess-3 code?

(*a*) It is also represented as XS-3 (*b*) It is a sequential code

(*c*) It cannot be used for arithmetic operations

(*d*) It is a self complementing code.

***80.** The gray code of binary 1101

(*a*) 1101 (*b*) 1100

(*c*) 1011 (*d*) 1110.

***81.** The binary code of gray code 1101

(*a*) 1010 (*b*) 1111

(*c*) 0110 (*d*) 1001.

**82.** The minimum number of NAND gate required to implement the Boolean function $A + \bar{A}B + A\bar{B}C$ is

(*a*) one (*b*) two

(*c*) three (*d*) four.

**83.** In a cyclic code

(*a*) each successive code word do not differ from its preceding code word

(*b*) each successive code word differs in only one digit portion from its preceding code word

(*c*) each successive code word differs in only two digit portion from its preceding code word

(*d*) none of the above.

***84.** The seven bit even-parity Hamming code for the data bits 1011 is

(*a*) 1110101 (*b*) 0010100

(*c*) 1010101 (*d*) 0110011.

***85.** In an even-parity scheme, which of the following words contains an error?

(*a*) 10101010 (*b*) 11110110

(*c*) 10111001 (*c*) 11111010.

***86.** In an odd-parity scheme, which of the following words contains no error?

(*a*) 10101010 (*b*) 11101010

(*c*) 10101111 (*d*) 11111111.

**87.** Hamming code can

(*a*) only detect errors (*b*) only correct errors

(*c*) only detect and correct errors (*d*) none of the above.

**88.** Choose the correct statement

(*a*) Gray code is weighted code (*b*) Gray code suitable for arithmetic

(*c*) Gray code is BCD code (*d*) Gray code is cyclic code.

**89.** To transmit four data bits, the number of parity required in a 7-bit hamming code is

(*a*) 1 (*b*) 2

(*c*) 3 (*d*) 4.

***90.** In hamming code to transmit eleven data bits, the parity bits are located at positions

(*a*) 1, 2, 4, 6 (*b*) 1, 2, 8, 12

(*c*) 1, 2, 4, 8 (*d*) 1, 2, 3, 4.

**91.** The simplest technique for detecting errors is by adding an extra bit is known as

(*a*) gray code (*b*) parity code

(*c*) hamming code (*d*) CRC.

**92.** Which of the following is not a mapping procedure?

(*a*) Associative mapping (*b*) Direct mapping

(*c*) Set associative mapping (*d*) Indirect mapping.

**93.** ASCII is basically

(*a*) 5-bit code (*b*) 6-bit code

(*c*) 7-bit code (*d*) 8-bit code.

***94.** What will be the equivalent ASCII code for the message HAI?

(*a*) 1001000 1000001 1001001 (*b*) 1001000 1000001 10010101

(*c*) 1001001 1000001 1001001 (*d*) 1001000 1000010 1001001.

***95.** Suppose a message is encoded in ASCII code. The ASCII code is 1001100 1001111 1010110 1000101. What is the message?

(*a*) LIFE (*b*) LOVE

(*c*) LONG (*d*) GOOD.

**96.** EBCDIC code is

(*a*) 4-bit alphanumeric code (*b*) 6-bit alphanumeric code

(*c*) 8-bit alphanumeric code (*d*) 10-bit alphanumeric code.

**97.** Which of the following is De Morgan's Theorem?

(*a*) $(\bar{A} + \bar{B}) = (\overline{A \cdot B})$ (*b*) $(A + B) = (\overline{A \cdot B})$

(*c*) $A \cdot B = A + B$ (*d*) $(\overline{A + B}) = (\bar{A} \cdot A)$

**98.** Which of the following theorems is correct for the expression A + A = A?

(*a*) Idempotence laws (*b*) Associative Law

(*c*) Distributive law (*d*) Commutative law.

**99.** Which of the following gates produces a constant LOW output when they are in the inhibited condition?

(*a*) NAND & NOR (*b*) AND & OR

(*c*) AND & NOR (*d*) NAND & OR.

**100.** Which of the following are the basic types of gates?

(*a*) AND, OR, NOT (*b*) AND, OR, NOR

(*c*) AND, NAND, NOT (*d*) NAND, OR, X-NOR.

**101.** Which of the following gates can be used as inverter?

(*a*) NAND (*b*) NOT

(*c*) OR (*d*) AND.

**102.** Choose the gate which produces HIGH output only if all the input is HIGH

(*a*) NAND (*b*) NOT.

(*c*) AND (*d*) None of the above.

**103.** A logic gate which produces a 1, even if one of its inputs is a 1

(*a*) AND (*b*) NOT

(*c*) OR (*d*) None of the above.

**104.** Which of the following are Universal Gates?

(*a*) NAND & AND (*b*) NAND & NOR

(*c*) NOR & OR (*d*) AND & NOT.

**105.** Choose the correct answer

(*a*) The NAND operation is commutative and not associative

(*b*) The NAND operation is commutative and associative

(*c*) The NAND operation is not commutative and not associative

(*d*) The NAND operation is associative and not commutative.

**106.** Which of the following gates produces an output 1 when the inputs are different and an output 0 when the inputs are same?

(*a*) OR (*b*) NAND

(*c*) NOR (*d*) EX-OR.

**107.** Choose the correct answer

(*a*) The OR operation is commutative and associative

(*b*) The OR operation is commutative and not associative

(*c*) The OR operation is not commutative and not associative

(*d*) The OR operation is associative and not commutative.

**108.** Which of the following gates is preferably used to check the parity of a digital word?

(*a*) AND (*b*) EX-OR

(*c*) OR (*d*) NAND.

**109.** AND gate is also called as

(*a*) nothing gate (*b*) any gate

(*c*) inverter (*d*) none of the above.

**110.** Exclusive-NOR (X-NOR) gate is also called as

(*a*) inequality detector (*b*) equality detector

(*c*) coincidence gate (*d*) anti-coincidence gate.

**111.** Choose the correct answer

(*a*) An X-OR gate is a two-input, one-output logic circuit

(*b*) An X-OR gate is a one-input, one-output logic circuit

(*c*) An X-OR gate is a two-input, two-output logic circuit

(*d*) None of the above.

**112.** An X-NOR gate is combination of an

(*a*) X-OR gate and a NOT gate (*b*) X-OR gate and a OR gate

(*c*) X-OR gate and AND gate (*d*) None of the above.

**113.** Choose the correct answer

(*a*) Conjunction of a variable with logic 0 always yields a constant

(*b*) Conjunction of a variable with logic 1 always yields a constant

(*c*) Disjunction of a variable with logic 1 always yields a constant

(*d*) None of the above.

**114.** An $n$-variable K-map usually have

(*a*) $n^2$ cells or squares (*b*) $2^n$ cells or squares

(*c*) $2^{n+1}$ cells or squares (*d*) none of the above.

**115.** A K-map is used to

(*a*) minimise the number of flip-flops in a digital circuit

(*b*) maximise the number of flip-flops in a digital circuit

(*c*) to maximise the number of gates

(*d*) to minimize the number of gates and fan-in requirements of the gates in a digital circuit.

**116.** The logic expression $(A + B)(\bar{A} + \bar{B})$ can be implemented by giving the inputs A and B to a two-input

(*a*) NOR gate (*b*) AND gate

(*c*) X-OR gate (*d*) X-NOR gate.

**117.** Choose the incorrect statement

(*a*) Karnaugh map is also represented as K-map

(*b*) Karnaugh map is a chart or graph

(*c*) Karnaugh map is a systematic method of simplifying Boolean expression

(*d*) Karnaugh map are composed of an arrangement of non-adjacent cells.

**118.** A four-variable K-map can have

(*a*) 4 possible combinations of input variables

(*b*) 8 possible combinations of input variables

(*c*) 16 possible combinations of input variables

(*d*) 32 possible combinations of input variables.

**119.** In a canonical SOP form, each one of the product terms is called

(*a*) minterm (*b*) maxterm

(*c*) both minterm and maxterm (*d*) none of the above.

**120.** The two minterms or maxterms can be combined, only if they are

(*a*) adjacent to each other (*b*) diagonal to each other

(*c*) hypotenuse to each other (*d*) all the above.

**121.** Choose the correct answer

(*a*) A minterm is the logical sum for all literals in the row

(*b*) A minterm is the logical sum and product for all literals in the row

(*c*) A maxterm is the logical sum for all literals in the row
(*d*) A maxterm is the logical product for all literals in the row.

**122.** The Quine-McClusky method, also known as
(*a*) K-map (*b*) tabular method
(*c*) N-map (*d*) column method.

**123.** A latch can be constructed only using two cross-coupled
(*a*) NAND gates (*b*) AND gates
(*c*) NOT gates (*d*) OR gate.

**124.** A flip-flop has
(*a*) one stable states (*b*) two stable states
(*c*) three stable states (*d*) none of the above.

**125.** The invalid state of NAND latch occurs when
(*a*) S = 0, R = 0 (*b*) S = 1, R = 0
(*c*) S = 0, R =1 (*d*) S = 1, R = 1.

**126.** The invalid state of NOR latch occurs when
(*a*) S = 0, R = 0 (*b*) S = 1, R = 0
(*c*) S = 0, R = 1 (*d*) S = 1, R = 1.

**127.** A J-K flip-flop is in toggle condition when
(*a*) J = 0, K = 0 (*b*) J = 0, K = 1
(*c*) J = 1, K = 0 (*d*) J = 1, K = 1.

**128.** Which of the following flip-flops is not widely available as commercial item?
(*a*) J-K flip-flop (*b*) S-R flip-flop
(*c*) T flip-flop (*d*) D flip-flop.

**129.** Flip-flop that can operate in the 'no change', 'set', 'reset' and 'toggle' modes is
(*a*) S-R flip-flop (*b*) J-K flip-flop
(*c*) T flip-flop (*d*) flip-flop.

**130.** The most versatile and most widely used flip-flop is
(*a*) S-R flip-flop (*b*) J-K flip-flop
(*c*) T flip-flop (*d*) D flip-flop.

**131.** Flip-flops are used for
(*a*) data storage (*b*) counting
(*c*) frequency division (*d*) all the above.

**132.** Clocked latches are also called as
(*a*) asynchronous latches (*b*) synchronous latches
(*c*) both a and b (*d*) none of the above.

**133.** Edge triggering is also called
(*a*) static triggering (*b*) dynamic triggering
(*c*) constant triggering (*d*) none of the above.

**134.** Which of the following flip-flops can be used as a delay switch?

(*a*) J-K flip-flop (*b*) T flip-flop
(*c*) D flip-flop (*d*) None of the above.

**135.** D flip-flop can be used as

(*a*) latch (*b*) divider circuit
(*c*) differentiator (*d*) none of the above.

**136.** The maximum number of states that a counter with a six flip-flop can count are

(*a*) 6 (*b*) 8
(*c*) 64 (*d*) 256.

***137.** A binary ripple counter is required to count up to $16{,}383_{10}$. How many flip-flops are required?

(*a*) 8 (*b*) 10
(*c*) 14 (*d*) 18.

**138.** A three-bit counter requires how many flip-flops and has how many states?

(*a*) 3 flip-flops and 6 states (*b*) 3 flip-flops and 8 states
(*c*) 3 flip-flops and 9 states (*d*) 3 flip-flops and 12 states.

***139.** Suppose a five bit binary counter starts in the 00000 state. What will be the counter state after 205 pulses?

(*a*) $(01101)_2$ (*b*) $(01110)_2$
(*c*) $(01111)_2$ (*d*) $(11101)_2$.

**140.** A twisted ring counter consisting of four flip-flops will have low array states?

(*a*) 6 (*b*) 8
(*c*) 10 (*d*) 12.

**141.** In which of the following, the race condition occurs?

(*a*) Asynchronous circuit (*b*) Synchronous circuit
(*c*) Both a and b (*d*) None of the above.

***142.** A college with 2000 strength requires a counter at the entrance gate to count the number of students enter the college each day. Each time a student enters the main gate a signal pulse is generated using a photo detector and a light source. How many flip-flops are required to construct the counter?

(*a*) 8 (*b*) 9
(*c*) 10 (*d*) 11.

**143.** In a bidirectional shift register, data can be shifted

(*a*) only from left-to-right (*b*) only from right-to-left
(*c*) left-to-right or right-to-left (*d*) none of the above.

**144.** Data can be changed from temporal code to special code and *vice-versa* by using

(*a*) shift register (*b*) counters
(*c*) A/D converter (*d*) D/A converter.

**145.** A twisted ring counter is also called

(*a*) basic ring (*b*) a switch-tail ring count

(*c*) simple ring counter (*d*) none of the above.

**146.** Asynchronous counters are also known as

(*a*) ring counter (*b*) ripple counter

(*c*) decade counter (*d*) hybrid counter.

**147.** In which of the following codes each succeeding code word is one binary number greater than its preceding code word?

(*a*) Sequential code (*b*) Self-complementing code

(*c*) Code converter (*d*) Unit distance code.

## The Next Two Questions (148–149) are Based on the Following Information

**A Binary Counter is Being Pulsed by a 256 kHz Clock Signal. The Output Frequency from the Last Flip-flop is 2 kHz**

***148.** What is the MOD number?

(*a*) 64 (*b*) 128

(*c*) 256 (*d*) 512.

***149.** What is the counting range?

(*a*) 31 (*b*) 61

(*c*) 127 (*d*) 255.

**150.** A BCD counter has

(*a*) 5 distinct states (*b*) 10 distinct states

(*c*) 15 distinct states (*d*) 20 distinct states.

**151.** Which of the following gates can be used to implement A + B?

(*a*) NAND gates alone (*b*) AND gates alone

(*c*) NOR gates alone (*d*) None of the above.

**152.** Which of the following comments about full adder is not true?

(*a*) Full-adder can be constructed using two half-adder

(*b*) There are three inputs in a full adder

(*c*) A full-adder has one output

(*d*) A full-adder can be realized using universal gates.

**153.** Which of the following gates combination produces a constant HIGH output when they are in the inhibited condition?

(*a*) NAND & NOR (*b*) AND & OR

(*c*) AND & NOR (*d*) NAND & OR.

**154.** An 8-bit binary adder has
(*a*) 8 half adder (*b*) 8 full adder
(*c*) 4 half adder and 4 full adder (*d*) 1 half adder and 7 full adder.

**155.** An I/O channel designed to operate with only one I/O device at a time is called
(*a*) block multiplexer channel (*b*) selector channel
(*c*) multiplexer channel (*d*) none of the above.

**156.** A half-adder circuit can be realized by using
(*a*) one X-OR gate and one AND gate
(*b*) one AND gate and one NAND gate
(*c*) one OR gate and one AND gate
(*d*) one NOR gate and one NAND gate.

**157.** How many inputs and outputs does a full-subtractor have?
(*a*) Two inputs and one output (*b*) One input and two outputs
(*c*) Three inputs and two outputs (*d*) Two inputs and three outputs.

**158.** A half-subtractor can be realized by using
(*a*) a X-OR gate together with one each NOT gate and AND gate
(*b*) AOI gates
(*c*) only NAND gates
(*d*) all the above.

**159.** The number of directed arcs terminating on any state of a state diagram is
(*a*) $2^n$ where $n$ is the number of gates
(*b*) $2^n$ where $n$ is the number of flip-flops in the circuit
(*c*) independent of the number of inputs
(*d*) dependent on the number of inputs.

**160.** The ICs used in calculators are of
(*a*) TTl (*b*) ECL
(*c*) CMOS (*d*) MOS.

**161.** An ALU performs
(*a*) only logical operations (*b*) only arithmetic operations
(*c*) both a and b (*d*) control operations.

**162.** A decoder
(*a*) only identifies a particular code
(*b*) only detects a particular code
(*c*) only recognizes a particular code
(*d*) does all the above

**163.** Which of the following display devices gives off a characteristic reddish glow when lit?

(a) LCD (b) LED
(c) Gas-discharge tube (d) Vacuum fluorescent.

**164.** A demultiplexer has
(a) one input and many outputs (b) many inputs and one output
(c) many inputs and many outputs (d) none of the above.

**165.** A multiplexer has
(a) one input and many outputs (b) many inputs and one output
(c) many inputs and many outputs (d) none of the above.

**166.** Choose the device which will change parallel data to serial data.
(a) Decoder (b) Serial Adder
(c) Multiplexer (d) Demultiplexer.

**167.** A device which does the opposite function of a decoder is
(a) multiplexer (b) demultiplexer
(c) encoder (d) none of the above.

**168.** A multiplexer with a 4-bit data select input is a
(a) 1 : 8 multiplexer (b) 8 : 1 multiplexer
(c) 1 : 16 multiplexer (d) 16 : 1 multiplexer.

**169.** Choose the device which will change serial data to parallel data.
(a) Parallel Adder (b) Serial Adder
(c) Multiplexer (d) Demultiplexer.

**170.** Suppose all the LEDs in a seven segment display are turned ON, the number displayed will be
(a) 0 (b) 4
(c) 6 (d) 8.

**171.** Choose the addressing mode which do not uses displacement addressing.
(a) Register-indirect addressing (b) Relative addressing
(c) Base-register addressing (d) Indexing addressing.

**172.** Which of the following registers is not essential during instruction execution?
(a) Program counter (b) Instruction register
(c) Memory address register (d) Index register.

**173.** An address in a computer language that identifies a storage location or device without the use of any intermediate reference is known as
(a) absolute address (b) base address
(c) direct address (d) logical address.

**174.** A block of data associated with a cache tag and the unit of transfer between cache and memory is known as
(a) cache miss (b) cache line
(c) cache hit (d) hit ratio.

**175.** The portion of the instruction cycle during which the CPU performs a memory access to convert an indirect address into a direct address is

(*a*) fetch cycle (*b*) indirect cycle
(*c*) execute cycle (*d*) none of the above.

**176.** Which of the following will execute a sequence of I/O command from a main memory without the need for CPU?

(*a*) I/O controller (*b*) I/O processor
(*c*) I/O channel (*d*) None of the above.

**177.** A computer that has two or more processors having common access to a main storage is called

(*a*) multiprogramming (*b*) multiprocessor
(*c*) multiplexer (*d*) multitasking.

**178.** Which of the following memories is volatile memory?

(*a*) RAM (*b*) ROM
(*c*) PROM (*d*) None of the above.

**179.** Choose the memory whose contents are stable and do not require a constant power source.

(*a*) ROM (*b*) DRAM
(*c*) SRAM (*d*) RAM.

**180.** Which of the following memories is also called as read/write memory?

(*a*) ROM (*b*) RAM
(*c*) PROM (*d*) None of the above.

**181.** Choose the correct answer.

(*a*) The power consumption of DRAM is same as SRAM
(*b*) The power consumption of DRAM is two times more than SRAM
(*c*) The power consumption of DRAM is less than SRAM
(*d*) The power consumption of DRAM is ten times more than SRAM.

**182.** Dynamic RAM has to periodically recharged at a regular interval of

(*a*) 1 to 2 milliseconds (*b*) 3 to 8 milliseconds
(*c*) 9 to 12 milliseconds (*d*) 13 to 18 milliseconds.

**183.** The periodic recharge of the memory cells at regular interval is required in

(*a*) ROM (*b*) PROM
(*c*) Static RAM (*d*) Dynamic RAM.

**184.** In sequential access memory

(*a*) the access time is constant
(*b*) the access time is not constant
(*c*) the access time is the same for any address in memory
(*d*) none of the above.

**185.** Which one of the floppy disks is not manufactured?

(*a*) 8 inch (*b*) 6 inch
(*c*) 5.25 inch (*d*) 3.5 inch.

**186.** A PLA is a

(*a*) SSI device (*b*) MSI device
(*c*) LSI device (*d*) VLSI device.

**187.** The size of PLA is specified by

(*a*) number of inputs (*b*) number of outputs
(*c*) number of product terms (*d*) all the above.

**188.** A modem converts

(*a*) only digital signal to analog signal
(*b*) only analog signal to digital signal
(*c*) both a & b
(*d*) none of the above..

**189.** A processor design that includes multiple instructions pipelines, so that more than one instructions can be executing in the same pipeline stage simultaneously, is

(*a*) pipeline processor (*b*) super pipelined processor
(*c*) superscalar processing (*d*) uniprocessing.

**190.** Choose the system which performs overlapped computations to exploit temporal parallelism.

(*a*) Array processor (*b*) Pipeline computer
(*c*) Multiprocessor system (*d*) None of the above.

**191.** The major difficulty that cause the instruction pipeline to deviate from its normal operation is

(*a*) resource conflicts (*b*) data dependency
(*c*) branch difficulty (*d*) all the above.

## The Next Three Questions (192–194) are Based on the Following Information
## A Certain Memory has a Capacity of 16k x 16

***192.** How many data input and output lines does it have?

(*a*) 8 (*b*) 16
(*c*) 32 (*d*) 64.

***193.** How many address lines does it have?

(*a*) 12 (*b*) 13
(*c*) 14 (*d*) 16.

*194. What is its capacity in bytes?

(a) 16 kb (b) 32 kb

(c) 64 kb (d) 128 kb.

195. Choose the correct sequence of steps that takes place while executing an instruction in a digital computer.

(a) instruction fetch, instruction decoding, operand fetch, execution

(b) instruction fetch, operand fetch, instruction decoding, execution

(c) operand fetch, instruction fetch, instruction decoding, execution

(d) instruction decoding, instruction fetch, operand fetch, execution.

196. Choose the command which activates the peripheral and inform it what to do.

(a) I/O command (b) Control command

(c) Status (d) Output data command.

197. Assume that the pipeline has 4 segments and 6 tasks in sequence. The time it takes to process a sub operation in each segment is 20 ns. What will be the total time to complete all tasks?

(a) 120 ns (b) 80 ns

(c) 180 ns (d) 240 ns.

198. In which of the following addressing modes, the address field contains the effective address of the operand?

(a) Immediate mode (b) Implied mode

(c) Indirect mode (d) Direct mode.

199. Which of the following is not a data transfer technique?

(a) Programmed I/O (b) Interrupt I/O

(c) DMA (d) DMAC.

200. Establishing the priority of simultaneous interrupt by software means is known as

(a) vectored interrupt (b) non-vectored interrupt

(c) polling (d) chaining priority.

201. Choose the memory which stores bootstrap loader.

(a) ROM (b) DRAM

(c) SRAM (d) Cache.

202. Which one of the following is not a mapping procedure?

(a) Associative mapping (b) Direct mapping

(c) Direct-Associative mapping (d) Set-Associative mapping.

203. A multiprocessor system with a common shared memory is classified as

(a) loosely coupled multiprocessor (b) distributed-memory

(c) tightly coupled system (d) none of the above.

204. Choose the memory system that employs separate buses between each memory module and each CPU.

(*a*) Multiport Memory (*b*) Crossbar Switch
(*c*) Multistage Switching network (*d*) Hypercube System.

**205.** Which of the following memories could be used to increase the speed of processing by making current program and data available to the CPU at a rapid rate?
(*a*) Magnetic tape (*b*) Cache
(*c*) Magnetic drum (*d*) Hard disk.

**206.** When data is transmitted, the receiving unit responds with a control signal to acknowledge the receipt of the data is referred to as
(*a*) strobe method (*b*) handshaking
(*c*) synchronous (*d*) asynchronous.

**207.** Which of the following does not hold good for an input-output interface unit?
(*a*) Placed between memory and processor
(*b*) Placed between CPU and peripherals
(*c*) Converts serial data to parallel data
(*d*) The interface must have necessary logic to interpret the device address generated by the processor.

**208.** Choose the CPU organization which supports zero addressing.
(*a*) Accumulator based CPU (*b*) GRO based CPU
(*c*) Stack-oriented CPU (*d*) None of the above.

**209.** Choose the register which contains the address of a location in the memory to be fetched.
(*a*) Program Counter (*b*) Instruction Register
(*c*) MBR (*d*) MAR.

**210.** The advantages of using stack is
(*a*) short instruction format
(*b*) simplicity of algorithm to convert formulae
(*c*) complicated algorithms to optimize register usage are not needed
(*d*) all the above.

**211.** When the locations of the memory is accessed in any order and access time is independent of the location being accessed, the memory is termed as
(*a*) sequential access (*b*) random access
(*c*) direct access (*d*) associative.

**212.** The rate at which the information can be read from or written into the memory is known as
(*a*) access time (*b*) memory-cycle time
(*c*) transfer rate (*d*) seek time.

**213.** Which of the following is not a characteristic of memory?
(*a*) Capacity (*b*) Access time
(*c*) Cost (*d*) Availability.

**214.** What is the main drawback of CD-ROM over magnetic disk?

(*a*) Greater storage capacity

(*b*) Removable and portable

(*c*) Mass replication of data along with disk is not costly

(*d*) Access time is longer.

***215.** A CPU refers cache memory 20 times for a word of which 17 times it has found the word. What will be the hit ratio in the above case?

(*a*) 0.90 (*b*) 0.92

(*c*) 0.80 (*d*) 0.85.

**216.** The procedure employed to handling of branch instruction in RISC processor is

(*a*) branch prediction (*b*) loop buffer

(*c*) delayed branch (*d*) branch target buffer.

**217.** Which of the following is not a method to handle data dependency conflict in a pipeline computer?

(*a*) Hardware interlocks (*b*) Operand forwarding

(*c*) Delayed load (*d*) Software interlocks.

**218.** Which of the following Programmable Logic Device (PLD), the inputs of both arrays of AND and OR gates need programming?

(*a*) Programmable Array Logic (PAL)

(*b*) PROM

(*c*) Programmable Logic Array (PLA)

(*d*) Generic Array Logic (GAL).

***219.** Assume memory access time of a computer system is 200 ns and the clock rate is 500 MHz (i.e. clock cycle = 1/clock rate). What will be the miss penalty for this system?

(*a*) 100 cycles (*b*) 200 cycles

(*c*) 300 cycles (*d*) 400 cycles.

**220.** Which of the following is not a characteristic of RISC?

(*a*) Relatively few instruction types and addressing

(*b*) Fixed and easily decoded instruction

(*c*) Different types of instruction/data formats of variable length

(*d*) Use of complier to optimize object code performance.

**221.** Choose the CPU register that will hold the address of the top most element in a stack.

(*a*) Stack base (*b*) Stack Pointer

(*c*) Stack limit (*d*) Instruction pointer.

## ANSWERS

| | | | | | | | |
|---|---|---|---|---|---|---|---|
| **1.** (*d*) | **2.** (*a*) | **3.** (*b*) | **4.** (*d*) | **5.** (*b*) | **6.** (*a*) | **7.** (*d*) | **8.** (*d*) |
| **9.** (*c*) | **10.** (*b*) | **11.** (*c*) | **12.** (*c*) | **13.** (*a*) | **14.** (*d*) | **15.** (*b*) | **16.** (*b*) |
| **17.** (*d*) | **18.** (*c*) | **19.** (*b*) | **20.** (*c*) | **21.** (*b*) | **22.** (*b*) | **23.** (*a*) | **24.** (*c*) |
| **25.** (*a*) | **26.** (*b*) | **27.** (*a*) | **28.** (*c*) | **29.** (*b*) | **30.** (*c*) | **31.** (*b*) | **32.** (*c*) |
| **33.** (*a*) | **34.** (*b*) | **35.** (*d*) | **36.** (*a*) | **37.** (*c*) | **38.** (*a*) | **39.** (*d*) | **40.** (*c*) |
| **41.** (*b*) | **42.** (*c*) | **43.** (*b*) | **44.** (*d*) | **45.** (*b*) | **46.** (*c*) | **47.** (*c*) | **48.** (*c*) |
| **49.** (*a*) | **50.** (*b*) | **51.** (*b*) | **52.** (*b*) | **53.** (*c*) | **54.** (*d*) | **55.** (*b*) | **56.** (*c*) |
| **57.** (*b*) | **58.** (*c*) | **59.** (*c*) | **60.** (*b*) | **61.** (*c*) | **62.** (*d*) | **63.** (*a*) | **64.** (*d*) |
| **65.** (*d*) | **66.** (*d*) | **67.** (*b*) | **68.** (*b*) | **69.** (*c*) | **70.** (*d*) | **71.** (*b*) | **72.** (*b*) |
| **73.** (*d*) | **74.** (*b*) | **75.** (*d*) | **76.** (*b*) | **77.** (*b*) | **78.** (*d*) | **79.** (*c*) | **80.** (*c*) |
| **81.** (*d*) | **82.** (*c*) | **83.** (*b*) | **84.** (*d*) | **85.** (*c*) | **86.** (*b*) | **87.** (*c*) | **88.** (*d*) |
| **89.** (*c*) | **90.** (*c*) | **91.** (*b*) | **92.** (*d*) | **93.** (*c*) | **94.** (*a*) | **95.** (*b*) | **96.** (*c*) |
| **97.** (*a*) | **98.** (*a*) | **99.** (*c*) | **100.** (*c*) | **101.** (*b*) | **102.** (*c*) | **103.** (*c*) | **104.** (*b*) |
| **105.** (*a*) | **106.** (*d*) | **107.** (*b*) | **108.** (*b*) | **109.** (*a*) | **110.** (*c*) | **111.** (*a*) | **112.** (*a*) |
| **113.** (*a*) | **114.** (*b*) | **115.** (*d*) | **116.** (*c*) | **117.** (*d*) | **118.** (*c*) | **119.** (*a*) | **120.** (*a*) |
| **121.** (*c*) | **122.** (*b*) | **123.** (*a*) | **124.** (*b*) | **125.** (*a*) | **126.** (*d*) | **127.** (*d*) | **128.** (*c*) |
| **129.** (*b*) | **130.** (*b*) | **131.** (*d*) | **132.** (*b*) | **133.** (*b*) | **134.** (*c*) | **135.** (*a*) | **136.** (*b*) |
| **137.** (*c*) | **138.** (*b*) | **139.** (*a*) | **140.** (*b*) | **141.** (*a*) | **142.** (*d*) | **143.** (*c*) | **144.** (*a*) |
| **145.** (*b*) | **146.** (*b*) | **147.** (*a*) | **148.** (*b*) | **149.** (*c*) | **150.** (*b*) | **151.** (*c*) | **152.** (*c*) |
| **153.** (*d*) | **154.** (*d*) | **155.** (*b*) | **156.** (*a*) | **157.** (*c*) | **158.** (*d*) | **159.** (*c*) | **160.** (*c*) |
| **161.** (*c*) | **162.** (*d*) | **163.** (*b*) | **164.** (*a*) | **165.** (*b*) | **166.** (*c*) | **167.** (*c*) | **168.** (*d*) |
| **169.** (*d*) | **170.** (*d*) | **171.** (*a*) | **172.** (*d*) | **173.** (*a*) | **174.** (*b*) | **175.** (*b*) | **176.** (*c*) |
| **177.** (*b*) | **178.** (*a*) | **179.** (*a*) | **180.** (*b*) | **181.** (*c*) | **182.** (*b*) | **183.** (*d*) | **184.** (*b*) |
| **185.** (*b*) | **186.** (*c*) | **187.** (*d*) | **188.** (*c*) | **189.** (*c*) | **190.** (*b*) | **191.** (*d*) | **192.** (*b*) |
| **193.** (*c*) | **194.** (*b*) | **195.** (*a*) | **196.** (*b*) | **197.** (*c*) | **198.** (*d*) | **199.** (*d*) | **200.** (*c*) |
| **201.** (*a*) | **202.** (*c*) | **203.** (*c*) | **204.** (*a*) | **205.** (*b*) | **206.** (*b*) | **207.** (*a*) | **208.** (*c*) |
| **209.** (*d*) | **210.** (*d*) | **211.** (*b*) | **212.** (*a*) | **213.** (*d*) | **214.** (*d*) | **215.** (*d*) | **216.** (*c*) |
| **217.** (*d*) | **218.** (*c*) | **219.** (*a*) | **220.** (*c*) | **221.** (*b*) | | | |

## EXPLANATIONS

**48.** The complete range of values that can be represented in the 2's complement system having $N$ magnitude bits is $-2^N$ to $+(2^N - 1)$. Therefore, $-2^{16} = -32768$ and $(2^{16} - 1) = 32767$

**51.** Given $16_{10} = 100_{(a)}$ By converting $100_a$ to decimal we get $1 \times a^2 + 0 \times a^1 + 0 \times a^0 = a^2$, i.e. $a = 4$

**53.** The given data is 10100110. After one bit arithmetic right shift the data = 11010011. After two bit arithmetic right shift the data = 11101001. After third bit arithmetic right shift the data = 11110100

**54.** The given data is 10100110. After one bit arithmetic right rotate the data = 01010011. After two bit arithmetic right rotate the data = 10101001. After third bit arithmetic right rotate the data = 11010100

**55.** The octal equivalent of 001,001,101.101,100 = $115.54_8$

**57.** Since each BCD bit requires a 4-bit code, a 4-digit thermometer display requires 4 × 2 = 8 bits.

**58.** Since it is a 3-digit thermometer it will have 3 × 4 = 12 bits. Therefore, to display temperature 98 Fahrenheit degree, we need to convert each digit to its 4-bit BCD code. Thus

| 0 | 9 | 8 |
|---|---|---|
| ↓ | ↓ | ↓ |
| 0000 | 1001 | 1000 |

**60.** The given expression (A – B) * (C*D) has to be converted into post fix form before executing in Stack. The post fix of the given expression = AB – CD**. Therefore, 8 – 6 = 2, 2*3 = 6, 2*6 = 12

**61.** A frequency division of $2^N$ can be achieved by using $N$ number of flip-flops.

Therefore $2^N = 64$ i.e $N = 6$

**63.**

| | | |
|---|---|---|
| | 1000 1010 .1001 | (57.6 in XS-3) |
| | –0101 1010 .1011 | (27.8 in XS-3) |
| | 0010 1111 . 1110 | (Correct 0010 by adding 0011 and correct 1111 and |
| i.e. | 0010 + 0011 = 0101, | 1110 by subtracting 0011) |
| | 1111 – 0011 = 1110 | |
| and | 1110 – 0011 = 1011 | |

**65.** The hexadecimal code for 0101, 1110, 1100 = $5EC_{16}$

**66.** The binary equivalent of the octal number 777 = 111111111

**67.** Decimal number 16 is represented in BCD as 1 = 0001 and 6 = 0110 i.e 0001 0110

**68.** The number of analog values in decimal = $2^{10}$ = 1024

**69.** The largest decimal value = $2^{10} - 1$ = 1023. The hexadecimal equivalent of 1023 is 3FF.

**71.** When 1 is added to the hexadecimal number 88F it becomes 890.

**72.** The 8-bit binary number for +49 = 00110001. In the sign magnitude system, –49 is produced by changing the sign-bit (MSB) to a 1 and leaving the other bits unchanged)

| | |
|---|---|
| | 0 0 1 1 0 0 0 1 |
| Sign bit | ↓ |
| | 1 0 0 0 0 0 0 1 |

**73.** The binary equivalent of 49 is 00110001. In one's complement 0 is changed as 1 and *vice-versa*.

| Therefore, | 0 | 0 | 1 | 1 | 0 | 0 | 0 | 1 |
|---|---|---|---|---|---|---|---|---|
| | ↓ | ↓ | ↓ | ↓ | ↓ | ↓ | ↓ | ↓ |
| | 1 | 1 | 0 | 0 | 1 | 1 | 1 | 0 |

**74.** By adding 1 to the one compliment of 49, we get two's complement of the number, i.e. 11001110 + 1 = 11001111

**77.** 2's Complement of 1011 is 0100 + 1 = 0101

2's Complement of 1000 is 0111 + 1 = 1000

2's Complement of 1101 is 0010 + 1 = 0011

2's Complement of 1001 is 0110 + 1 = 0111

Therefore, 2's Complement of 1000 = 1000

**78.** In one's complement system, 1 is converted to 0 and 0 is converted to 1. Therefore 1's complement of 1010 is 0101

**80.**

| Binary | 1 | $-\oplus\rightarrow$ | 1 | $-\oplus\rightarrow$ | 0 | $-\oplus\rightarrow$ | 1 |
|---|---|---|---|---|---|---|---|
| | \|\| | | \|\| | | \|\| | | \|\| |
| Gray | 1 | | 0 | | 1 | | 1 |

**81.**

| Gray 1 | 1 | | 1 | | 0 | | 1 |
|---|---|---|---|---|---|---|---|
| | \|\| | $\otimes\nearrow$ | \|\| | $\otimes\nearrow$ | \|\| | $\otimes\nearrow$ | \|\| |
| Binary | 1 | | 0 | | 0 | | 1 |

**84.** The bit pattern is $P_1$, $P_2$, $D_3$, $P_4$, $D_5$, $D_6$, $D_7$

Bits 1, 3, 5, 7 (i.e $P_1$ 1 0 1) must have even parity. So, $P_1$ must be a 0.

Bits 2, 3, 6, 7 (i.e $P_2$ 1 1 1) must have even parity. So, $P_2$ must be a 1.

Bits 4, 5, 6, 7 (i.e $P_4$ 0 1 1) must have even parity. So, $P_4$ must be a 0.

Therefore, the final code is 0110011.

**85.** (*a*) The number of 1s in the word 10101010 is even (4), so there is no error.

(*b*) The number of 1s in the word 11110110 is even (6), so there is no error.

(*c*) The number of 1s in the word 10111001 is odd (5), so there is error.

(*d*) The number of 1s in the word 11111010 is even (6), so there is no error.

**86.** (*a*) The number of 1s in the word 10101010 is even (4), so there is error.

(*b*) The number of 1s in the word 11101010 is odd (5), so there is no error

(*c*) The number of 1s in the word 10101111 is even (6), so there is error.

(*d*) The number of 1s in the word 11111111 is even (8), so there is error.

**90.** To transmit eleven data bits, four parity bits located at positions $2^0$, $2^1$, $2^2$, $2^3$, i.e. in 15 bit code the parity bits are placed at 1, 2, 4, 8 positions.

**94.** The equivalent decimal number for the letter "H" = 72, "A" = 65 and "I" = 73. The binary equivalent of 72 = 1001000, 65 = 1000001 and 73 = 1001001

**95.** The decimal equivalent of 1001100 = 76, 1001111 = 79, 1010110 = 86 and 1000101 = 69. The equivalent ASCII character for 76 is L, 79 is O, 86 is V and 69 is E.

**137.** The number of flip-flops '$n$' is to be selected such that the number of states N ≤ $2^n$. With '$n$' flip-flops, the largest count possible is $2^n - 1$. Therefore, $2^n - 1$ = 16,383, $n = \log_2 16384 = 14$.

**139.** The five bit counter will reset after every 32 pulses. The counter will reset at 32, 64, 96, 128, 160 and after resetting at 192[nd] pulse the count until 205[th] pulse will be in binary equivalent to 205 – 192 = 13, i.e = $01101_2$

**142.** To construct a counter which counts up to 2000, we need a counter that goes through at least 2000 states, i.e. $2^N \geq 2000$. Therefore, we need 11 flip-flops.

**148.** MOD number = frequency of the Input clock signal/Output frequency. Therefore, MOD number = $256 \times 10^3/2 \times 10^3 = 128$

**149.** The MOD number = 128 = $2^N$ (where $N$ is the number of flip-flops). Therefore, the maximum count = $2^N - 1 = 127$

**192.** Since the word size is 16 bits, data input and data output will be 16 lines each.

**193.** The memory stores 16K = 16 × 1024 = 16384 words. Therefore, there are 16384 memory addresses.

Since 16384 = $2^{14}$, it requires 14 address lines.

**194.** Since a byte is 8 bit, the memory has a capacity of 32 kb.

**215.** CPU refers cache memory 20 times for a word and 17 times it has found the word. Therefore, the bit ratio will be 17/20 = 0.85.

**219.** Miss penalty = memory access time/clock cycle. The clock cycle = $1(500*10^6)$ sec = 2 ns.

Therefore, miss penalty = 200 ns/2 ns = 100 cycles.

CHAPTER 2

# C PROGRAMMING

**1.** C program was developed by

(*a*) Pascal (*b*) Dennis Ritchie

(*c*) Charles Babbage (*d*) Bill Gates.

**2.** C language was developed in the year

(*a*) 1972 (*b*) 1973

(*c*) 1974 (*d*) 1975.

***3.** What will be the output of the following code?

```
void main()
{
printf("%d",3==4?7:8);
}
```

(*a*) 3 (*b*) 4

(*c*) 7 (*d*) 8.

***4.** Choose the valid identifier.

(*a*) far (*b*) near

(*c*) close (*d*) entry.

**5.** Which of the following statements will exactly reproduce the line "I Love C!"

(*a*) `printf("\"I Love C\!\"\n");`

(*b*) `printf("I Love C\n");`

(*c*) `printf(" I Love 'C'!\n");`

(*d*) `printf("I Love C!");`

**6.** C language was developed at

(*a*) IBM, USA (*b*) AT & T Bell Labs, USA

(*c*) borland International, USA (*d*) infosys, India.

**7.** C language is

(*a*) High-level language (*b*) Low-level language

(*c*) Assembly language (*d*) Middle level language.

**8.** Suppose a particular computer uses a *n*-bit word. What will be the range for unsigned integer quantity?

(*a*) $-2^{n-1}$ to $+2^{n-1}-1$ (*b*) 0 to $2^{n-1}$

(*c*) –128 to 127 (*d*) $-2^{n-1}$ to $+2^{n-1}$.

***9.** Choose the invalid floating-point constant.

(*a*) 1. (*b*) 3E-8

(*c*) 2.66E+8 (*d*) 2,000.0.

***10.** Choose the incorrect hexadecimal integer constant.

(*a*) 0xABCD (*b*) 0Xabcd

(*c*) 0X777 (*d*) 0xEFG.

***11.** Which of the following octal escape sequences represents the character constant 'C'?

(*a*) '\101' (*b*) '\102'

(*c*) '\103' (*d*) none of the above.

***12.** What will be the value of *a* and *b* if the following code is executed?

```
main()
{
int  a, b, c=5,  d=10;
a=c*++d;
b=c*d++;
}
```

(*a*) a = 50 b = 50 (*b*) a = 50 b = 55

(*c*) a = 55 b = 55 (*d*) a = 55 b = 50.

**13.** Choose the best answer

(*a*) C is the first high level language

(*b*) C is a object oriented language

(*c*) C is structured language

(*d*) C language are not efficient and fast.

**14.** The enumerated data type is a

(*a*) primary (*b*) user defined

(*c*) derived (*d*) empty data set.

**15.** The default extension of C program files is

(*a*) '.exe' (*b*) '.doc'

(*c*) '.c' (*d*) '.d'.

***16.** What will be the value of x when the statement *int x = 2 * 3 + 5 * 5;* is executed?

(*a*) 30 (*b*) 31

(*c*) 80 (*d*) 81.

***17.** What will be the output of the following program?

```
main()
{
int  x, y;
x  =  25;  y  =  50;
printf("%d  ",x,y);
}
```

(*a*) 25 (*b*) 50

(*c*) 25 50 (*d*) none of these.

**18.** The C language is closely associated with

(*a*) MS-Windows (*b*) Unix

(*c*) Linux (*d*) MS-DOS.

**19.** A software which reads the source program one line at a time and converts it to object program is called

(*a*) compiler (*b*) interpreter

(*c*) assembler (*d*) none of the above.

***20.** What will be the output of the following program?

```
main()
{
printf("\n100!=100  :  %5d",100!=100);
printf("\n100<=1000  :  %5d",100<=1000);
}
```

(*a*) 0 0 (*b*) 0 1

(*c*) 1 0 (*d*) 1 1.

**21.** What will be the output of the following statement?

```
int  z,x=5,y=-10,a=4,b=2;
z=x++ - --y*b/a;
```

(*a*) 4 (*b*) 6

(*c*) 8 (*d*) 10.

**22.** The smallest individual units of a C program are called

(*a*) identifiers (*b*) constants

(*c*) tokens (*d*) keywords.

**23.** Which of the following is right associative operator in C?

(*a*) , (*b*) =

(*c*) [ ] (*d*) >.

**24.** C does not have an operator for

(*a*) addition (*b*) modulus operation
(*c*) assignment (*d*) exponentiation.

***25.** Consider the expression `((int) (a) % 3)`, where *a* is a floating-point variable whose value is 10.5. What will result if this expression is executed?

(*a*) 1.5 (*b*) 1
(*c*) 2 (*d*) invalid expression.

***26.** What will be the output of the following code?

```
int i=4;
int x=6;
double z;
z=x/i;
printf("z=%.2f\n",z);
```

(*a*) 1.50 (*b*) 1.00
(*c*) 0.00 (*d*) 2.00.

**27.** The *int* data type is a

(*a*) primary data type (*b*) user defined data type
(*c*) derived data type (*d*) empty data set.

**28.** The function used for reading a single character from the keyboard is

(*a*) `putchar()` (*b*) `getchar()`
(*c*) `gets()` (*d*) `scanf()`.

***29.** What will be the output of the following program?

```
main()
{
printf("\n8>6 ||8<3:  %5d",8>6||8<3);
printf("\n10>6 &&  10<9:  %5d",10>6 && 10<9);
}
```

(*a*) 0 0 (*b*) 0 1
(*c*) 1 0 (*d*) 1 1.

**30.** The format conversion specification used for a floating point number is

(*a*) %d (*b*) %f
(*c*) %c (*d*) %s.

**31.** Choose the non unary arithmetic operator.

(*a*) % (*b*) ++
(*c*) & (*d*) sizeof.

**32.** The symbol used to terminate every C statement is

(*a*) : (colon) (*b*) ; (semicolon)

(*c*) . (full stop) (*d*) */.

***33.** What will be the output of the following statement?

```
int x = 0;
for(x=1; x<=4; x++);
printf("x=%d\n",x);
```

(*a*) 2 (*b*) 3

(*c*) 4 (*d*) 5.

**34.** "?:" is known as

(*a*) Conditional operator (*b*) Assignment operator

(*c*) Arithmetic operator (*d*) Relational operator.

**35.** Which of the following is a bitwise operator?

(*a*) > (*b*) @

(*c*) >> (*d*) %.

**36.** What will be the output *(a* and *b)* of the following program?

```
void main()
{
int a=7,b=9;
a=a+b;
b=a-b;
a=a-b;
printf("%d%d",a,b);
}
```

(*a*) a = 12 b = 2 (*b*) a = 2 b = 2

(*c*) a = 5 b = 7 (*d*) a = 7 b = 5.

**37.** Which of the following preprocessor directives replace tokens in the current file with specified replacement tokens?

(*a*) Macro definition directives (*b*) File inclusion directives

(*c*) Message generation directives (*d*) Pragma directives.

***38.** What will be the output of the following statement?

```
main()
{
unsigned i=0xabcd;
printf ("~i=%x", ~i);
}
```

(*a*) DCBA (*b*) ABCD

(*c*) 2345 (*d*) 5432.

## The Next Five Questions (39–43) are Based on the Following Information

**Suppose *x* and *y* are unsigned integer variables of values 0xabcd and 0xdcba.**

***39.** What will be the result (in hexadecimal) if the bitwise operation `(x & y)` is executed?

(*a*) ABCD (*b*) 8888
(*c*) DCBA (*d*) 7777.

***40.** What will be the result (in hexadecimal) if the bitwise operation `(x ^ y)` is executed?

(*a*) ABCD (*b*) 8888
(*c*) DCBA (*d*) 7777.

***41.** What will be the result (in hexadecimal) if the bitwise operation `(x | y)` is executed?

(*a*) ABCD (*b*) ABAB
(*c*) DDDD (*d*) FFFF.

***42.** What will be the value of *z* (in hexadecimal), `if z = x << 5?`

(*a*) F340 (*b*) F240
(*c*) F140 (*d*) F040.

***43.** What will be the value of *z* (in hexadecimal), `if z = x >> 4?`

(*a*) CBA (*b*) ABC8
(*c*) ABC (*d*) ABB7.

**44.** Any violation of rules of C language results in

(*a*) syntax error (*b*) run-time error
(c) logical error (*d*) latent error.

**45.** Which of the following operators is used for manipulating data at bit level?

(*a*) Relational (*b*) Bitwise
(c) Arithmetic (*d*) Increment.

**46.** What is the purpose of using conversion group %1s in *scanf* function?

(*a*) To skip over whitespace character and read the next statement non whitespace character.
(*b*) Indicate the length of the corresponding arguments.
(*c*) Specify the field width.
(*d*) To indicate the data item is short integer.

**47.** What will be the output of the following program if the value of '*a*' is entered as 8?

```
main()
{
```

```
int  a,b;
scanf("%d", &(a);
a>>=2;
b=a;
printf("%d",b);
}
```

(*a*) 0 (*b*) 1

(*c*) 2 (*d*) 3.

***48.** Which of the following statements is incorrect with respect to flag?

(*a*) Flag must appear immediately after the % (per cent sign)

(*b*) Two or more flags can occur consecutively

(*c*) Flag '–' right justifies the data item

(*d*) Flag '0' causes leading zero to appear instead of leading blanks.

**49.** The process of executing one instruction at a time by pressing a function key is called

(*a*) break points (*b*) tracing

(*c*) watch value (*d*) stepping.

***50.** What will be the value of' '*x*' when the following code is executed?

```
int  x  =  3;
if(x  ==  2);
x  =  0;
if(x  ==  3)
x++;
else  x  +=  2;
```

(*a*) 1 (*b*) 2

(*c*) 3 (*d*) 4.

**51.** A statement `include<stdio.h>` without the # sign in a program will result in

(*a*) overflow error (*b*) syntactic error

(*c*) execution error (*d*) underflow error.

**52.** What will be the output of the following statements?

```
int  x,y;
scanf("%d",  &x);
y=(x  >  7  ?  5:  4);
```

(*a*) The statement will store 5 in *y* if *x* is greater than 7, otherwise it will store 4 in *y*

(*b*) The statement will store 4 in *y* if *x* is greater than 7, otherwise it will store 5 in *y*

(c) The statement will store 5 in $y$ if $x$ is less than 4, otherwise it will store 7 in $y$

(d) None of the above.

**53.** What will be the value of 'a' if the following code is executed?

```
main()
{
int a =6;
(a++ - a++);
printf("%d",a);
}
```

(a) 5 (b) 6

(c) 7 (d) 8.

**54.** A string constant is enclosed within

(a) double quotes (b) single quotes

(c) parenthesis (d) none of the above.

***55.** Consider the following code

```
int i,j;
int x = 0;
int a[2][3];
for(i=0; i<3; i++)
for(j=0; j<2; j++)
{
a[j][i] = x;
++x;
}
```

What is the value of `a[1][1]` in the code given above?

(a) 1 (b) 2

(c) 3 (d) 4.

**56.** Choose the incorrect among the following.

(a) A variable in C can start with underscore symbol

(b) A variable name in C should not start with a digit

(c) A variable should not be a C keyword

(d) A variable in C can start with a character.

**57.** Choose the incorrect statement among the following.

(a) *String* in C is represented internally by the ASCII character

(b) There is no operator in C which manipulates entire *string* at once (*c*) *Strings* are terminated by the null character

(*d*) A character string is stored in an array of string type.

**58.** What will be the output of the following program?

```
main()
{
int i = 1;
while(i <= 32767)
{
printf("%d\n", i);
i = i+ 1;
}
}
```

(*a*) 1 to 32767 (*b*) 1 to 32777

(*c*) 1 to 32768 (*d*) indefinite loop.

**59.** Which of the following string functions appends a maximum of *n* characters from the string source to the end of the string destination?

(*a*) `strncmp(a,b,n)` (*b*) `strncpy(dest,source,n)`

(*c*) `strncat(dest,source, n)` (*d*) `strcat(dest,source)`.

**60.** What will be the output of the following?

```
void main()
{
if (-1)
printf("\nhai");
}
```

(*a*) Error (*b*) 1

(*c*) –1 (*d*) hai.

***61.** If text is '*London*' what will be the output of the following statement?

```
printf("%.3s\n",text);
```

(*a*) London (*b*) Londo

(*c*) Lond (*d*) Lon.

**62.** The string always ends with

(*a*) '\' (*b*) '0\'

(*c*) '\0' (*d*) ;.

**63.** If s1 is '*kumar*' and s2 is '*shiva*', what will be the output for the following statement?

```
strcpy(s2, s1);
printf ("%s", s2);
```

(*a*) shiva (*b*) kumar

(*c*) shivakumar (*d*) none of the above.

*64. How many bytes of memory will be reserved for the statement int a[5]

(a) 4 byte (b) 6 bytes

(c) 8 bytes (d) 10 bytes.

65. What will be the output of the following program?

```
void main()
{
char b[20];
sprintf(b,"%s","hello world");
printf("%.5s",b);
}
```

(a) hello world (b) hello

(c) world (d) error.

66. The function used to join two strings is

(a) strcat() (b) strcmp()

(c) strcpy() (d) strcoll().

67. What will be the output of the following statement?

```
void main()
{
clrscr();
printf("%s",strupr("hello world"));
}
```

(a) hello world (b) Hello World

(c) HELLO WORLD (d) Error.

68. The function that compares two strings, where string may be in lower or upper case is

(a) stricmp() (b) strcspn()

(c) strcmp() (d) strncmp().

*69. What will be the output of the following program?

```
void main()
{
clrscr();
printf("%s",strlwr(strrev("HELLO")));
}
```

(a) HELLO (b) hello

(c) olleh (d) OLLEH.

**70.** The `printf()` function is an example of

(*a*) user defined function (*b*) library function

(*c*) multi function program (*d*) none of the above.

**71.** Consider the following statements

```
int x[] = {1, 2, 3, 4, 5};
int u;
int *ptr = x;
****
for( u = 0; u < 5; u++ )
{
printf("%d-", x[u]);
}
printf( "\n" );
```

Which of the following statements could replace the **** in the above code to cause the string 1-2-3-10-5-to be printed when the code is executed?

(*a*) *ptr + 3 = 10; (*b*) *ptr[ 3 ] = 10;

(*c*) *(ptr + 3) = 10; (*d*) (*ptr)[ 3 ] = 10;.

**72.** Which of the following statements is an example for decision making and branching?

(*a*) For statement (*b*) If statement

(*c*) Do....while statement (*d*) While statement.

**73.** What value will the variable counter have when the following statements are executed?

```
int x = 5, counter = 0;
while ((x-1))
{
++counter;
x—;
}
```

(*a*) 4 (*b*) 3

(*c*) 2 (*d*) 1

**74.** What will be the output of the following statement?

```
printf("hello how are you"+6);
```

(*a*) hello how are you (*b*) how are you

(*c*) hello (*d*) none of the above

**75.** Which of the following conditional statements tests the continuation of the loop at the end of each pass?

(*a*) While statement (*b*) Do.....while statement

(*c*) For statement (*d*) None of the above.

**76.** What will be the output of the following program?

```
void main()
{
int i;
for( i=0; i<8;i++, i+=2, i-=1)
{
printf("welcome to c");
}
}
```

(*a*) *welcome to c* will be printed once

(*b*) *welcome to c* will be printed two times

(*c*) *welcome to c* will be printed three times

(*d*) *welcome to c* will be printed four times.

**77.** Which of the following is a *unary negation* operator?

(*a*) &&  (*b*) | |

(*c*) !  (*d*) ?:.

**78.** Which of the following operators is equivalent to a simple *if – else* statement?

(*a*) &&  (*b*) ?|

(*c*) !  (*d*) ?:.

***79.** What will be the outcome when the following statements are executed?

```
void main()
{
int a=10, *b;
float *f=(float *)&a;
b=(int *)f;
printf("%d",*b);
}
```

(*a*) 0  (*b*) 10

(*c*) Syntax error  (*d*) Runtime error.

**80.** What will be the output if the following codes are executed?

```
#define GOOD 0
while(GOOD)
{
printf("hai");
}
printf("welcome");
```

(*a*) hai (*b*) welcome

(*c*) hai welcome (*d*) error.

**81.** What will be the outcome of the following program?

```
void main()
{
if(printf("Welcome to MCQs"))
{ }
}
```

(*a*) Syntax error (*b*) Compilation error

(*c*) Welcome to MCQs (*d*) Execution error.

**82.** What will be the value of *y*, when the codes given below are executed?

```
int y = 0;
for ( ; ; )
{
if (y++ == 4)
break;
continue;
}
printf("y=%d\n", y);
```

(*a*) 4 (*b*) 5

(*c*) 6 (*d*) 7.

***83.** What will be the output when the following statements are executed?

```
void main ()
{
int x = 0;
if(x=5)
printf("Love Peace")
else printf("Hate Violence");
}
```

(*a*) Love Peace (*b*) Hate Violence

(*c*) Syntax error (*d*) Compilation error.

**84.** Which of the following streams identifies the standard input text and its association with our terminal?

(*a*) `stdin` (*b*) `stdout`

(*c*) `stderr` (*d*) None of the above.

***85.** What will be the output of the following program?

```
void main()
```

```
        {
        int  a[7];
        printf("%d",sizeof(int));
        printf("%d",sizeof(x));
    }
```

(*a*) 7 7 (*b*) 2 7

(*c*) 2 14 (*d*) 0 7.

**86.** A character in an array always ends with

(*a*) semicolon (;) (*b*) null character (0\)

(*c*) full stop (.) (*d*) colon (:).

**87.** Which of the following loops is generally used when the number of passes is known in advance?

(*a*) `While` (*b*) `Do - while`

(*c*) `For` (*d*) None of the above.

**88.** What will be the output of the following program?

```
void  main()
{
char  x[]={'l','o','v','e',NULL};
printf("%d",sizeof(x));
}
```

(*a*) Error (*b*) love

(*c*) 4 (*d*) 5.

**89.** Assuming a short is four bytes long, what will be printed for the below codes?

```
short  x[4][3]  =  {  {1},  {2,  3},  {4,  5,  6}  };
printf("%d\n",  sizeof(x));
```

(*a*) 12 (*b*) 24

(*c*) 48 (*d*) 96

***90.** Which statement in the following program has an error?

```
//1    #include  "stdio.h"
//2    void  main()
//3    {
//4    int  a[5],  b[5];
//5    if(printf("hai"))
//6    {  }
//7    a=b;
//8    }
```

(*a*) Line 1 (*b*) Line 5

(*c*) Line 6 (*d*) Line 7.

**91.** Which of the following does not hold good for an array?

(*a*) While declaring an array, the size may be omitted

(*b*) Selected elements in an array can be initialized

(*c*) Array must be declared before they are used

(*d*) Individual array element can be used anywhere like a normal variable.

***92.** What will be the output when the following codes are executed?

```
int x = 5;
int y = 2;
char op = '*';
switch (op)
{
default : x += 1;
case '+' : x += y;
case '-' : x -= y;
}
```

(*a*) 5 (*b*) 6

(*c*) 7 (*d*) 8.

***93.** Suppose *a* is assigned value 2, what will be the output of the following statements?

```
int main()
{
int a;
printf("%d, scanf("%d", &(a));
return 0;
}
```

(*a*) 0 (*b*) 1

(*c*) 2 (*d*) error.

***94.** What is the value of the expression `6["COIMBATORE"]`?

(*a*) Error (*b*) A

(*c*) T (*d*) O.

***95.** Which of the following is an incorrect statement for the keyword '*auto*'?

(*a*) Auto variable is visible only in the block in which it is blocked

(*b*) The auto storage-class specific declares a local variable

(*c*) It is the default storage-class specific for block-scoped variable declaration

(*d*) The variable with auto storage class is initialized automatically.

**96.** What will be the output of the following program?

```
int * func1()
```

```
{
int b=10, *a;
a = &b;
return a;
}
main()
{
printf("%d", *(func1()));
}
```

(*a*) 10

(*b*) Returns the address of the memory location

(*c*) Syntax Error

(*d*) Run time error.

**97.** Which of the following statements forms a ladder?

(*a*) If
(*b*) If ...Else
(*c*) If... Else ...If
(*d*) None.

**98.** Let x = 20, y = 10 what will be the output of the statement `z = x * y++`

(*a*) 20
(*b*) 10
(*c*) 100
(*d*) 200.

**99.** *#define* is used to define __________ constants.

(*a*) real
(*b*) integer
(*c*) symbolic
(*d*) string.

**100.** Consider the following statements

```
int y[4] = {6, 7, 8, 9};
int *ptr = y + 2;
printf("%d\n", ptr[1]); /*ptr+1 == ptr[1]*/
```

What will be the output when the above code is executed?

(*a*) Error in the program
(*b*) 7
(*c*) 8
(*d*) 9.

**101.** What will be the output of the following program?

```
main()
{
int b, a =9;
b=(a++-a++ - a++, a++);
printf("%d",b);
}
```

(*a*) 8
(*b*) 9
(*c*) 11
(*d*) 12.

**102.** What will be the output of the following program?

```
main()
{
int  a=  66;
printf("%c%d",a,a);
return  0;
}
```

(*a*) A 66 (*b*) 66 66

(*c*) B 66 (*d*) b 66.

**103.** The While loop is an example for ____________ controlled loop.

(*a*) entry (*b*) exit

(*c*) switch (*d*) none.

**104.** The switch statement is used for

(*a*) switches between functions in a program

(*b*) switch from one variable to another variable

(*c*) choose from multiple possibilities

(*d*) use switching variable.

**105.** What will be the output of the following program?

```
main()
{
int  a-2,  b=a+2,  c-b+2
printf("\tA=%d\nB=%d\'C=%d\'",   a,b,c);
}
```

(*a*) A=2, B=4' C=6' (*b*) A=2, B=4 C=6'

(*c*) A=2, B=4' C=6 (*d*) A=2, B=4 C=6.

**106.** If *label:* is used before the statement *goto label;* then it is called ___________.

(*a*) forward jump (*b*) backward jump

(*c*) conditional jump (*d*) none of the above.

**107.** What will be the output of the following program?

```
main  ()
{
double  a  =  3.0,  b=  2.0;
printf  ("%.2lf",  pow(a,b));
}
```

(*a*) 8.00 (*b*) 9.00

(*c*) 8.000000 (*d*) 9.000000.

**108.** Which of the following statements is correct?

(*a*) Each element in an array is not unique

(*b*) Array is a collection of different data

(*c*) Each element in an array are located in a same memory location

(*d*) Array is a collection of similar data.

**109.** What will be the value of x and y when the following program is executed?

```
main()
{
int  x=4, y=5;
x=x+y;
y=x-y;
x=x-y;
printf("%d%d",x,y);
}
```

(*a*) x = 5, y = 4 (*b*) x = 4, y = 5

(*c*) x = 9, y = 5 (*d*) x = 9, y = 4.

**110.** What will be the output of the following statements?

```
struct  x
{
int  *x;
}  a;
main()
{
struct  x  *struct_pointer;
int  temp=10;
a.x=&temp;
struct_pointer=&a;
printf("%d  %d",  *(struct_pointer->x),  *(a.x));
}
```

(*a*) 10 0 (*b*) 0 10

(*c*) 10 10 (*d*) None of the above.

**111.** Which of the following is a macro/function that forces the character in the output buffer to be written to the file?

(*a*) rewind ( ) (*b*) fflush ( )

(*c*) ftell ( ) (*d*) fseek ( ).

**112.** A character array always ends with

(*a*) question mark (?) (*b*) semicolon (;)

(*c*) null character (\0) (*d*) full stop (.).

**113.** Which of the following statement about `scanf()` is true?

(*a*) Function allow to read character from a character array writes them to another array

(*b*) Function allow to read character from a character array writes them to the same array

(*c*) both a and b

(*d*) None of the above.

**114.** $a - = b + 1$ is equivalent to

(*a*) `a = a - b + 1` (*b*) `a = - b - 1`

(*c*) `a = a - b - 1` (*d*) illegal expression.

**115.** The arguments specified in the called function are known as

(*a*) actual arguments (*b*) formal arguments

(*c*) reference arguments (*d*) none of these.

**116.** Global variables are also known as ___________ variables.

(*a*) internal (*b*) automatic

(*c*) external (*d*) register.

**117.** A C function returns a value of type ________ as a default case, when no other type is specified explicitly.

(*a*) int (*b*) float

(*c*) char (*d*) none of the above.

***118.** What will be the output of the following program?

```
void main()
{
int *b;
int a[10]={1,2,3,4,5,6,7,8,9,10};
b=a;
printf("%d", *(b+2));
}
```

(*a*) 1 (*b*) 3

(*c*) 5 (*d*) 7.

**119.** The ___________ of a variable determines the variable availability in the program.

(*a*) lifetime (*b*) scope

(*c*) longevity (*d*) none of these.

**120.** When there is a mismatch of data type while executing a statement will result in

(*a*) syntax error (*b*) run-time error

(*c*) logical error (*d*) latent error.

**121.** To pass an array as argument to a function, which of the following is needed?

(*a*) Array name, subscript

(*b*) Array name, size

(*c*) Subscript, size

(*d*) None of the above.

**122.** Choose the correct statement

(*a*) The library functions are user-defined functions

(*b*) The user can understand the internal working of library functions

(*c*) The user can modify the library functions

(*d*) Library functions task is limited.

**123.** Choose the correct statement

(*a*) A functions can be without argument and return value

(*b*) A function can be with argument but without return values

(*c*) A function can be with argument and with return values

(*d*) All the above statements are false.

**124.** Which of the following is a user-defined function?

(*a*) `sqrt( )` (*b*) `main( )`

(*c*) `printf( )` (*d*) `scanf( )`.

**125.** What will be the output for the following code?

```
char* myFunc (char *ptr)
{
ptr += 3;
return (ptr);
}
int main()
{
char *x, *y;
x = "ABOVE";
y = myFunc(x);
printf ("y = %s \n", y);
return 0;
}
```

(*a*) ABOVE (*b*) BOVE

(*c*) OVE (*d*) VE.

**126.** The statement `x = (a + b)/(c - d)`, and *c* and *d* are equal will results in

(*a*) syntax error (*b*) run-time error

(*c*) latent error (*d*) logical error.

**127.** Recursion is a process in which a function calls

(*a*) another functions (*b*) main ( )

(*c*) itself (*d*) none of the above.

**128.** The operator used to find the size of structures is

(*a*) size operator (*b*) sizeof operator

(*c*) byte operator (*d*) none of the above.

**129.** Structure and Union is a

(*a*) primary data type (*b*) user-defined data type

(*c*) derived data type (*d*) none of the above.

**130.** What will be the output when the following code is executed?

```
int x[] = { 1, 4, 8, 5, 1, 4 };
int *ptr, y;
ptr = x + 4;
y = ptr - x;
```

(*a*) 0 (*b*) 1

(*c*) 4 (*d*) 5.

**131.** Members of the structure can be accessed with

(*a*) left arrow option (*b*) comma operator

(*c*) semicolon operator (*d*) dot operator.

**132.** A variable that contains the address of another variable in memory is called

(*a*) array (*b*) structure

(*c*) Pointer (*d*) union.

**133.** In which of the following do all the members use the same location?

(*a*) Array (*b*) Structure

(*c*) Union (*d*) None of the above.

**134.** The operator used to determine the address of a variable is called

(*a*) address operator (*b*) indirection operator

(*c*) arrow operator (*d*) none of the above.

**135.** The hidden error that shows up only when a particular set of data is used is

(*a*) syntax error (*b*) run-time error

(*c*) logical error (*d*) latent error.

**136.** What will be the output of the following program?

```
void main()
{
char a[]="computer technology";
int i;
printf("%c",toupper(a[0]));
```

```
        for(i=1;i<strlen(a);i++)
        {
        if  (a[i-1]  ==  '  ')
        printf("%c",toupper(a[i]));
        else
          printf("%c",a[i]);
    }
    }
```

(*a*) computer technology (*b*) Computer Technology

(*c*) COMPUTER TECHNOLOGY (*d*) Computer technology.

**137.** The keyword used to declare a structure is ___________.

(*a*) `struc` (*b*) `struct`

(*c*) `structure` (*d*) None of the above.

**138.** The function used for creating a new file or opening an existing file is

(*a*) `fclose()` (*b*) `fopen()`

(*c*) `fseek()` (*d*) `ftell()`.

**139.** Which function gives the current position in the file?

(*a*) `ftell()` (*b*) `fseek()`

(*c*) `rewind()` (*d*) `fopen()`.

**140.** To open a file for adding data to it, the mode is specified as

(*a*) r (*b*) w

(*c*) a (*d*) none of the above.

**141.** Which one of the following function will read a character from the keyboard and will store it in the variable *c*?

(*a*) `c=getch();` (*b*) `getc(&c);`

(*c*) `c=getchar(&c)` (*d*) `c=getchar()`.

**142.** The function that writes a character in a file is

(*a*) `getc()` (*b*) `putc()`

(*c*) `getchar()` (*d*) `putchar()`.

**143.** Which function is used to reset the file pointer to the start of the file?

(*a*) `fseek()` (*b*) `ftell()`

(*c*) `rewind()` (*d*) `fprintf()`.

**144.** The function used to write group of data in a file is

(*a*) `fprintf()` (*b*) `putc()`

(*c*) `putchar()` (*d*) none of the above.

**145.** The `int(*X)[]` indicates

(*a*) X is a pointer to an array of int

(*b*) X is a pointer to the int

(*c*) X is an array of pointers to the int

(*d*) None of these.

**146.** Consider the following statements

```
void *ptr;
myStruct myArray[10];
ptr = myArray;
```

Which of the following is the correct way to increment the variable "ptr" in the above statement?

(*a*) ptr = ptr + sizeof(myStruct); (*b*) ++(int*)ptr ;

(*c*) ptr = ptr + sizeof(myArray); (*d*) increment(ptr);.

**147.** The void pointer is a

(*a*) generic pointer (*b*) address pointer

(*c*) logical pointer (*d*) none of the above.

**148.** Pointers are of

(*a*) integer data type (*b*) character data type

(*c*) unsigned integer data type (*d*) any data type.

**149.** `float *p = &x` means

(*a*) *p* contains value of *x* (*b*) *p* contains address of *x*

(*c*) *p* contains float value (*d*) none of these.

**150.** The process of calling a function using pointers to pass the address of variable is known as

(*a*) call by reference (*b*) call by value

(*c*) call by parameter (*d*) call by function.

**151.** What will be the value of i when the following code is executed?

```
#include <stdio.h>
int i;
void increment(int i)
{
i++;
}
int main()
{
for( i = 0; i <= 10; i++)
{
}
printf("i=%d\n", i);
```

```
return 0;
}
```

(*a*) 8 (*b*) 9
(*c*) 10 (*d*) none of the above.

***152.** What will be the output of the following program?

```
void main()
{
struct student
{
int id;
char name[20];
} x,*new_student;
clrscr();
x.id = 10;
strcpy(x.name,"Mr.X");
new_student=&x;
printf("%x, %s", new_student->id, new_student->name);
}
```

(*a*) 10 Mr.X (*b*) a Mr.X
(*c*) 1010 Mr.X (*d*) none of the above.

**153.** Choose the incorrect statement

(*a*) Pointers save the memory space
(*b*) Execution time with pointer is faster
(*c*) The memory is accessed efficiently with pointers
(*d*) Pointers cannot be used with data structures.

**154.** Incase both external and auto variables are declared with the same name in a program the first priority is given to the

(*a*) auto variable (*b*) external variable
(*c*) whichever is declared first (*d*) none.

**155.** Variable declared in C must be

(*a*) only automatic (*b*) only External
(*c*) only Register (*d*) any one of the above.

**156.** A static variable is one that

(*a*) cannot be initialized
(*b*) returns its value throughout the life of the programs
(*c*) is same as an automatic variable but is placed at the head of the program
(*d*) none of the above.

**157.** Which file function is used to read as integer from the file?

(*a*) gets( ) (*b*) getw( )

(*c*) fget( ) (*d*) fread( ).

**158.** What will be the output of the following statement?

```
char *ptr;
char myString[] = "ABCDEFG";
ptr = myString;
ptr += 5;
```

(*a*) FG (*b*) EFG

(*c*) DEFG (*d*) CDEFG.

**159.** Which of the following sets the pointer position anywhere in the file?

(*a*) ftell() (*b*) rewind()

(*c*) fseek() (*d*) none of the above.

**160.** What will be the output of the following statement?

```
printf("\n date: %s", _DATE_);
```

(*a*) displays the system date in string format

(*b*) displays the date in which the program was compiled

(*c*) displays the date in which program is created

(*d*) none of the above.

**161.** Which of the following functions allocates request size of bytes and returns a pointer to the first byte of the allocated space?

(*a*) calloc (*b*) malloc

(*c*) free (*d*) realloc.

**162.** What will be the output when the following code is executed?

```
int x[] = { 1, 4, 8, 5, 1, 4 };
int *ptr, y;
ptr = x + 4;
y = ptr - x;
```

(*a*) 0 (*b*) 1

(*c*) 4 (*d*) 5.

**163.** What will be the output of the following program?

```
#define say(m) printf(m)
{
void main( )
{
Say("welcome");
} }
```

(a) wel (b) come
(c) welcome (d) error.

*164. What will be the output of the following program?

```
void main()
{
int a=5, b=10, c=4, i;
clrscr();
i=a<b>c;
printf("%d", i);
}
```

(a) 0 (b) 1
(c) 5 (d) 10.

165. What will be the output of the following program?

```
void main()
{
int a=3;
switch(a)
{
default: printf("hai");
case 1:
printf("welcome");
break;
case 2:
printf("to C");
}
}
```

(a) hai (b) hai welcome
(c) welcome to C (d) hai welcome to C.

166. Which of the following preprocessor directives used to test for macro definition?

(a) #define (b) #include
(c) #ifdef (d) #if.

167. Which of the following function modifies the size of previously allocated space?

(a) calloc (b) malloc
(c) free (d) realloc.

168. What will be the output of the following program?

```
#define FUN(a,b) a##b
void main()
```

```
{
int  val1=3;
int  val12=4;
clrscr();
printf("%d",  FUN(val1,2));
}
```

(*a*) 3 4 (*b*) 4 3

(*c*) 3 (*d*) 4

***169.** What will be the output of the following?

```
#define  SAMPLE(x, y)  x  *  y
void  main()
{
printf("%d",  SAMPLE(4+2,  5+1);
}
```

(*a*) 36 (*b*) 14

(*c*) 22 (*d*) 56

**170.** Choose the incorrect statement

(*a*) Preprocessor is a program that process the source code before it passes through the compiler

(*b*) Preprocessor directive can be placed anywhere in a C program

(*c*) Preprocessor operates under the control of what is known as preprocessor command lines

(*d*) Preprocessor directives follow a special syntax rules that are different from the normal C syntax.

**171.** What will be the output of the following program?

```
main()
{
char  s[]="ab";
int  i;
for(i=0;s[i];i++)
printf("\n%c%c",s[i],i[s]);
return  0;
}
```

(*a*) a<br>b

(*b*) aa<br>b

(*c*) a<br>bb

(*d*) aa<br>bb.

**172.** What will be the output when the following statement is executed?

```
printf("%x",-1<<1);
```

(*a*) fffe (*b*) fff8

(*c*) ffff (*d*) fff0.

**173.** Which of the following preprocessor directives is used to test a compile-time condition?

(*a*) #define (*b*) #include

(*c*) #ifdef (*d*) #if.

**174.** Which of the following functions frees previously allocated space?

(*a*) calloc (*b*) malloc

(*c*) free (*d*) realloc.

**175.** Which of the following directives allows a section of a program to be compiled only if the macro that is specified as the parameter has been defined?

(*a*) #if (*b*) #endif

(*c*) #ifdef (*d*) #elif.

## ANSWERS

| **1.** (*b*) | **2.** (*a*) | **3.** (*d*) | **4.** (*c*) | **5.** (*d*) | **6.** (*b*) | **7.** (*d*) | **8.** (*b*) |
|---|---|---|---|---|---|---|---|
| **9.** (*d*) | **10.** (*d*) | **11.** (*c*) | **12.** (*c*) | **13.** (*c*) | **14.** (*b*) | **15.** (*c*) | **16.** (*b*) |
| **17.** (a) | **18.** (*b*) | **19.** (*b*) | **20.** (*b*) | **21.** (*d*) | **22.** (*c*) | **23.** (*b*) | **24.** (*d*) |
| **25.** (*b*) | **26.** (*b*) | **27.** (*a*) | **28.** (*b*) | **29.** (*c*) | **30.** (*b*) | **31.** (*a*) | **32.** (*b*) |
| **33.** (*d*) | **34.** (*a*) | **35.** (*c*) | **36.** (*c*) | **37.** (*a*) | **38.** (*d*) | **39.** (*b*) | **40.** (*d*) |
| **41.** (*d*) | **42.** (*a*) | **43.** (*c*) | **44.** (*a*) | **45.** (*b*) | **46.** (*a*) | **47.** (*c*) | **48.** (*c*) |
| **49.** (*d*) | **50.** (*b*) | **51.** (*b*) | **52.** (*a*) | **53.** (*d*) | **54.** (*a*) | **55.** (*c*) | **56.** (*a*) |
| **57.** (*d*) | **58.** (*d*) | **59.** (*c*) | **60.** (*d*) | **61.** (*d*) | **62.** (*c*) | **63.** (*b*) | **64.** (*d*) |
| **65.** (*b*) | **66.** (*a*) | **67.** (*c*) | **68.** (*a*) | **69.** (*c*) | **70.** (*b*) | **71.** (*c*) | **72.** (*b*) |
| **73.** (*a*) | **74.** (*b*) | **75.** (*b*) | **76.** (*d*) | **77.** (*c*) | **78.** (*d*) | **79.** (*b*) | **80.** (*b*) |
| **81.** (*c*) | **82.** (*b*) | **83.** (*a*) | **84.** (*a*) | **85.** (*c*) | **86.** (*b*) | **87.** (*c*) | **88.** (*d*) |
| **89.** (*c*) | **90.** (*d*) | **91.** (*b*) | **92.** (*b*) | **93.** (*b*) | **94.** (*c*) | **95.** (*d*) | **96.** (*a*) |
| **97.** (*c*) | **98.** (*d*) | **99.** (*c*) | **100.** (*d*) | **101.** (*d*) | **102.** (*c*) | **103.** (*a*) | **104.** (*c*) |
| **105.** (*a*) | **106.** (*b*) | **107.** (*b*) | **108.** (*d*) | **109.** (*a*) | **110.** (*c*) | **111.** (*b*) | **112.** (*c*) |
| **113.** (*a*) | **114.** (*a*) | **115.** (*b*) | **116.** (*c*) | **117.** (*a*) | **118.** (*b*) | **119.** (*b*) | **120.** (*b*) |
| **121.** (*b*) | **122.** (*d*) | **123.** (*d*) | **124.** (*b*) | **125.** (*d*) | **126.** (*c*) | **127.** (*c*) | **128.** (*b*) |
| **129.** (*b*) | **130.** (*c*) | **131.** (*d*) | **132.** (*c*) | **133.** (*c*) | **134.** (*a*) | **135.** (*d*) | **136.** (*b*) |
| **137.** (*b*) | **138.** (*b*) | **139.** (*a*) | **140.** (*c*) | **141.** (*d*) | **142.** (*b*) | **143.** (*c*) | **144.** (*a*) |
| **145.** (*c*) | **146.** (*a*) | **147.** (*a*) | **148.** (*d*) | **149.** (*b*) | **150.** (*a*) | **151.** (*c*) | **152.** (*b*) |
| **153.** (*d*) | **154.** (*a*) | **155.** (*d*) | **156.** (*d*) | **157.** (*b*) | **158.** (*a*) | **159.** (*c*) | **160.** (*a*) |

**161.** (*b*) **162.** (*c*) **163.** (*c*) **164.** (*a*) **165.** (*a*) **166.** (*c*) **167.** (*d*) **168.** (*d*)
**169.** (*b*) **170.** (*b*) **171.** (*d*) **172.** (*a*) **173.** (*d*) **174.** (*c*) **175.** (*c*)

## EXPLANATIONS

**3.** In the conditional expression `(3==4 ? 7 : 8)`, the expression `(3==4)` is evaluated first. Since 3 is not equal to 4, the entire expression takes on the value 8.

**4.** The identifiers *far, near* and *entry* are reserved word in C compiler.

**9.** Illegal character `(,)` is found in 2,000.0

**10.** A hexadecimal integer constant must begin with either 0x or 0X and followed by any combination of digits taken from the sets 0 to 9 and A through F (either upper or lower case). Since G is a illegal character 0xEFG is an invalid hexadecimal integer constant.

**11.** The letter C is represented by the decimal value 067 in the ASCII character set. Therefore, the octal equivalent of the value 067 is 103. Hence the character constant 'C' can be expressed as the octal escape sequence '\103'.

**12.** Initially `c` and `d` are assigned value 5 and 10 respectively. When the expression `a=c*++d` is executed the d value is pre incremented and the value of *d* becomes 11. Therefore, $a = 5 \times 11 = 55$. Similarly when expression `b=c*d++;` the *d* value is post incremented.

**16.** When the expression $x = 2 * 3 + 5 * 5$ is executed, according to operator precedence first 2 x 3 is executed followed by 5 x 5, and 6 is added with 25 to get 31.

**17.** Since there is one format specifier `(%d)` in the `printf` statement, only the value of $x$ is printed.

**20.** Since the condition `100!=100` is false it returns a value 0 and the condition `100<=1000` is true it returns a value 1.

**25.** The expression `((int)(a)%3)` contains two integer operands which will result in integer remainder 1.

**26.** 6/4 results in fractional output. A field width specification .2 is applied to double data.

**29.** Since the first comparison in the `printf` which has a *OR* function satisfies the condition, therefore, it returns a value 1 (true). Whereas in the second `printf` statement *AND* function is used and the condition does not satisfy which results in a output value 0 (false).

**33.** The *for* loop is repeated 4 times and at the end of the loop $x$ is assigned a value *5*.

**38.** The unary operator (~)is a *one complement operator* that causes the bits of its operand to be inverted. Therefore, the binary value of hexadecimal value *abcd* is 1010 1011 1100 1101. The one's complement of 1010 1011 1100 1101 is 0101 0100 0011 0010, which is equivalent to hexadecimal value 5432.

**39.** The bitwise operator (&) will return a 1 if both bits have a value 1. Otherwise it will return 0. (*and operation)* The binary equivalent of hexadecimal value x = 1010 1011 1100 1101, and y = 11011100 1011 1010. By performing AND operation we get 1000 1000 1000 1000, which is equivalent to 8888 in hexadecimal.

**40.** The bitwise operator (^) will return a 1 if both bits have a different value. Otherwise it will return 0.*(exclusive operation)* The binary equivalent of hexadecimal value x = 1010 1011 1100 1101, and y = 1101 1100 1011 1010.By performing X-OR operation we get 0111 0111 0111 0111, which is equivalent to 7777 in hexadecimal.

**41.** The bitwise operator (|) will return a 1 if one or more bits have the value 1.*(or operation)* The binary equivalent of hexadecimal value x = 1010 1011 1100 1101, and y = 1101 1100 1011 1010. By performing OR operation we get 1111 1111 1111 1111, which is equivalent to FFFF in hexadecimal.

**42.** The operator '<<' performs shift left. The binary equivalent of x = 1010 1011 1100 1101. By performing shift left by six places we get x = 1111 0011 0100 0000, which is equivalent to F340 in hexadecimal.

**43.** The operator '>>' performs shift right. The binary equivalent of x = 1010 1011 1100 1101. By performing shift right by four places we get x = 0000 1010 1011 1100 , which is equivalent to ABC in hexadecimal.

**47.** Flag '–' left justifies the data item.

**50.** Initially 3 is assigned to *x*. The *if* statement terminates after making comparing value of *x* (*i.e.* 3) with 2. Next 0 is assigned to *x* and compared with 3, which is false. Therefore, the *else* part of the *if* statement is executed which increments x by 2.

**55.** The value in the array *a* (2 x 3) will be stored in the following manner: a[0][0]=0, a[1][0]=1, a[0][1]=1, a[1][1]=3, a[0][2]=4, a[1][2]=5.

**61.** Since the field width specification `(.3s)` is applied the first three character is displayed.

**64.** Each integer data type requires 2 bytes of memory. Since, the array size is 5 a total of (5 × 2 = 10) 10 bytes of memory is reserved.

**69.** The string function `strrev` will reverse the string and `strlwr` will convert the upper case character to lower case.

**77.** Execution will not go into the loop since GOOD is defined as 0.

**78.** The `printf()` function is returns any number of character that is to be printed. This return value can be used in `"if"` condition expression and can print the required string without using a semicolon.

**78.** 10 will be printed because address of a is stored in f as float address, but it is re casted to integer pointer to b.

**79.** The *for* loop will be terminated when the value of *y* is 4. Since *y* is incremented by using post increment operator, the value of *y* become 5.

**83.** In the *if* statement the value of '*x*' is assigned to 5, therefore the *if* statement will return true and the statement `printf("Love Peace")` will be executed.

**85.** To find the total size in bytes for a single dimensional array is *Total bytes = sizeof(data type) x size of the array.* Since integer data type requires 2 bytes, Total bytes = 2 x 7 = 14

**90.** Can't assign arrays to each other.

**92.** The default case can be placed anywhere inside the switch statement. The default case is executed only when all other cases do not match.

**93.** `scanf()` function returns the number of items successfully read. i.e. the number of item read.

**94.** The string literal `"COIMBATORE"` is an array, and the expression is equivalent to `"COIMBATORE"[6]`. The inside-out expression is equivalent because `x[y]` is equivalent to `*(x+y)`, which is equivalent to `(*y+x)` which is equivalent to `y[x]`.

**95.** The auto variable should either explicitly initialized when it is declared or assign initial values to them in statements within blocks.

**118.** 3 will be printed because array address + 2 points to the third element in the array i.e. b+2 points to a[2].

**152.** prints the value 10 in hexadecimal and Mr. X

**164.** Since *a<b* is true, it is replaced by 1. This 1 is compared with the value of c. i.e. *(1>4)*. Since this condition turns to be false it is replaced by 0. Thus 0 is assigned to i.

**169.** The macro is expanded as *4+2x3+4* and * operator is executed first since it has the highest precedence.

CHAPTER 3

# DATA STRUCTURES AND ALGORITHMS

1. Which one of the following is not true for an algorithm?
   (a) Algorithm must not terminate after a finite number of steps
   (b) The steps of algorithm must be precisely defined
   (c) Algorithm must be generic enough to solve all problems of a particular class
   (d) Algorithm should not be too complex to warrant writing another algorithm for operation.
2. The data types of integer, real, character, boolean are inherently referred as
   (a) abstract data type (b) primitive data type
   (c) string data type (d) none of the above.
3. Which of the following focuses on what a data structure does rather than how it does?
   (a) Data Abstraction (b) Data Encapsulation
   (c) Data Integration (d) None of the above.
4. Two main measures for the efficiency of an algorithm are
   (a) processor and memory (b) complexity and capacity
   (c) time and space (d) data and space.
5. The empirical approach of finding the time complexity of an algorithm is also known as
   (a) theoretical approach (b) apriori approach
   (c) posteriori approach (d) none of the above.
6. Mathematically determining the resources such as time and space needed by the algorithm, as a function of a parameter related to the instances of the problems are known as
   (a) theoretical approach (b) apriori approach
   (c) posteriori approach (d) empirical approach.

7. The time factor when determining the efficiency of algorithm is measured by
   (*a*) counting the number of key operations
   (*b*) counting the number of statements
   (*c*) counting the size of the algorithm
   (*d*) counting the number of modules.
8. Which of the following operations is supported by an array ADT?
   (*a*) Insertion and delete (*b*) Store and retrieve
   (*c*) Copy and delete (*d*) Append and copy.
9. The algorithm reporting 0(1) time complexity indicate
   (*a*) linear time complexity (*b*) quadratic time complexity
   (*c*) cubic time complexity (*d*) constant running time.
10. The space vector when determining the efficiency of an algorithm is measured by
   (*a*) counting the maximum disk space needed by the algorithm
   (*b*) counting the minimum disk space needed by the algorithm
   (*c*) counting the maximum memory needed by the algorithm
   (*d*) counting the minimum memory needed by the algorithm.
11. Which of the following is a quadratic time complexity?
   (*a*) O(n) (*b*) $O(n^2)$
   (*c*) $O(n^3)$ (*d*) O(log n).
12. Which of the following case does not exist in complexity theory?
   (*a*) Best case (*b*) Worst case
   (*c*) Null case (*d*) Average case.
13. Which of the following is a polynomial time complexity?
   (*a*) $O(n^k)$ (*b*) $O(k^n)$
   (*c*) O(log n) (*d*) O(log k).
14. If P is a procedure containing a call statement to another procedure that results in a call to itself, than it is termed as
   (*a*) direct recursion (*b*) indirect recursion
   (*c*) recurrence relations (*d*) none of the above.
15. Consider a one-dimensional array *A [1:5]*. The 1 in the above array is referred as
   (*a*) low bounds (*b*) upper bounds
   (*c*) upper indexes (*d*) none of the above.
16. Which of the following abstract data types are NOT used by Integer Abstract Data type group?
   (*a*) Short (*b*) Int
   (*c*) float (*d*) long.

**17.** Value of the first linked list index is ______ .

(*a*) one (*b*) zero

(*c*) –1 (*d*) none of these.

**18.** Two dimensional arrays are also called

(*a*) tables arrays (*b*) matrix arrays

(*c*) both of the above (*d*) none of the above.

**19.** Arrays are best data structure for

(*a*) relatively permanent collection of data

(*b*) relatively for large collections of data

(*c*) the data in the structure are constantly changing

(*d*) the size of the structure constantly changing.

**20.** Which of the following data structure store the homogeneous data elements?

(*a*) Arrays (*b*) Records

(*c*) Pointers (*d*) None of the above.

**21.** Each data item in a record may be a group item composed of sub-items; those items which are indecomposable are called

(*a*) elementary items (*b*) atoms

(*c*) scalars (*d*) all of above.

**22.** Each array declaration need not give, implicitly or explicitly, the information about

(*a*) the name of the array

(*b*) the data type of the array

(*c*) the first data from the set to be stored

(*d*) the index set of the array.

**23.** Which one of the following is not true for ordered list?

(*a*) Ordered list is also known as linear list

(*b*) Ordered list cannot be empty

(*c*) The elements of the list is known as atoms

(*d*) Operations such as retrieval, insertion etc can be performed in a list.

**24.** Which of the following properties does not hold good for a stack?

(*a*) Stack obeys the principle LIFO

(*b*) The element insertion/ deletion can be done in both the side of the stack

(*c*) Insertion of elements known as PUSH

(*d*) Deletion of elements known as POP.

**25.** What is the equivalent prefix expression of ( a * b – f * h)

(*a*) –*ab*fh (*b*) *–ab*fh

(*c*) *–ab–fh (*d*) *ab*fh–.

**26.** Post fix notation is also known as

(*a*) reverse polish notation (*b*) polish notation

(*c*) prefix (*d*) infix.

**27.** Prefix notation is also known as

(*a*) reverse polish notation (*b*) polish notation

(*c*) postfix (*d*) infix.

**28.** Which of the following properties does not hold good for a queue?

(*a*) It is a non-linear list

(*b*) Insertion is done at the rear end of the queue

(*c*) Deletion is done at the front of the queue

(*d*) The insertion operation is also referred as enqueuing a queue.

**29.** When insertion/deletion of items from any position in the queue are done based on some property is called

(*a*) linear queues (*b*) circular queues

(*c*) priority queues (*d*) deques.

## The Next Three Questions (30–32) are Based on the Following Stack Diagram, Which is Implemented as an Array?

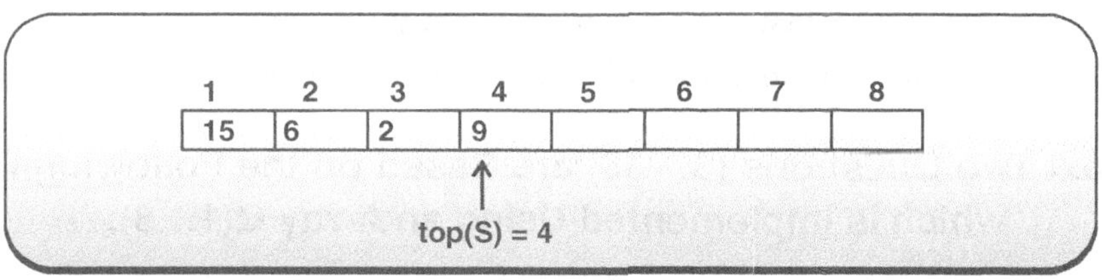


***30.** Suppose the following operation PUSH(S, 17), PUSH (S, 3), POP(S) takes place, what will be the value of top?

(*a*) 4 (*b*) 5

(*c*) 6 (*d*) 7.

***31.** Suppose the following operation POP(S), POP(S), POP(S), POP(S), PUSH (S, 5), POP(S), POP(S) takes place, what will be the state of the stack?

(*a*) 0 (*b*) 1

(*c*) Overflow (*d*) Underflow.

***32.** Suppose the following operation PUSH (S, 5), PUSH(S, 17), PUSH (S, 3), PUSH (S, 19), POP(S),PUSH (S, 3), PUSH (S, 3) takes place, what will be the state of the stack?

(*a*) 0 (*b*) 1

(*c*) Overflow (*d*) Underflow.

**33.** Which of the following properties does not hold good in a queue?

(*a*) Queue supports the principle of FCFS

(*b*) The rear end of the queue is affected when item is added in a queue

(*c*) The front end of the queue is affected when item is deleted in a queue

(*d*) The enqueuing operation shrinks the queue length.

**34.** Which of the following property does not hold good for a linked data structures?

(*a*) Efficient implementation of insertion operation

(*b*) Efficient implementation of deletion operation

(*c*) Efficient use of storage memory

(*d*) Contiguous memory allocation.

**35.** The worst case in linear search algorithm when

(*a*) item is somewhere in the middle of the array

(*b*) item is in the first of the array

(*c*) item is in the last element in the array

(*d*) item is last element in the array or is not there at all.

**36.** The average case in linear search algorithm when

(*a*) item is somewhere in the middle of the array

(*b*) item is in the first of the array

(*c*) item is in the last element in the array

(*d*) item is last element in the array or is not there at all.

## The Next Two Questions (37–38) are Based on the Following Queue which is Implemented Using an Array Q(1...8).

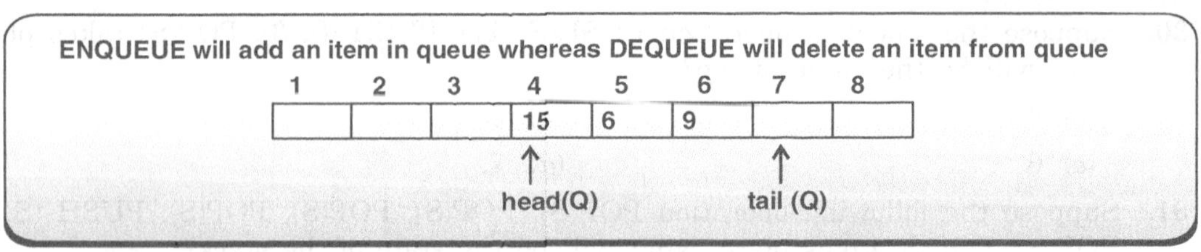


***37.** Where will tail points when the following operation takes place?
ENQUEUE (Q,17), ENQUEUE (Q,17), ENQUEUE (Q,17)

(*a*) 8 (*b*) 1

(*c*) 2 (*d*) 3.

***38.** Where will head points when DEQUEUE (Q) happens?

(*a*) 2 (*b*) 3

(*c*) 4 (*d*) 5.

**39.** Which one of the following is a linear list in which all insertions and deletion are made at the end of the list?

(*a*) Linear Queues

(*b*) Circular Queues

(*c*) Priority Queues

(*d*) Deques.

**40.** The complexity of the average case of an algorithm is

(*a*) much more complicated to analyze than that of worst case

(*b*) much more simpler to analyze than that of worst case

(*c*) much more complicated to analyze than that of best case

(*d*) much more simpler to analyze than that of best case.

**41.** The indirect change of the values of a variable in one module by another module is called

(*a*) internal change (*b*) inter-module change

(*c*) side effect (*d*) side-module update.

**42.** The operation of processing each element in the list is known as

(*a*) traversal (*b*) updating

(*c*) sorting (*d*) searching.

**Let the following diagram represent a circular queue with a capacity of three elements**

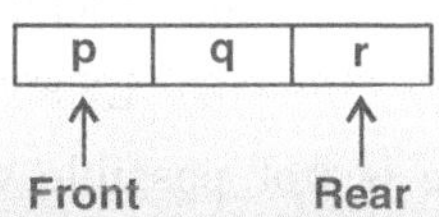


***43.** Which of the following is correct, if two deletions are performed followed by insertions of 'x' and 'y' in the above circular queue?

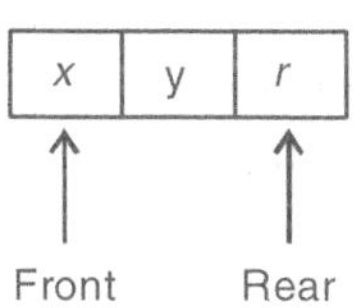


(*a*)

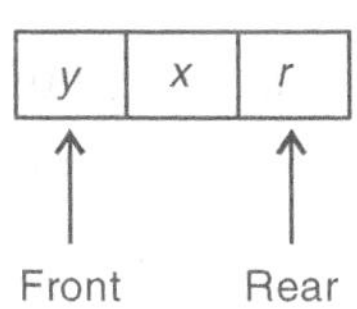


(*b*)

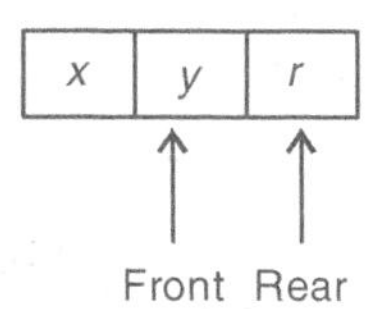


(*c*)

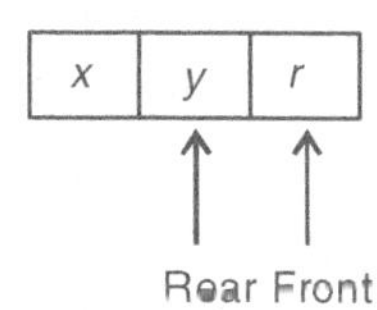


(*d*)

**44.** Finding the location of the element with a given value is

(*a*) traversal (*b*) updating

(*c*) sorting (*d*) searching.

## The Next Three Questions (45–47) are Based on The following Information

**Let A[1:6] be a deque implemented as a circular array and LEFT and RIGHT are active ends of the deque. The contents of A and that of LEFT and RIGHT are given below**

| | 1 | 2 | 3 | 4 | 5 | 6 | |
|---|---|---|---|---|---|---|---|
| A: | | P | Q | R | | | LEFT: 2 RIGHT: 4 |

***45.** Which of the following is correct if three elements S, T, U are inserted at the left end?

| | 1 | 2 | 3 | 4 | 5 | 6 | | |
|---|---|---|---|---|---|---|---|---|
| (*a*) | S | T | U | P | Q | R | LEFT : 2 | RIGHT : 5 |
| | 1 | 2 | 3 | 4 | 5 | 6 | | |
| (*b*) | P | Q | R | S | T | U | LEFT : 2 | RIGHT : 4 |
| | 1 | 2 | 3 | 4 | 5 | 6 | | |
| (*c*) | S | P | Q | R | U | T | LEFT : 5 | RIGHT : 4 |
| | 1 | 2 | 3 | 4 | 5 | 6 | | |
| (*d*) | S | P | Q | R | T | U | LEFT : 2 | RIGHT : 6 |

***46.** Where will LEFT and RIGHT point?

(*a*) LEFT : 1 RIGHT : 4 (*b*) LEFT : 2 RIGHT : 4

(*c*) LEFT : 4 RIGHT : 5 (*d*) LEFT : 5 RIGHT : 4.

***47.** Insertion of new item in deque is not possible when

(*a*) LEFT = RIGHT (*b*) LEFT = RIGHT – 1

(*c*) LEFT = RIGHT + 1 (*d*) None of the above.

**48.** A linked list with two links each pointing to the predecessor and successor of a node is known as

(*a*) singly linked list (*b*) circularly linked list

(*c*) doubly linked list (*d*) multiply linked list.

**49.** If the null pointer in a singly linked list is replaced with the address of the first node in the list then it is called as

(*a*) circularly linked list (*b*) circular linked list

(*c*) circular list (*d*) all the above.

**The following diagram represents stack with four elements**

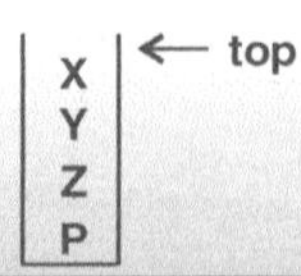

**50.** Which of the following is the linked representation of the above stack?

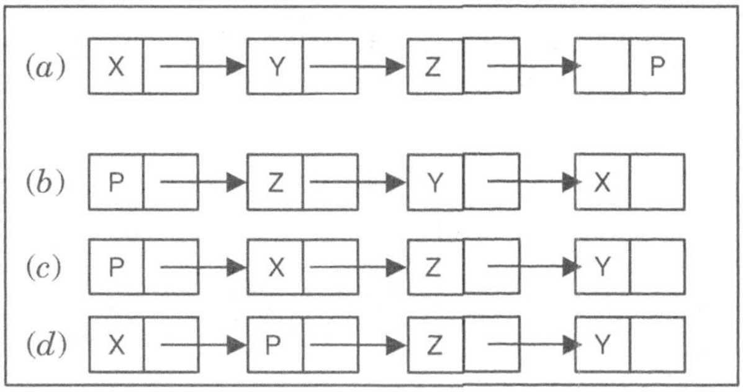


**51.** Which of the following data structures is a linear data structure?

(*a*) Trees

(*b*) Graphs

(*c*) Arrays

(*d*) None of the above.

**52.** Which of the following is a linear list of element commonly implemented as singly linked list with two pointers?

(*a*) Linked stack

(*b*) Linked Queue

(*c*) Stack

(*d*) Queue.

**53.** The automatic recycling of dynamically allocated memory is known as

(*a*) garbage collection

(*b*) memory Compaction

(*c*) fragmentation

(*d*) none of the above.

**54.** Which of the following is a disadvantage of circularly linked list?

(*a*) The accessibility of a node is simple

(*b*) Deletion of a node is simple

(*c*) Concatenation of two lists possible

(*d*) Possibility of entering into infinite loop.

**55.** Which of the following is true for a node in a tree?

(*a*) A node in a tree represents an item of information

(*b*) The links between nodes are termed as branches

(*c*) Node represents an association between the items of information

(*d*) All the above.

***56.** What will be the array representation of the following binary tree?

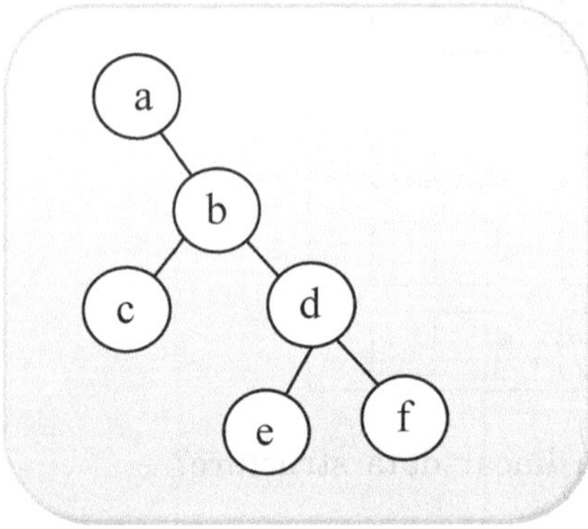


| a | b | | | c | d | | c | f | | |
|---|---|---|---|---|---|---|---|---|---|---|

(a)

| a | b | c | d | e | f | | | | | |
|---|---|---|---|---|---|---|---|---|---|---|

(b)

| a | | b | | | c | d | | | e | f |
|---|---|---|---|---|---|---|---|---|---|---|

(c)

| a | b | | c | d | | | | | e | f |
|---|---|---|---|---|---|---|---|---|---|---|

(d)

**57.** The depth of a tree is defined to be maximum level of any node in the tree, which yields the relation

(*a*) depth of the tree = height of the tree – 1

(*b*) depth of the tree = height of the tree – 2

(*c*) depth of the tree = height of the tree – 3

(*d*) depth of the tree = height of the tree – 4.

**58.** Nodes that have zero degree are called

(*a*) leaf nodes (*b*) non-terminal nodes

(c) parent node (*d*) none of the above.

**59.** Which of the following observation with regard to binary tree is not correct?

(*a*) In binary tree all the nodes have a degree of at most 2

(*b*) A binary tree can be empty

(*c*) In a binary tree the distinction of left and right sub tree are very clearly maintained

(*d*) All the above.

**60.** What will be the equivalent expression for the binary tree given below?

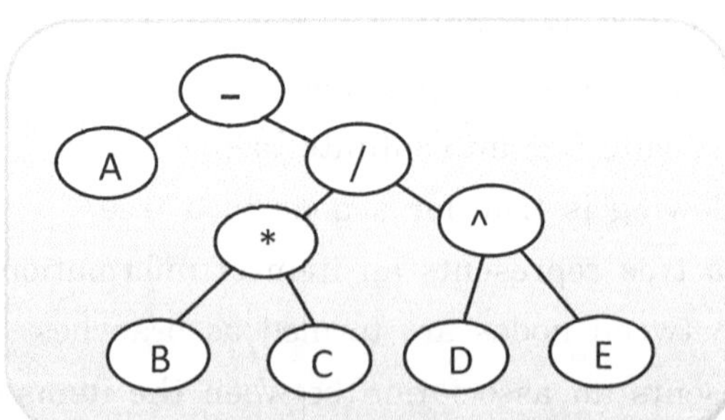

(a) B*C /D^E–A (b) A–D^E/B*C
(c) A–B*C/D^E (d) B*C /A–D^.

**61.** A binary tree which is dominated solely by the left child nodes or right child nodes is called
(a) full binary tree of height h (b) complete binary tree
(c) skewed binary tree (d) none of the above.

## The Next Eight Questions (62–69) are Based on the Tree Diagram Given below

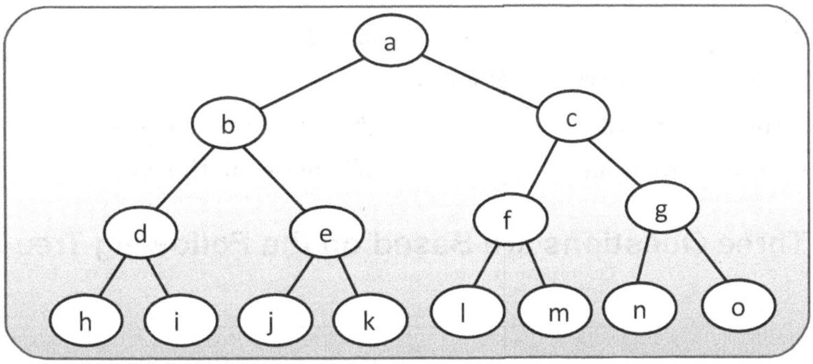


***62.** The tree is an example of
(a) complete binary tree (b) full binary tree
(c) left skewed (d) right skewed.

***63.** What is the height of the tree?
(a) 2 (b) 3
(c) 4 (d) 5.

***64.** What is the depth of the node h?
(a) Depth 1 (b) Depth 2
(c) Depth 3 (d) Depth 4.

***65.** How many external nodes are there?
(a) 4 (b) 8
(c) 7 (d) 15.

***66.** How many internal nodes are there?
(a) 1 (b) 7
(c) 8 (d) 15.

***67.** How many forests can be formed?
(a) 1 (b) 7
(c) 8 (d) 15.

***68.** Suppose the binary tree height is extended to 6, how many nodes will be there in the tree?
(a) 31 (b) 32
(c) 63 (d) 64.

*69. Suppose the binary tree is extended, how many nodes will be there in the level 5?

(a) 4 (b) 8
(c) 12 (d) 16.

70. The number of sub trees of a node is known as the

(a) terminal nodes (b) degree of the nodes
(c) non-terminal node (d) parent node.

71. The maximum number of nodes on level j of a binary tree is

(a) 2j (b) $2^{j-1}$
(c) $2^{j+1}$ (d) $2^{j-2}$.

72. In a binary tree traversal, LPR is a

(a) inorder traversal (b) postorder traversal
(c) preorder traversal (d) none of the above.

## The Next Three Questions are Based on the Following Tree Diagram

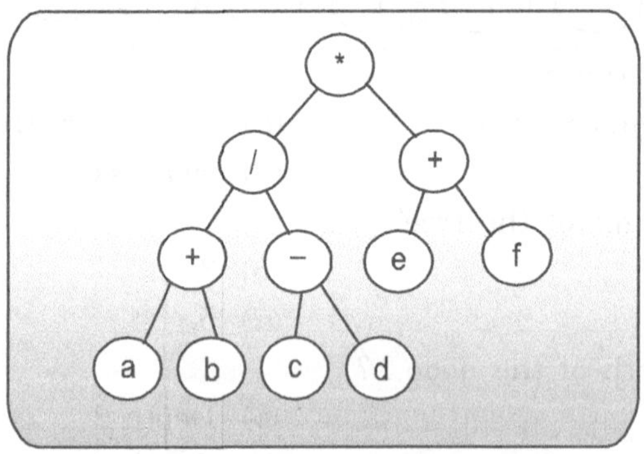


73. What will be the Preorder Traversal of expression for the above tree?

(a) + /*ab – cd + ef (b) */ + ab – cd + ef
(c) +*/ab–cd + ef (d) + /*ab + ef – cd.

74. What will be the Inorder Traversal of expression for the above tree?

(a) a + b/c – d*e + f (b) c – d/a + b*e + f
(c) e + f*a + b/c – d (d) e + f/c – d*a + b.

75. What will be the Postorder Traversal of expression for the above tree?

(a) cd – ab + /ef +* (b) ab + cd/ – ef +*
(c) ab + cd – /ef +* (d) ab + cd – *ef + /.

76. Threaded binary tree was devised by

(a) niklaus Wirth (b) trembly
(c) AJ Perlis and C Tharston (d) none of the above.

**77.** The maximum number of nodes in binary tree of height L is

(*a*) $2^L - 1$ (*b*) $2^{L-1}$

(*c*) $2^{L+1}$ (*d*) $2^L$.

**78.** Which is an example of non-linear data structures

(*a*) linked list (*b*) array

(*c*) graphs (*d*) queues.

**79.** Which of the following is not a linear sequential data structures?

(*a*) Linked list (*b*) Array

(*c*) Graphs (*d*) Queues.

**80.** Which of the following is a non-linear data structure which consists of a finite non empty set of vertices, and finite set of unordered pairs of distinct vertices called edges?

(*a*) Tree (*b*) Graph

(*c*) Linked list (*d*) Circular linked list.

***81.** The below graph is an example of

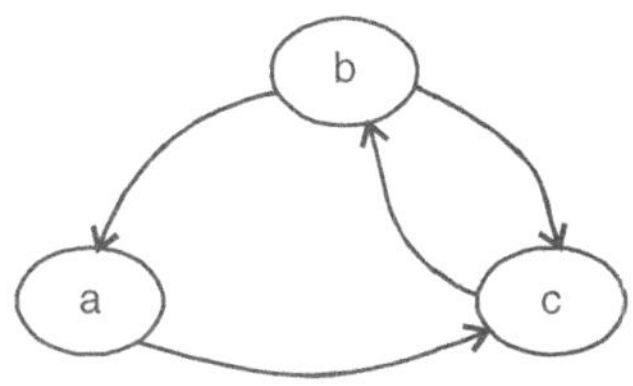


(*a*) undirected graph (*b*) a complete digraph

(*c*) not complete diagraph (*d*) none of the above.

**82.** Consider the following linked list

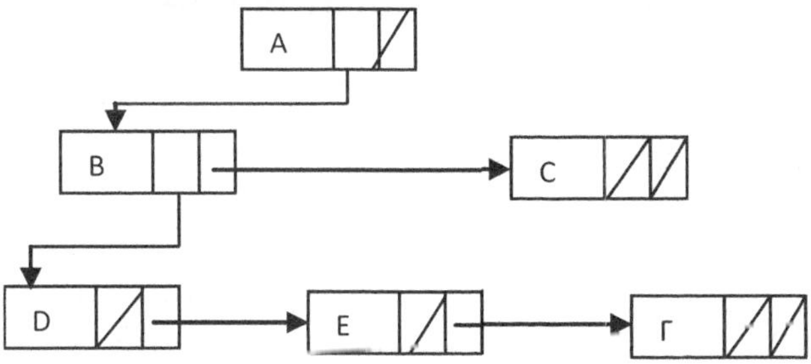


What will be the resulting tree if the above linked list is transformed into a tree?

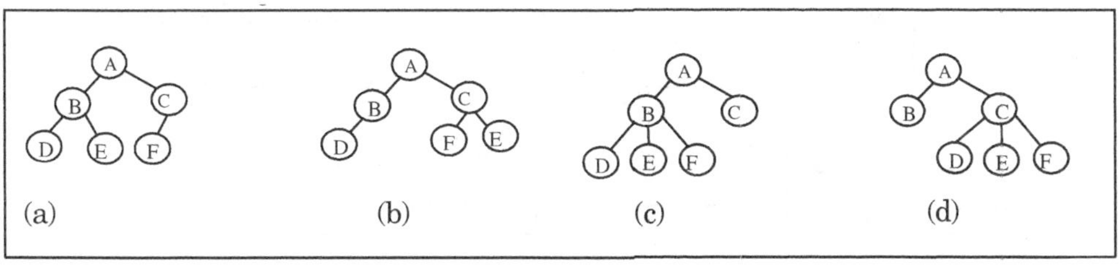

**83.** Which of the following observation with regard to connected graph is not true?

(*a*) Two vertices $V_i$, $V_j$ in a graph G are said to be connected only if there is a path in G between $V_i$ and $V_j$

(*b*) A undirected graph is said to be a connected graph if every pair of distinct vertices $V_i$, $V_j$ are connected

(*c*) In the case of an undirected graph which is not connected, the maximal connected subgroups is called as a component

(*d*) A directed graph is said to be not strongly connected if every pair of distinct vertices $V_i$, $V_j$ are connected.

Consider the following directed graph

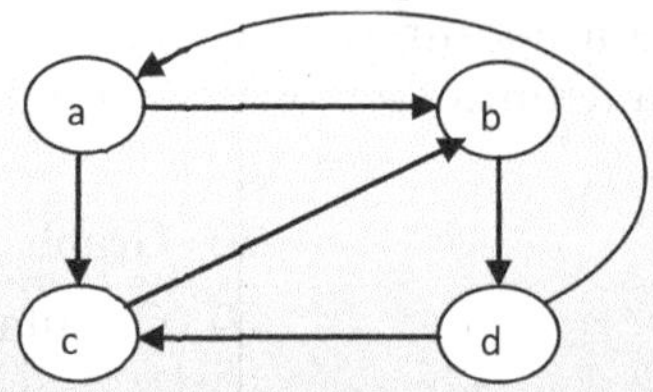


**84.** What will be the adjacency matrix of the above given graph.

(*a*)

| | a | b | c | d |
|---|---|---|---|---|
| a | F | T | F | F |
| b | F | F | F | T |
| c | T | T | F | F |
| d | T | F | T | F |

(*b*)

| | a | b | c | d |
|---|---|---|---|---|
| a | F | T | T | F |
| b | F | F | F | T |
| c | F | T | F | F |
| d | T | T | T | F |

(*c*)

| | a | b | c | d |
|---|---|---|---|---|
| a | F | T | T | F |
| b | F | F | F | T |
| c | F | T | F | F |
| d | T | F | T | F |

(*d*)

| | a | b | c | d |
|---|---|---|---|---|
| a | F | T | T | T |
| b | F | F | F | T |
| c | F | T | F | F |
| d | F | F | T | F |

## The Next Three Questions (85–87) are Based on the Graph (G) Given Below, where the Graph Node's Data Structure is as Follows

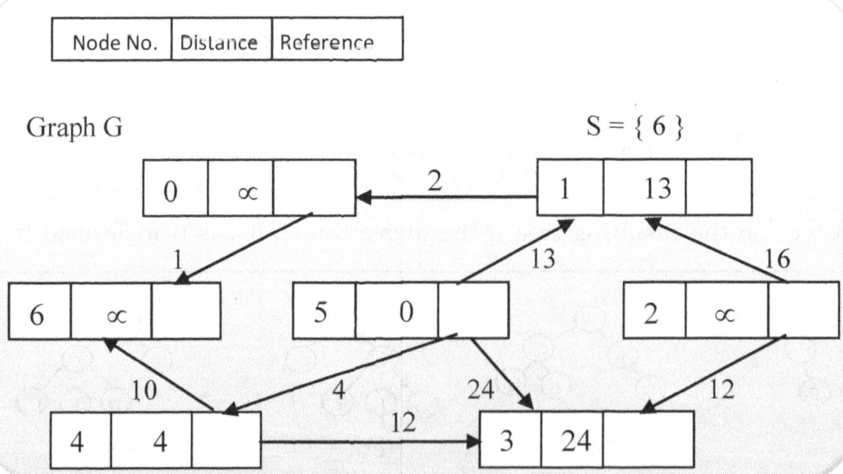

What will be the shortest distance from vertex 5 to the other vertices given below?

***85.** To the vertices 5

(*a*) 0 (*b*) 4

(*c*) 13 (*d*) 24.

***86.** To the vertices 6

(*a*) 0 (*b*) 16

(*c*) 14 (*d*) ∝.

***87.** To the vertices 3

(*a*) 12 (*b*) 13

(*c*) 16 (*d*) 24.

## The Next Three Questions (88–90) are Based on the Heap Diagram Given Below

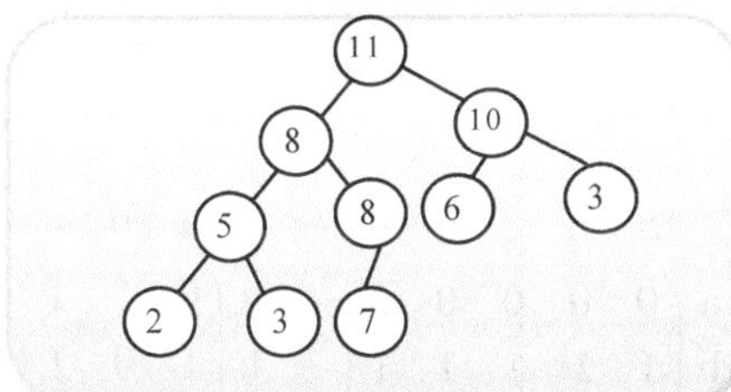

**88.** What will be the equivalent array for the above heap?

(*a*) [11 8 10 5 8 6 3 3 2] (*b*) [11 10 8 5 8 6 3 3 2]

(*c*) [11 8 10 8 5 6 3 3 2] (*d*) [11 10 8 5 8 6 3 3 2].

**89.** Suppose the value 2 is modified so that it becomes 9, what will be the heap after percolating 9 to its place?

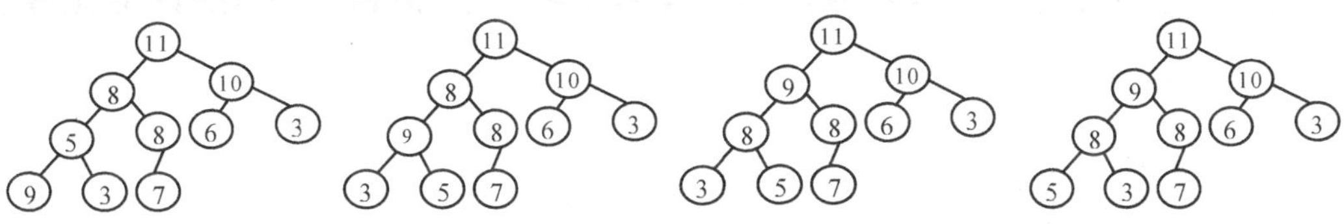

(*a*) (*b*) (*c*) (*d*)

**90.** Suppose 11 in the heap is modified to 3

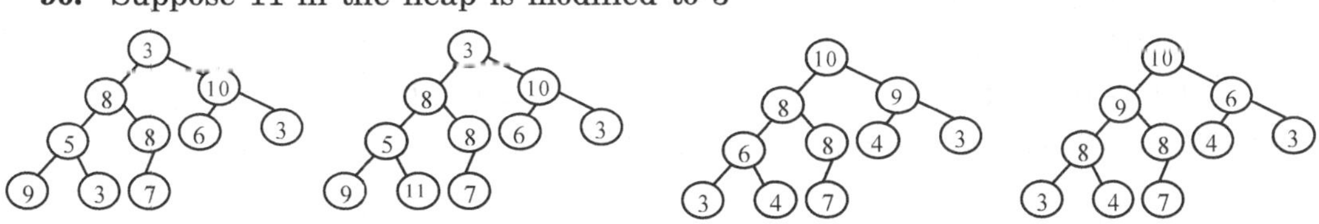

(*a*) (*b*) (*c*) (*d*)

**91.** If a Graph has a Vertex with degree zero and hence has no incident edges is called

(*a*) pendant vertex (*b*) end vertex

(*c*) isolated vertex (*d*) none of the above.

**92.** A cut set in a connected graph is also known as

(*a*) proper cut set (*b*) cocycle

(*c*) minimal cut set (*d*) all the above.

**93.** Choose the search technique that favors efficient storage and retrieval of linear data elements.

(*a*) Hash tables (*b*) Binary search tree

(*c*) AVL trees (*d*) B trees.

**94.** What will be the transitive closure of the undirected graph given below?

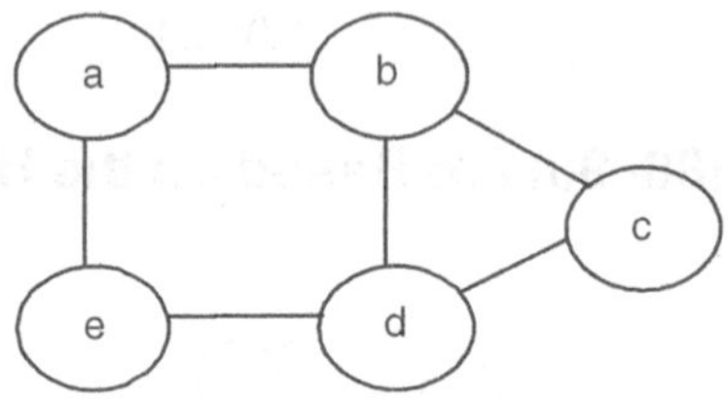


$$\begin{array}{c} \\ a\\ b\\ c\\ d\\ e \end{array}\!\!\begin{array}{c} \begin{array}{ccccc} a & b & c & d & e \end{array}\\ \begin{pmatrix} 1&1&1&1&1\\ 1&1&1&1&1\\ 1&1&1&1&1\\ 1&1&1&1&1\\ 1&1&1&1&1 \end{pmatrix} \end{array}$$

(*a*)

$$\begin{array}{c} \\ a\\ b\\ c\\ d\\ e \end{array}\!\!\begin{array}{c} \begin{array}{ccccc} a & b & c & d & e \end{array}\\ \begin{pmatrix} 0&0&0&0&0\\ 1&1&1&1&1\\ 1&1&1&1&1\\ 1&1&1&1&1\\ 1&1&1&1&1 \end{pmatrix} \end{array}$$

(*b*)

$$\begin{array}{c} \\ a\\ b\\ c\\ d\\ e \end{array}\!\!\begin{array}{c} \begin{array}{ccccc} a & b & c & d & e \end{array}\\ \begin{pmatrix} 0&1&1&1&1\\ 1&0&1&1&1\\ 1&1&0&1&1\\ 1&1&1&0&1\\ 1&1&1&1&0 \end{pmatrix} \end{array}$$

(*c*)

$$\begin{array}{c} \\ a\\ b\\ c\\ d\\ e \end{array}\!\!\begin{array}{c} \begin{array}{ccccc} a & b & c & d & e \end{array}\\ \begin{pmatrix} 0&1&0&0&1\\ 0&0&1&1&0\\ 0&1&0&1&0\\ 0&1&1&0&1\\ 1&0&0&1&0 \end{pmatrix} \end{array}$$

(*d*)

## The Next Two Questions (95–96) are Based on the Following Directed Graph

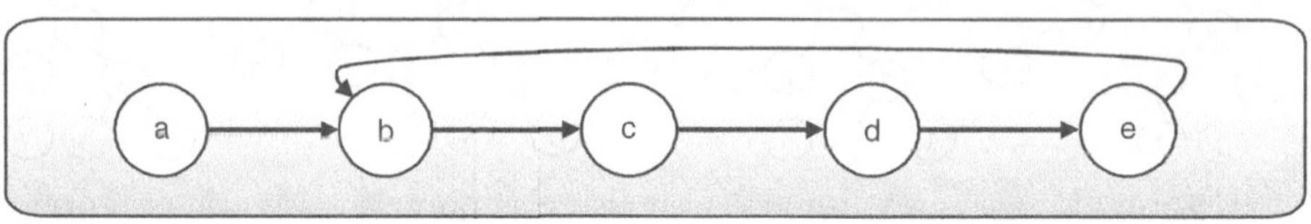


***95.** What will be the value in the second row of the transitive closure?

(*a*) {1 1 1 1 1} (*b*) {0 1 1 1 1}

(*c*) {1 0 1 1 1} (*d*) {0 0 1 1 1}.

***96.** What will be the value in the first column of the transitive closure?

(*a*) $\begin{bmatrix} 0\\0\\0\\0\\0 \end{bmatrix}$ (*b*) $\begin{bmatrix} 0\\1\\1\\1\\1 \end{bmatrix}$

(c) $\begin{bmatrix}1\\0\\1\\1\\1\end{bmatrix}$ (d) $\begin{bmatrix}1\\1\\1\\1\\1\end{bmatrix}$.

**97.** Which of the following method is not a sequential representation?

(a) Adjacency list representation (b) Adjacency matrix representations

(c) Incidence matrix representation (d) Path matrix representation.

**98.** Which of the following statement holds good for isomorphic graphs?

(a) They have the same number of vertices

(b) They have the same number of edges

(c) They have an equivalent number of vertices with a given degree

(d) All the above.

**99.** Which of the following rotations node u inserted in the right subtree of left subtree of ancestor node

(a) LL rotation (b) LR rotation

(c) RR rotation (d) RL rotation.

## The Next Three Questions (100–102) are Based on the Graph Given Below

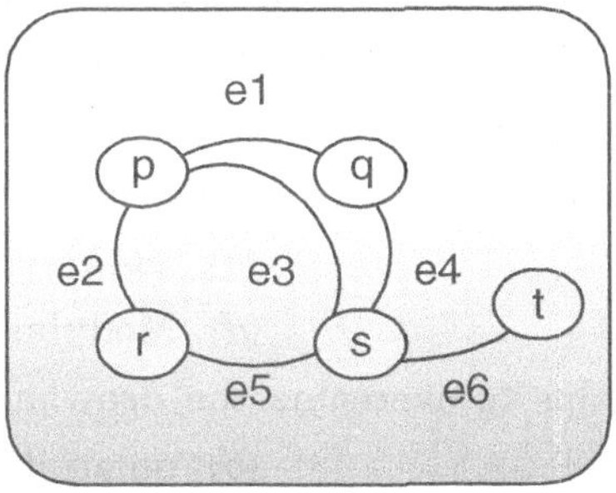


***100.** What would be the fourth row of the incidence matrix for the graph?

(a) [1 1 1 0 0 0] (b) [ 0 0 1 1 1 1]

(c) [0 0 0 1 1 1] (d) [ 1 0 0 1 0 0].

***101.** What would be the value of the third row of the circuit matrix of the graph?

(a) [1 1 1 0 0 0] (b) [ 0 0 1 1 1 1]

(c) [0 0 0 1 1 1] (d) [ 1 1 0 1 1 0].

***102.** What would be the value of the first row of the path set matrix of the graph between the vertices p and t?

(a) [1 1 1 0 0 0] (b) [ 0 0 1 1 1 1]

(c) [1 0 0 1 0 1] (d) [ 1 1 0 1 1 0].

**103.** Which of the following norms is not satisfied by a binary search tree T?

(*a*) All keys of the binary search tree must be distinct

(*b*) All keys in the left subtree of T are greater than the root element

(*c*) All keys in the right subtree of T are greater than the root element

(*d*) The left and right subtree of T are also binary search trees.

**104.** Which of the following deteriorates the performance of a binary search tree T with *n* nodes?

(*a*) When the height of T becomes n

(*b*) When there is large number of deletions to T

(*c*) The number of external nodes becomes (n+1)

(*d*) When the height of T becomes $\log_2$ n.

**105.** Choose the incorrect answer

(*a*) a red-black tree is an extended binary search tree

(*b*) the root node and the external nodes are always red nodes

(*c*) no two red nodes can occur consecutively on the paths from the root node to an external node

(*d*) the number of black nodes on path from the root to an external node must be the same for all external nodes.

**106.** Which of the following property that will not satisfy Splay tree?

(*a*) Splay trees are binary search tree

(*b*) Splay trees like AVL trees are always remain height balanced

(*c*) Splay trees move frequently accessed nodes towards the root

(*d*) The time complexity is O(n).

**107.** Which one of the following is not a method of obtaining hash functions?

(*a*) folding (*b*) ISAM

(*c*) Truncation (*d*) Modular Arithmetic.

**108.** The technique that helps to overcome the drawbacks of linear probing is

(*a*) rehashing (*b*) quadratic

(*c*) random probing (*d*) all the above.

**109.** Hash tables are ideal data structure for

(*a*) dictionaries (*b*) graphs

(*c*) B tree (*d*) binary search tree.

**110.** A linked implementation of a hash table is known as

(*a*) Chaining (*b*) open hashing

(*c*) separate chaining (*d*) all the above.

**111.** The secondary storage devices that stores data in serial order is called

(*a*) random access storage device (*b*) sequential storage devices

(*c*) DASD (*d*) none of the above.

**112.** Choose the storage which is volatile

(*a*) magnetic tape (*b*) magnetic drum

(*c*) RAM (*d*) floppies.

**113.** Which is a sequential access storage device?

(*a*) Magnetic tape (*b*) Magnetic drum

(*c*) Magnetic disk (*d*) Floppies.

**114.** Which of the following statement is more suitable for file?

(*a*) It is the logical collection of fields

(*b*) It is the logical collection of information

(*c*) It is the logical collection of records

(*d*) It is the logical collection of data base.

**115.** What would be the index of the hash table for a six digit numerical key 719532 using flooding method?

(*a*) 98 (*b*) 96

(*c*) 97 (*d*) 95.

**116.** Which is **NOT** a indexing technique?

(*a*) Primary (*b*) Multilevel

(*c*) Secondary (*d*) Super.

**117.** Choose the technique which is suitable for list of data elements represented using non-linear structures?

(*a*) Interpolation search (*b*) Depth-first search

(*c*) Fibonacci search (*d*) Binary search.

**118.** The worst case complexity in terms of comparisons for finding a specific key in the list L in transpose sequential search is

(*a*) O(1) (*b*) O(n)

(*c*) O(log n) (*d*) none of the above.

**119.** Which of the search technique applicable on files those are too large to be accommodated in the internal memory of the computer?

(*a*) ISAM (*b*) Graph search

(*c*) Tree (*d*) Binary search.

**120.** The worst case the number of comparisons needed to search for a key in a binary search is

(*a*) $O(\log_2 \log_2 n)$ (*b*) $O(\log_2 n)$

(*c*) O(n) (*d*) O(1).

**121.** A sorting technique is said to be stable if

(*a*) the keys that are equal return their relative orders of occurrence even after sorting

(*b*) the keys that are unequal, return their relative orders of occurrence even after sorting (*c*) the keys that are equal, do not return their relative orders of occurrence even after sorting

(*d*) the keys that are equal, return their relative orders of occurrence even before sorting.

**122.** The worst case time complexity of quick sort is

(*a*) O(n) (*b*) O(1)

(*c*) $O(n^2)$ (*d*) $O(n^3)$.

**123.** Which of the sorting technique belongs to family of sorting by exchange?

(*a*) Quick (*b*) Heap

(*c*) Shell (*d*) Radix.

**124.** Initially a queue has the element in the following order *k,l,m,n* (where *k* is in the front). To get the configuration *n,m,l,k*, which of the following has to be done?

(*a*) 3 deletion and 4 addition (*b*) 4 deletion and 4 addition

(*c*) 3 deletion and 3 addition (*d*) 4 deletion and 3 addition.

**125.** Which of the sorting technique belongs to family of sorting by selection?

(*a*) Quick (*b*) Heap

(*c*) Shell (*d*) Radix.

**126.** The depth-first order is same as

(*a*) breadth-first order (*b*) preorder

(*c*) linear order (*d*) post order.

**127.** Which of the sort procedure is built as the design principle of divide and conquer?

(*a*) Recursive merge sort (*b*) Selection sort

(*c*) Quick sort (*d*) Insertion sort.

**128.** To sort on-line telephone directory, which of the following sort technique is more suitable?

(*a*) Bubble sort (*b*) Quick sort

(*c*) Radix sort (*d*) Polyphase merge sort.

**129.** The sorted batches of records are referred as

(*a*) runs (*b*) merge

(*c*) source reel (*d*) platters.

### The Next Four Questions (130–133) are Based the Following Set of Integers {43, 24, 75, 12, 66, 59, 95, 37, 99, 88}

***130.** If one uses selection sort algorithm, what would be the intermediate result at Pass1?

(*a*) {12, 24, 43, 59, 66, 37, 75, 88, 95, 99}

(*b*) {24, 43, 12, 66, 59, 75, 37, 95, 88, 99}

(*c*) {12, 24, 43, 59, 37, 66, 75, 88, 95, 99}

(*d*) {12, 24, 75, 43, 66, 59, 95, 37, 99, 88}.

***131.** If one uses selection sort algorithm to sort the above set of integers, how many pass is required to completely sort the file?

(*a*) 7 (*b*) 9

(*c*) 11 (*d*) 12.

***132.** If one uses Bubble sort algorithm, what would be the intermediate result at Pass 2?

(*a*) {24, 12, 43, 59, 66,37, 75, 88, 95, 99}

(*b*) {24, 43, 12, 66, 59, 75, 37, 95, 88, 99}

(*c*) {12, 24, 43, 59, 37, 66, 75, 88, 95, 99}

(*d*) {12, 24, 43, 37, 59,66, 75, 88, 95, 99}.

***133.** If one uses selection bubble algorithm to sort the above set of integers, how many pass is required to completely sort the file?

(*a*) 4 (*b*) 6

(*c*) 8 (*d*) 10.

**134.** The method of repeated partitioning until every pivot element settles down to its appropriate position thereby sorting the list is

(*a*) recursive merge sort (*b*) selection sort

(*c*) quick sort (*d*) insertion sort.

**135.** Which of the following is an unstable sort?

(*a*) Quick sort (*b*) Bubble sort

(*c*) Insertion sort (*d*) Merge sort.

**136.** Which of the following statement does not hold good for quick sort?

(*a*) It was invented by C.A.R. Hoare

(*b*) It is based on the principle of insertion

(*c*) It is better sorting technique compared to bubble sort

(*d*) It is an internal sorting technique.

**137.** In a magnetic tape, IBG refers to

(*a*) International Block Group (*b*) Insert Block Gap

(*c*) Inter Block Gap (*d*) Inter Block Group.

**138.** In a magnetic tape the smallest addressable segment of a track is known as

(*a*) cylinder (*b*) sectors

(*c*) track index (*d*) cylinder index.

**139.** Which of the following is a complete binary tree which serves to obtain the smallest key from a set of keys?

(*a*) Selection tree (*b*) B tree

(*c*) Binary tree (*d*) None of the above.

**140.** The technique that uses (k+1) tapes to perform the *k-way* merge is

(*a*) bubble sort (*b*) quick sort

(*c*) radix sort (*d*) polyphase merge sort.

## The Next Two Questions (141–142) are Based on the Unordered List L and the Information Followed

**L = { 35, 21, 90, 49, 18, 95, 60, 73}. Assume that the search for the elements in the order of their appearance 95, 60, 49 is done using Transpose sequential search technique.**

***141.** What would be the final list after all searches?

(*a*) {35, 21, 90, 49, 18, 95, 60, 73} (*b*) {35, 21, 90, 49, 18, 95, 60, 73}

(*c*) {35, 21, 49, 90, 95, 60, 18, 73} (*d*) {35, 21, 90, 49, 18, 95, 60, 73}.

***142.** What is the total number of element comparison made during the entire search?

(*a*) 15 (*b*) 17

(*c*) 19 (*d*) 21.

**143.** Latency time is

(*a*) the time taken for a right sector to appear under the read/write head

(*b*) time taken for a transfer of data to and from the disk

(*c*) the time taken to position the read/write head on the cylinder

(*d*) the time taken to write data in a disk.

**144.** Transfer time is

(*a*) the time taken for a right sector to appear under the read/write head

(*b*) time taken for a transfer of data to and from the disk

(*c*) the time taken to position the read/write head on the cylinder

(*d*) the time taken to rotate the disk.

**145.** Seek time is

(*a*) the time taken for a right sector to appear under the read/write head

(*b*) time taken for a transfer of data to and from the disk

(*c*) the time taken to position the read/write head on the cylinder

(*d*) time taken to store data on disk.

**146.** Which one of the following systems the final outcome can be predicted?

(*a*) Continuous system (*b*) Discrete systems

(*c*) Deterministic system (*d*) Stochastic system.

**147.** A node, in the longest path in both of its subtree is equal then it is called as

(*a*) balanced node (*b*) left heavy

(*c*) right heavy (*d*) none of the above.

**148.** Which of the following algorithm design method that can be used when the solution to a problem can be viewed as the result of a sequence of decisions?

(*a*) Static Programming (*b*) dynamic Programming

(*c*) Backtracking (*d*) None of the above.

**149.** Which method searches a state space tree using a search mechanism in which the children of the E-node are generated before another node becomes the E-node?

(*a*) Branch-bound method (*b*) Bound method

(*c*) Branch method (*d*) Breadth-first method.

**150.** The algorithm with the property that the result of every operation is uniquely defined are termed as

(*a*) nondeterministic algorithm (*b*) decision algorithm

(*c*) deterministic algorithm (*d*) approximation algorithm.

**151.** A directed Hamiltonian cycle in a directed graph G=(V,E) is a directed cycle of length

(*a*) $n = |V|$ (*b*) $n = |V| + 1$

(*c*) (*b* $n = |V| + 2$ (*d*) $n = |V| + 3$.

**152.** Which of the following technique combines radix search trees and hashing?

(*a*) Dynamic hashing (*b*) Modified hashing

(*c*) Extendible hashing (*d*) Spiral hashing.

**153.** Virtual hashing technique was proposed by

(*a*) litwin (*b*) larson

(*c*) fagin (*d*) scholl.

**154.** Which one of the following is not a hash technique?

(*a*) Linear hashing (*b*) Virtual hashing

(*c*) Dynamic hashing (*d*) Parallel hashing.

**155.** Which one is not a distribution dependent hashing function?

(*a*) Digit analysis

(*b*) Single frequency distribution function

(*c*) Piece-wise linear functions

(*d*) Multiple frequency distribution function.

**156.** If the edges or vertices are assigned sommw data it is called as

(*a*) empty graph (*b*) multigraph

(*c*) trivial graph (*d*) labled graph.

## ANSWERS

| | | | | | | | |
|---|---|---|---|---|---|---|---|
| **1.** (*a*) | **2.** (*b*) | **3.** (*a*) | **4.** (*c*) | **5.** (*c*) | **6.** (*b*) | **7.** (*a*) | **8.** (*a*) |
| **9.** (*d*) | **10.** (*c*) | **11.** (*b*) | **12.** (*c*) | **13.** (*a*) | **14.** (*b*) | **15.** (*a*) | **16.** (*c*) |
| **17.** (*b*) | **18.** (*c*) | **19.** (*a*) | **20.** (*b*) | **21.** (*d*) | **22.** (*c*) | **23.** (*a*) | **24.** (*b*) |
| **25.** (*a*) | **26.** (*a*) | **27.** (*b*) | **28.** (*a*) | **29.** (*c*) | **30.** (*b*) | **31.** (*d*) | **32.** (*c*) |
| **33.** (*d*) | **34.** (*d*) | **35.** (*d*) | **36.** (*a*) | **37.** (*c*) | **38.** (*d*) | **39.** (*d*) | **40.** (*a*) |
| **41.** (*c*) | **42.** (*a*) | **43.** (*d*) | **44.** (*d*) | **45.** (*c*) | **46.** (*d*) | **47.** (*c*) | **48.** (*c*) |
| **49.** (*d*) | **50.** (*a*) | **51.** (*c*) | **52.** (*b*) | **53.** (*a*) | **54.** (*d*) | **55.** (*d*) | **56.** (*c*) |
| **57.** (*a*) | **58.** (*a*) | **59.** (*d*) | **60.** (*c*) | **61.** (*c*) | **62.** (*b*) | **63.** (*c*) | **64.** (*c*) |
| **65.** (*b*) | **66.** (*b*) | **67.** (*b*) | **68.** (*c*) | **69.** (*d*) | **70.** (*b*) | **71.** (*b*) | **72.** (*a*) |
| **73.** (*b*) | **74.** (*a*) | **75.** (*c*) | **76.** (*c*) | **77.** (*a*) | **78.** (*c*) | **79.** (*a*) | **80.** (*c*) |
| **81.** (*c*) | **82.** (*c*) | **83.** (*d*) | **84.** (*c*) | **85.** (*a*) | **86.** (*c*) | **87.** (*c*) | **88.** (*a*) |
| **89.** (*c*) | **90.** (*d*) | **91.** (*c*) | **92.** (*d*) | **93.** (*a*) | **94.** (*d*) | **95.** (*b*) | **96.** (*a*) |
| **97.** (*a*) | **98.** (*d*) | **99.** (*b*) | **100.** (*b*) | **101.** (*d*) | **102.** (*c*) | **103.** (*b*) | **104.** (*a*) |
| **105.** (*b*) | **106.** (*b*) | **107.** (*b*) | **108.** (*d*) | **109.** (*a*) | **110.** (*d*) | **111.** (*b*) | **112.** (*c*) |
| **113.** (*a*) | **114.** (*c*) | **115.** (*a*) | **116.** (*d*) | **117.** (*b*) | **118.** (*b*) | **119.** (*a*) | **120.** (*b*) |
| **121.** (*a*) | **122.** (*c*) | **123.** (*a*) | **124.** (*c*) | **125.** (*b*) | **126.** (*b*) | **127.** (*a*) | **128.** (*d*) |
| **129.** (*a*) | **130.** (*d*) | **131.** (*b*) | **132.** (*a*) | **133.** (*b*) | **134.** (*c*) | **135.** (*a*) | **136.** (*b*) |
| **137.** (*c*) | **138.** (*b*) | **139.** (*a*) | **140.** (*d*) | **141.** (*c*) | **142.** (*b*) | **143.** (*a*) | **144.** (*b*) |
| **145.** (*c*) | **146.** (*c*) | **147.** (*c*) | **148.** (*a*) | **149.** (*b*) | **150.** (*a*) | **151.** (*c*) | **152.** (*a*) |
| **153.** (*c*) | **154.** (*a*) | **155.** (*d*) | **156.** (*d*) | | | | |

## EXPLANATIONS

**30.** Various stages of Stack for the operations PUSH(S, 17), PUSH (S, 3), POP(S)

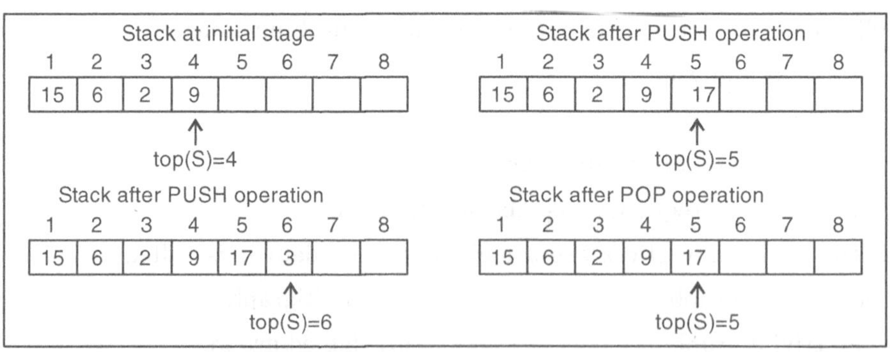


After the operation PUSH(S, 17), PUSH (S, 3), POP(S), top will point to 5

**31.** Stages of Stack for the operations POP(S), POP(S), POP(S), POP(S), PUSH (S, 5), POP(S), POP(S).

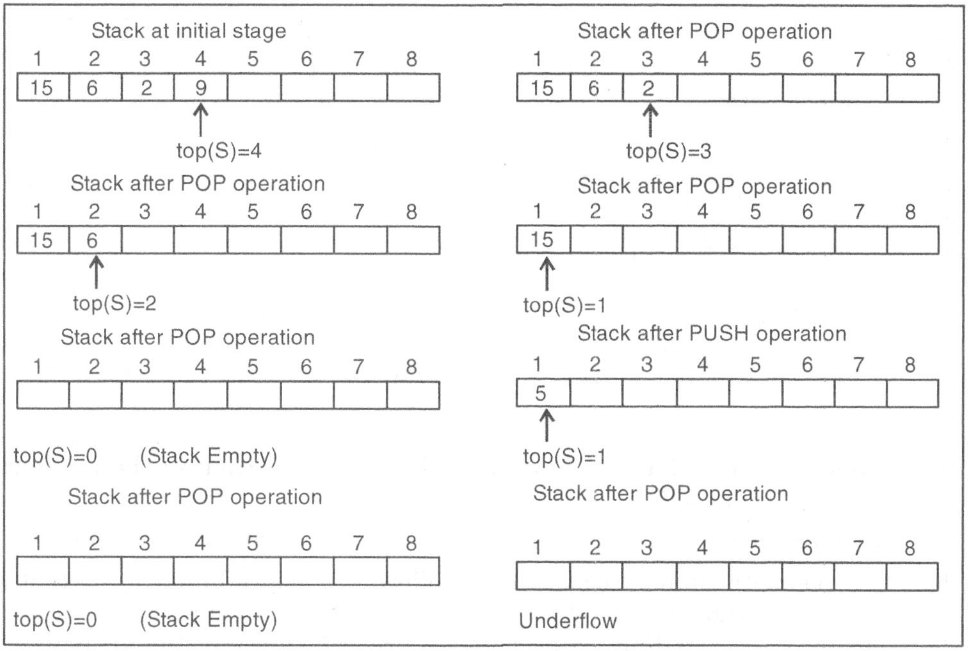


**32.** When a empty stack is popped, normally referred as underflow, which is an error.

**37.** Various stages of Queue for the operations ENQUEUE (Q,17), ENQUEUE (Q,17), ENQUEUE (Q,17)

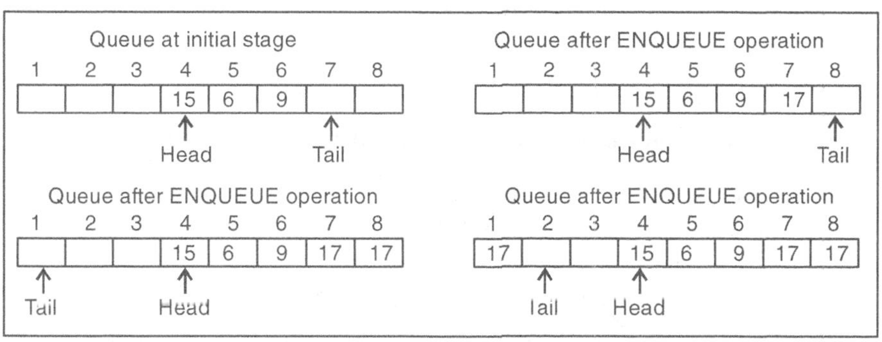


**38.** Various stages of Queue.

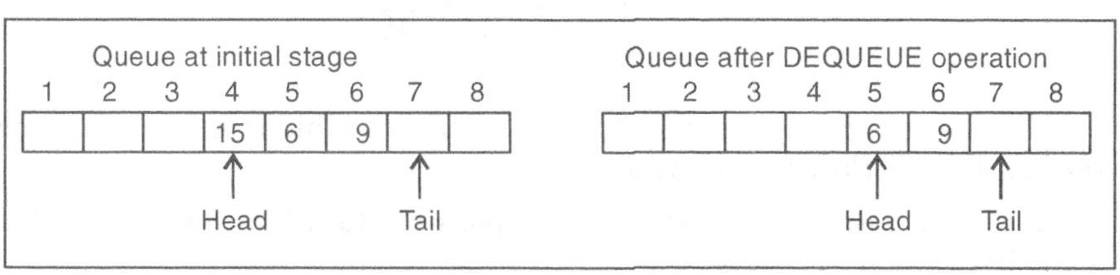

**43.** Various stages of Circular Queue.

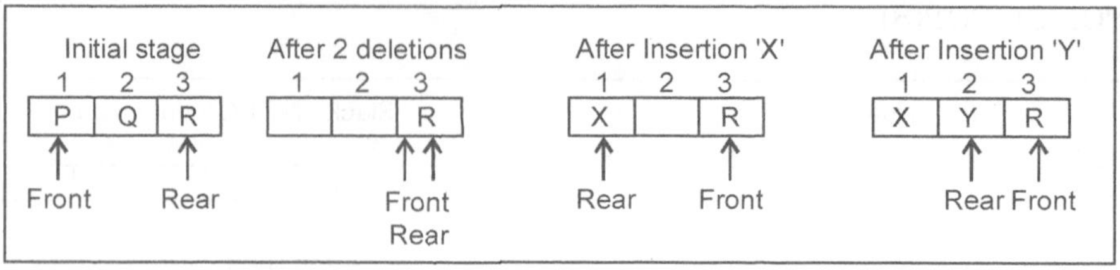


**45.**

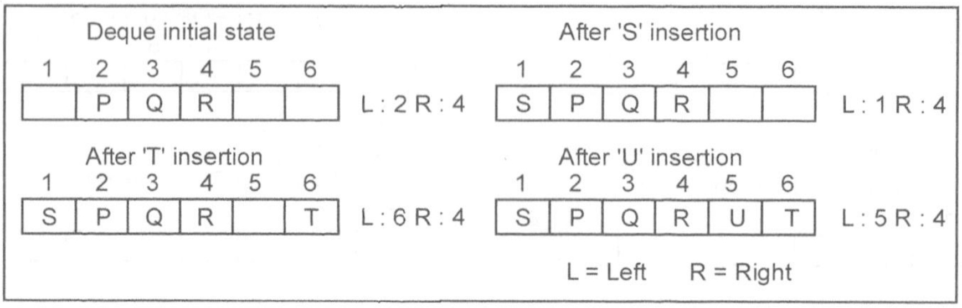


**46.** From the above diagram it is clear that after insertion of the elements S, T, U Left = 5, Right = 5.

**47.** Insertion of new item in deque is not possible when Left = Right + 1.

**56.** In a complete binary tree the nodes follow a sequential numbering that increment from left-to-right and top-to-bottom fashion. The missing nodes in the binary tree and the corresponding array locations are left empty in the array.

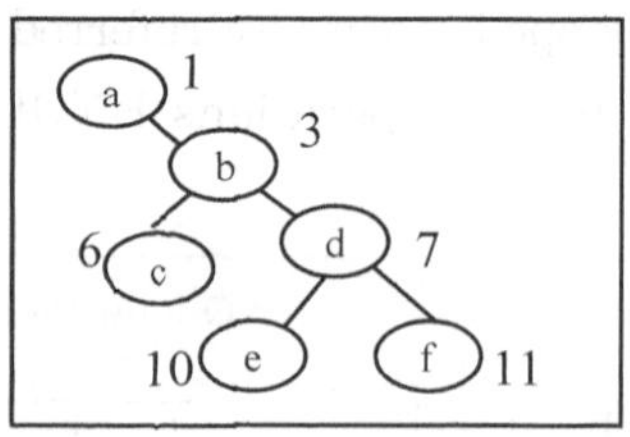


**Answers based on the following tree diagram**

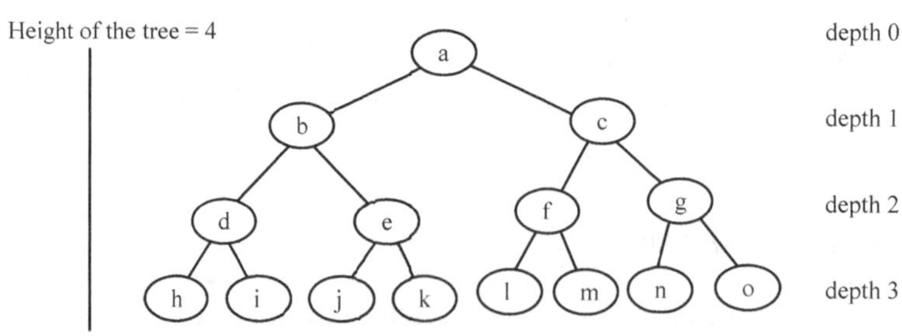


**62.** Since the binary tree of height 4 has all its permissible maximum number of nodes intact so it is a Full binary tree.

**63.** The maximum number of nodes that is possible to a leaf node from the root node is called height of the tree.

**64.** The depth of node is the number of edges in the longest path from the root to the node questions. The depth of node h is 3

**65.** The nodes with no children are an external node or leaf. The nodes in depth 3 has no children. Therefore, the tree has 8 external nodes.

**66.** The non-leaf nodes are internal nodes. Therefore, the tree contains 7 internal nodes.

**67.** The number of sub tree (forest) that can be formed are 7.

**68.** The maximum number of nodes in a binary tree of height $h$ is $2^h - 1$. Suppose the tree is extended to an height 6 then the number of nodes in the tree = $2^6 - 1 = 64 - 1 = 63$.

**69.** The maximum number of nodes on a level of a binary tree is given by $2^{i-1}$. Therefore, the number of node at level 5 = $2^{5-1} = 2^4 = 16$

**81.** A graph with $n(n - 1)$ edges is said to be a complete diagraph. Whereas the graph has only four edges, therefore it is not a complete digraph.

**85.** The distance from a node to itself is always zero

**86.** There are two paths from node 5 to node 6

(*i*) Node 5 → Node 1 → Node 0 → Node 6 (13+2+1=16)

(*ii*) Node 5 → Node 4 → Node 6 (4+10 = 14)

**87.** There are two paths from Node 5 to Node 3

(*i*) Node 5 directly to Node 3 (24)

(*ii*) Node 5 → Node 4 → Node 3 (4+12=16)

**95&96.** The transitive closure for the graph is

$$\begin{array}{c} \\ a \\ b \\ c \\ d \end{array} \begin{array}{c} \begin{matrix} a & b & c & d & e \end{matrix} \\ \begin{bmatrix} 0 & 1 & 0 & 0 & 0 \\ 0 & 1 & 1 & 1 & 1 \\ 0 & 1 & 1 & 1 & 1 \\ 0 & 1 & 1 & 1 & 1 \end{bmatrix} \end{array}$$

**100.** The incidence matrix representation of the graph is

$$\begin{array}{c} \\ p \\ q \\ r \\ s \\ t \end{array} \begin{array}{c} \begin{matrix} e1 & e2 & e3 & e4 & e5 & e6 \end{matrix} \\ \begin{bmatrix} 1 & 1 & 1 & 0 & 0 & 0 \\ 1 & 0 & 0 & 1 & 0 & 0 \\ 0 & 1 & 0 & 0 & 1 & 0 \\ 0 & 0 & 1 & 1 & 1 & 1 \\ 0 & 0 & 0 & 0 & 0 & 1 \end{bmatrix} \end{array}$$

**101.** Circuit 1: $e2$, $e3$, $e5$ Circuit 2 : $e1$, $e3$, $e4$ Circuit 3: $e1$, $e2$, $e5$, $e4$

$$\begin{array}{c} \\ 1 \\ 2 \\ 3 \end{array} \begin{array}{c} \begin{matrix} e1 & e2 & e3 & e4 & e5 & e6 \end{matrix} \\ \begin{bmatrix} 0 & 1 & 1 & 0 & 1 & 0 \\ 1 & 0 & 1 & 1 & 0 & 0 \\ 1 & 1 & 0 & 1 & 1 & 0 \end{bmatrix} \end{array}$$

**102.** Paths between vertices p and t are 1: { e1, e4, e6} 2: {e2, e5, e6} 3: {e3, e6}

$$P(p,t) = \begin{array}{c} \\ 1 \\ 2 \\ 3 \end{array} \begin{array}{c} e1\ e2\ e3\ e4\ e5\ e6 \\ \begin{bmatrix} 1 & 0 & 0 & 1 & 0 & 1 \\ 0 & 1 & 0 & 0 & 1 & 1 \\ 0 & 0 & 1 & 0 & 0 & 1 \end{bmatrix} \end{array}$$

**130 and 131.** Trace of selection sort

| | Unsorted | Pass Number | | | | | | | | |
|---|---|---|---|---|---|---|---|---|---|---|
| | | 1 | 2 | 3 | 4 | 5 | 6 | 7 | 8 | 9 |
| 1 | 43 | 12 | 12 | 12 | 12 | 12 | 12 | 12 | 12 | 12 |
| 2 | 24 | 24 | 24 | 24 | 24 | 24 | 24 | 24 | 24 | 24 |
| 3 | 75 | 75 | 75 | 37 | 37 | 37 | 37 | 37 | 37 | 37 |
| 4 | 12 | 43 | 43 | 43 | 43 | 43 | 43 | 43 | 43 | 43 |
| 5 | 66 | 66 | 66 | 66 | 66 | 59 | 59 | 59 | 59 | 59 |
| 6 | 59 | 59 | 59 | 59 | 59 | 66 | 66 | 66 | 66 | 66 |
| 7 | 95 | 95 | 95 | 95 | 95 | 95 | 95 | 75 | 75 | 75 |
| 8 | 37 | 37 | 37 | 75 | 75 | 75 | 75 | 95 | 88 | 88 |
| 9 | 99 | 99 | 99 | 99 | 99 | 99 | 99 | 99 | 99 | 95 |
| 10 | 88 | 88 | 88 | 88 | 88 | 88 | 88 | 88 | 95 | 99 |

**132 and 133.** Trace of Bubble sort

| | Unsorted | Pass Number | | | | | |
|---|---|---|---|---|---|---|---|
| | | 1 | 2 | 3 | 4 | 5 | 6 |
| 1 | 43 | 24 | 24 | 12 | 12 | 12 | 12 |
| 2 | 24 | 43 | 12 | 24 | 24 | 24 | 24 |
| 3 | 75 | 12 | 43 | 43 | 43 | 37 | 37 |
| 4 | 12 | 66 | 59 | 59 | 37 | 43 | 43 |
| 5 | 66 | 59 | 66 | 37 | 59 | 59 | 59 |
| 6 | 59 | 75 | 37 | 66 | 66 | 66 | 66 |
| 7 | 95 | 37 | 75 | 75 | 75 | 75 | 75 |
| 8 | 37 | 95 | 88 | 88 | 88 | 88 | 88 |
| 9 | 99 | 88 | 95 | 95 | 95 | 95 | 95 |
| 10 | 88 | 99 | 99 | 99 | 99 | 99 | 99 |

**141.** Searching for elements 95, 60 and 49 in the list L = { 35, 21, 90, 49, 18, 95, 60, 73}.

After searching for 95 L={ 35, 21, 90, 49, 95, 18, 60, 73} Number of search : 06

After searching for 60 L={ 35, 21, 90, 49, 18, 60, 95, 73} Number of search : 07

After searching for 49 L={ 35, 21, 49, 90, 18, 60, 95, 73} Number of search : 04

**142.** The total number of search = 6 + 7 + 4 = 17

CHAPTER 4

# SOFTWARE ENGINEERING

**1.** Which of the following is not a characteristic of software?

(*a*) Software doesn't *wear out* (*b*) Software is flexible

(*c*) Software is manufactured (*d*) Most software is custom built.

**2.** Who develop software products?

(*a*) Programmers (*b*) Software engineers

(*c*) Data Base Administrator (*d*) Customer.

**3.** What could be the type of software for a Rocket Launching System?

(*a*) Business software (*b*) Real Time software

(*c*) Scientific software (*d*) Embedded software.

**4.** What could be the type of software for braking system?

(*a*) Business software (*b*) System software

(*c*) Scientific software (*d*) Embedded software.

**5.** Choose the maintenance which results in modification to the software to accommodate changes to its external environment?

(*a*) Corrective maintenance (*b*) Adaptive maintenance

(*c*) Perfective maintenance (*d*) Preventive maintenance.

**6.** Which of the following is not true with regard to the spiral model of software development?

(*a*) It is an evolutionary model

(*b*) Spiral model is divided into number of frameworks

(*c*) It uses prototyping

(*d*) has strict standards for software development.

**7.** Which one of the following is not correct with regard to Waterfall model?

(*a*) It is linear model

(*b*) It is systematic and sequential

(*c*) There is risk analysis

(*d*) It involves heavy documentation.

**8.** Choose the manual which provides information about system scope, design, architecture, system flow, technology details and the variety of interfaces used in the system.

(*a*) Operations manual (*b*) System maintenance Model

(*c*) User manual (*d*) System Manual.

***9.** A software firm called Banthumy involves in a software project which has 6000 SLOC and requires 600 working days to implement. What would be the productivity of software project?

(*a*) 8 SLOC/days (*b*) 10 SLOC/days

(*c*) 12 SLOC/days (*d*) Insufficient data.

**10.** Which of the following is true with regard to RAD model?

(*a*) It is non-linear sequential software development process model

(*b*) Product can be developed within a short period of time

(*c*) RAD is appropriate when technical risks are high

(*d*) RAD emphasizes the development of non-reusable program model.

**11.** Chose the statement, which does not hold good for prototype?

(*a*) A prototype is a toy implementation of the system

(*b*) It exhibits unlimited functional capabilities compared to actual software

(*c*) It is the crude version of the actual system

(*d*) It is used when the technical solutions are unclear to the development team.

**12.** Consider the following flowchart.

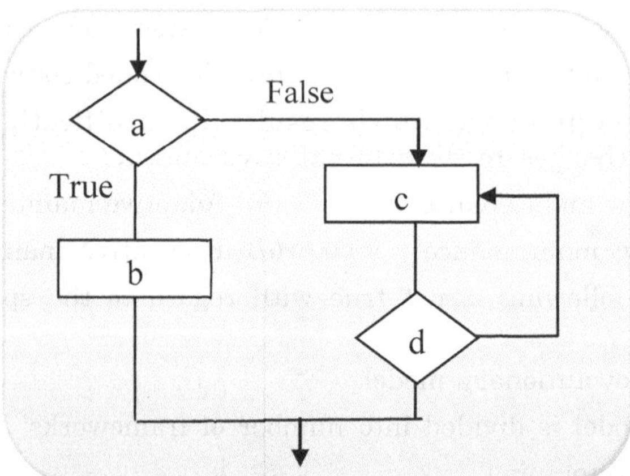


Choose the correct code fragment which shows its logic.

(*a*) if *a* then *b* else repeat *c* until *d*

(*b*) if *a* then repeat *c* until *d* else *b*

(*c*) if *a* then repeat *c* until *d* else *b*

(*d*) if *a* then *b* else while *d* do *c*.

**13.** Which of the following model is proposed when users, customers and stakeholders are not sure about their requirement.

(*a*) Linear Sequential Model

(*b*) The Prototype Model

(*c*) The Rapid Application Development Model

(*d*) The Incremental Model.

***14.** What will be the extendibility of the software project which consist 4750 SLOC and it took 380 work days to implement and some problem increases 100 SLOC and which took 25 work days to implement this?

(*a*) 25 % (*b*) 32 %

(*c*) 38 0 % (*d*) 44 %.

**15.** Which of the following system is self contained and self reliant, and not influenced by the external environment?

(*a*) Deterministic System (*b*) Probabilistic System

(*c*) Open System (*d*) Closed System.

**16.** Software reliability is defined as

(*a*) the probability of failure-free operation of a computer program in a specified environment for a specified time

(*b*) the probability of failure-free operation of a computer program in any environment for a unlimited period

(*c*) a software program with minimum errors

(*d*) the ability to deliver software on time with good quality.

**17.** Which of the following testing technique is done at the customer site, with user actually using the system?

(*a*) Application test (*b*) Unit test

(*c*) Beta testing (*d*) Alpha testing.

***18.** An organisation has 6 developers and the estimated time of software development is 30 months and the time given by the customer is 3 months. The available time per person is 0.9 and the effective time is 0.8. How many persons required for completing the project in time?

(*a*) 5 persons (*b*) 6 persons

(*c*) 7 persons (*d*) 8 pesons.

**19.** Which of the following risk arises on account of operational, organisational and contractual software development factors?

(*a*) Software Process Risks (*b*) Software Project Risks

(*c*) Software Product Risks (*d*) None of the above.

**20.** Which step in Risk Management helps to meet the challenges of risk occurrence in effective implementation of specific of Risk management?

(*a*) Risk Identification (*b*) Risk Analysis

(*c*) Risk Assessment (*d*) Risk Mitigation.

**21.** Which of the following is a predictable risk in software development?

(*a*) People (*b*) Technology

(*c*) Business (*d*) Obsolescence.

**22.** Which of the following testing technique ensures that the corrective steps taken to resolve problem that occur due to the error and also ensures that the errors are not created elsewhere?

(*a*) Stress test (*b*) Regression testing

(*c*) System testing (*d*) Alpha testing.

**23.** Which of the following strategy is chosen to reduce the risk by seeking more information about it for better evaluation and to deal with it effectively?

(*a*) Risk Avoidance (*b*) Risk Protection

(*c*) Risk Research (*d*) Risk Transfer.

**24.** The acronym of CASE is

(*a*) Computer Aided Software Engineering

(*b*) Continuously Aimed Software Engineering

(*c*) Computer Aided Structured Engineering

(*d*) None of the above.

***25.** Mean Repair Time (MRT) is directly relevant to which one of the following?

(*a*) System reliability (*b*) Availability

(*c*) System reliability (*d*) Feed back.

***26.** A system is made up of two components. The probability of each component operating correctly is 0.7 and 0.8. What will be the probability that the system will operate correctly?

(*a*) .50 (*b*) 0.72

(*c*) 0.70 (*d*) 0.80.

**27.** The Arithmetic Logic Unit (ALU) and Control Unit are two major components of Central Processing Unit (CPU). Intel and Motorola are two types of Processors which are widely used in computers. Generally, the user of the computer may be an expert or novices. Consider the following design classes.

(*i*) CPU and Motorola (*ii*) User and Computer (*iii*) CPU and Control Unit

The correct relationship between the above classes is

(*a*) inheritance, association, inheritance

(*b*) aggregation, association, inheritance

(*c*) inheritance, aggregation, association

(*d*) inheritance, association, aggregation.

**28.** Process definition risk is associated with

(*a*) the overall size of the software to b built or modified

(*b*) the overall technical and project experience of the software engineers who will carry out the work (*c*) the degree to which the software process has been defined and is followed by the department organisation

(*d*) none of the above.

**29.** Which of the following statement do not hold good for debugging?

(*a*) It involves code checking to locate the cause of defect.

(*b*) Code may be updated during debugging

(*c*) The test cases are defined for debugging

(*d*) Generally covers positive cases.

**30.** Choose the error that is identified by White Box testing.

(*a*) Incorrect or missing function

(*b*) Error in data model

(*c*) Logical decisions are tested on true or false criteria

(*d*) Error in access to external data source.

**31.** The usage of *modelling* CASE Tool in the software development cycle helps in

(*a*) analysing risks, functions, features

(*b*) to create WBS and its network estimates efforts and cost

(*c*) to represent process, functions and data for understanding and analysing

(*d*) to find structure, design and design information.

**32.** Which of the following diagram identify the relationship between various entities of the system?

(*a*) Workflow Diagram (*b*) Dataflow Diagram

(*c*) Entity Relation Diagrams (*d*) System Flow Charts.

**33.** A module is said to have coincidental cohesion if

(*a*) it performs a set of tasks that relate to each other very closely

(*b*) all elements of the module perform similar operations

(*c*) all functions of the module refer to or update the same data structure

(*d*) the elements of a module form the parts of a sequence.

**34.** When two modules communicate using an elementary data item that is passed as a parameter between the two is called

(*a*) stamp coupling (*b*) control coupling

(*c*) content coupling (*d*) data coupling.

**35.** Which of the following concept is not true with regard to Data Flow Diagram?

(*a*) When the two bubbles in DFD are connected directly by a data flow arrow, then it is said to be synchronous

(*b*) When the two bubbles in DFD are connected through a data store by a data flow arrow, then it is said to be asynchronous

(*c*) Every DFD model of a system must be accompanied by a data dictionary

(*d*) A data store could be connected either to another data store or to an external entity.

36. Which of the following information gathering technique are widely used to obtain information in a structured manner?

(a) Interviewing (b) Observation

(c) Brainstorming (d) Prototyping.

37. Which of the following information gathering technique helps to narrow down the number of alternatives, debate them and select one in consensus?

(a) Interviewing (b) Observation

(c) Brainstorming (d) Prototyping.

38. The behavioural property of software product measures the usefulness of the product is

(a) reliability (b) utility

(c) performance (d) robustness.

39. Which of the following architecture is also known as 'data transform architecture'?

(a) Call and return to the control architecture

(b) Data flow driven architecture

(c) Systems layer driven architecture

(d) Data store driven architecture.

40. Choose the testing method which is designed to evaluate the software system performance in rare and abnormal conditions.

(a) White box testing (b) Black box testing

(c) Stress testing (d) Alpha testing.

41. Which of the following method uses class diagrams, object diagrams, state transition and interaction diagram to develop a system?

(a) Rambaugh Methodology (b) Booch Methodology

(c) Jacobson Methodology (d) None of the above.

42. Which of the following object modeling technique encompasses a design activity that encourages design to be conducted at two different levels of abstraction?

(a) Rambaugh Method (b) Coad and Yourdon Method

(c) Jacobson Method (d) Wirfs-Brock method.

43. A system model created during the analysis process which shows entities have common characteristics is called

(a) data flow model (b) composition model

(c) architecture model (d) classification model.

44. What is the disadvantage of using distributed approach to system development?

(a) Concurrency (b) Scalability

(c) Fault tolerance (d) Security.

45. COCOTS is an acronym for

(a) common commercial off the shelf

(*b*) constructive commercial off the shelf

(*c*) common commercial off the system

(*d*) common commercial the system.

**46.** In which of the following, all the models of the system are simply linked together and tested?

(*a*) Big-ban Integration Testing (*b*) Bottom-up Integration Testing

(*c*) Top-down Integration Testing (*d*) Mixed Integration Testing.

**47.** Choose the debugging method which is most common and also least efficient?

(*a*) Brute force method (*b*) Backtracking method

(*c*) Cause elimination method (*d*) Program slicing.

**48.** Which of the following is **NOT** a phase in software life cycle?

(*a*) Project initiation and planning (*b*) Maintenance

(*c*) Project management (*d*) Testing.

**49.** Which of the following is **NOT** common to software engineering and hardware engineering?

(*a*) Project deadline (*b*) Risk management

(*c*) Planning (*d*) Use of CASE tools.

**50.** Consider the following table

| | **Column A** | | **Column B** |
|---|---|---|---|
| 1 | FORTRAN | A | System programming |
| 2 | C++ | B | Scientific programming |
| 3 | C | C | Business programming |
| 4 | COBOL | D | Expert system development |
| 5 | Prolog | E | Object Oriented programming |

Which of the following is the proper match?

(*a*) 1 & B 2 & A 3 & D 4 & C 5 & E

(*b*) 1 & D 2 & A 3 & B 4 & E 5 & C

(*c*) 1 & B 2 & E 3 & A 4 & C 5 & D

(*d*) 1 & D 2 & E 3 & B 4 & C 5 & A.

**51.** A system which was developed was taken to the customer site and the user checked whether it works according to the requirement. What did he do?

(*a*) Application test (*b*) Beta test

(*c*) Stress test (*d*) Alpha test.

**52.** An program module which had errors was handed over to the developer. After correcting the errors and other test, the enterprise system software was tested in the development site before it was taken to the customer site. What did he do?

(*a*) Application test (*b*) Beta test

(*c*) Stress test (*d*) Alpha test.

**53.** Choose the tool which is not used in the requirement analysis.

(*a*) Data Flow Diagram (*b*) Flow Graphs

(*c*) Activity Network (*d*) Module Dependency Diagram.

**54.** The three types of maintenance of a software product are corrective maintenance, adaptive maintenance and perfective maintenance. Which of the following sets represent a decreasing ordering of the types of maintenance with respect to their cost?

(*a*) Corrective Maintenance, Adaptive Maintenance and Perfective Maintenance

(*b*) Adaptive Maintenance, Perfective Maintenance and Corrective Maintenance

(*c*) Perfective Maintenance, Adaptive Maintenance and Corrective Maintenance

(*d*) Perfective Maintenance, Corrective Maintenance and Adaptive Maintenance.

**55.** Which of the following debugging approach manifested by induction or deduction and introduces the concept of binary partitioning?

(*a*) Brute force (*b*) Backtracking

(*c*) Cause elimination (*d*) None of the above.

**56.** Which of the following is not true about Data Flow Diagram (DFD)?

(*a*) Processes should be named and numbered for easy reference

(*b*) The direction of flow is from top to bottom and from right to left

(*c*) When the process is exploded into lower-levels details, they are numbered

(*d*) The names of data stores, sources and destinations are to written in capital letters.

**57.** Choose the design which transforms structural elements of the software architecture into procedural description of software components.

(*a*) Data design (*b*) Architectural design

(*c*) Interface design (*d*) Component-level design.

**58.** The following table gives information about the symbol used in DFD.

| | **Column A** | | **Column B** |
|---|---|---|---|
| 1 | Square | A | Data Store |
| 2 | Arrow | B | Source/Destination |
| 3 | Circle | C | Process |
| 4 | Open rectangle | D | Data flow |

Which of the following is the proper match?

(*a*) 1 & B, 2 & C, 3 & D, 4 & A (*b*) 1 & C, 2 & D, 3 & B, 4 & A

(*c*) 1 & B, 2 & A, 3 & D, 4 & C (*d*) 1 & B, 2 & D, 3 & C, 4 & A.

59. Choose the statement which is not correct about project metrics.
   (*a*) It helps to determine the size of the project
   (*b*) Helps to track potential risk
   (*c*) Adjust the work flow
   (*d*) To assess the status of the ongoing project.

## The Next Three Questions (60–62) are Based on the Following Diagram

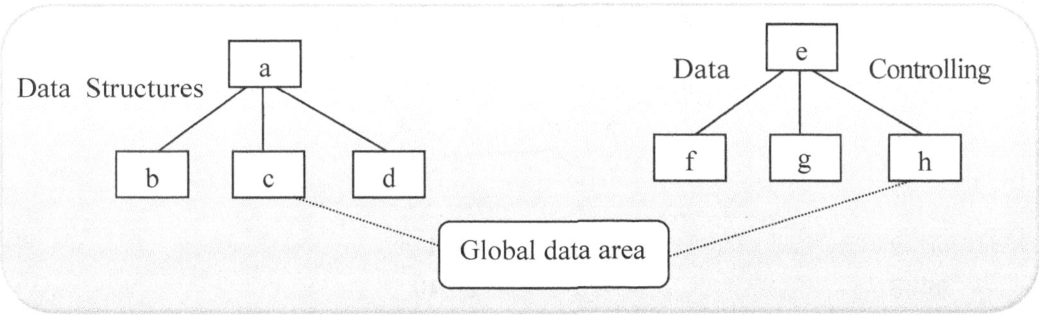


60. What is the name given to the level of coupling exhibited between the modules *b* and *a*?
   (*a*) Data coupling (*b*) Stamp coupling
   (*c*) Control coupling (*d*) Common coupling.

61. What is the name given to the level of coupling exhibited between the modules c and h?
   (*a*) Data coupling (*b*) Stamp coupling
   (*c*) Control coupling (*d*) Common coupling.

62. What is the name given to the level of coupling exhibited between the modules e and h?
   (*a*) Data coupling (*b*) Stamp coupling
   (*c*) Control coupling (*d*) Object coupling.

63. Which of the following phase involves more effort in software system development?
   (*a*) Information gathering (*b*) Software design
   (*c*) Software testing (*d*) Software maintenance.

*64. Find the odd man from the following programming languages: C, C++, Smalltalk, Java, Eiffel, Ada95
   (*a*) C (*b*) Java
   (*c*) C++ (*d*) Smalltalk.

65. Which of the following is not an internal software quality attribute?
   (*a*) Cyclomatic complexity (*b*) Program size
   (*c*) Number of procedure parameter (*d*) Reliability.

**66.** Which of the following is not a strategy form data re-engineering?

(*a*) Data Extension (*b*) Data Cleanup

(*c*) Data Mining (*d*) Data Migration.

***67.** What is the Cyclomatic Complexity of the flowing flow graph?

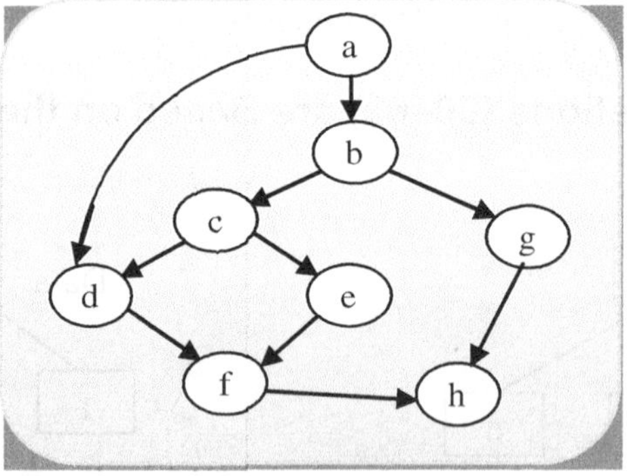


(*a*) 2 (*b*) 4

(*c*) 8 (*d*) 10.

**68.** Which among the following is the most important quality attribute of a web based transaction processing system?

(*a*) Security (*b*) Reusability

(*c*) Modularity (*d*) Efficiency.

**69.** What is the most suitable architecture to develop a web based system?

(*a*) Repository Model (*b*) Island Model

(*c*) Distributed System Model (*d*) Client-Server Model.

***70.** Choose the statement which is not correct about chief programmer.

(*a*) The nucleus of the chief programmer team is consists of a senior engineer, technical staff and backup engineer

(*b*) The chief programmer structure was first proposed by Harlan Mills and described by Baker

(*c*) They are built around a highly skilled chief programmer

(*d*) The specialist pool consists of a chief programmer and senior analyst.

**71.** Which of the following statement is more appropriate for problem decomposition?

(*a*) Not possible for human beings to find solution for complex problem

(*b*) Smaller problems are more manageable

(*c*) Cost involved in solving smaller problem is low

(*d*) projects can be delivered on time.

## ANSWERS

| | | | | | | | |
|---|---|---|---|---|---|---|---|
| **1.** (*c*) | **2.** (*b*) | **3.** (*b*) | **4.** (*d*) | **5.** (*b*) | **6.** (*d*) | **7.** (*c*) | **8.** (*d*) |
| **9.** (*b*) | **10.** (*b*) | **11.** (*b*) | **12.** (*a*) | **13.** (*b*) | **14.** (*b*) | **15.** (*d*) | **16.** (*a*) |
| **17.** (*c*) | **18.** (*c*) | **19.** (*b*) | **20.** (*d*) | **21.** (*a*) | **22.** (*b*) | **23.** (*c*) | **24.** (*a*) |
| **25.** (*b*) | **26.** (*b*) | **27.** (*d*) | **28.** (*d*) | **29.** (*c*) | **30.** (*c*) | **31.** (*c*) | **32.** (*a*) |
| **33.** (*a*) | **34.** (*d*) | **35.** (*d*) | **36.** (*a*) | **37.** (*c*) | **38.** (*b*) | **39.** (*c*) | **40.** (*c*) |
| **41.** (*b*) | **42.** (*b*) | **43.** (*d*) | **44.** (*d*) | **45.** (*b*) | **46.** (*a*) | **47.** (*a*) | **48.** (*c*) |
| **49.** (*d*) | **50.** (*c*) | **51.** (*b*) | **52.** (*d*) | **53.** (*a*) | **54.** (*c*) | **55.** (*c*) | **56.** (*b*) |
| **57.** (*d*) | **58.** (*d*) | **59.** (*a*) | **60.** (*b*) | **61.** (*d*) | **62.** (*c*) | **63.** (*d*) | **64.** (*a*) |
| **65.** (*d*) | **66.** (*c*) | **67.** (*b*) | **68.** (*a*) | **69.** (*d*) | **70.** (*d*) | **71.** (*b*) | |

## EXPLANATIONS

**9.** Productivity of original system = 4750 / 380 = 12.5 SLOC / staff day. Productivity after maintenance = 100/25 = 4 SLOC / staff day. Therefore, the extendibility = (4/ 12.5) × 100 % = 32 %

**14.** Productivity of the software project = total line of code / implementation days. Therefore, 6000/600 = 10 SLOC/days.

**18.** Manpower required = estimated time/available time *i.e.*, 30/6 = 5 persons. Considering the available time per person (0.9) and effective time (0.7), the actual manpower requirement is Manpower / (Available time per person x effective time). *i.e.*, 5/(0.9 × 0.8) = 7 persons.

**25.** Availability = MTBF/(MTBF+MRT).

**26.** The probability is computed as the product of the two. *i.e.*, 0.70 × 0.80 = 0.72.

**64.** Expect C programming languages all the remaining are Object-oriented programming languages.

**67.** Cyclomatic complexity is a software metric that provides a quantitative measure of the logical complexity of a program. Cyclomatic complexity, V(G), for a flow graph G is defined V(G) = E – N + 2. Where E is the number of flow graph edges and N is the number of flow graph nodes. *i.e.*, 10 – 8 + 2 = 4.

**70.** The specialist pool consists of database designer, telecommunication expert, support staff and a software librarian.

CHAPTER 5

# OPERATING SYSTEM

**1.** OS is a/an

(*a*) Application software (*b*) System software

(*c*) Compiler (*d*) Editor.

**2.** When more than jobs are in main memory then it is called as

(*a*) simple programming (*b*) multiprogramming

(*c*) dual programming (*d*) background processing.

**3.** Systems developed to multiprogram large numbers of simultaneous interactive users are known as

(*a*) timesharing systems (*b*) batch processing system

(*c*) distributed system (*d*) none of the above.

### The Next Five Questions (4 – 8) are Based on the Below Problem and FCFS Scheduling Technique

| **Consider a case in which the process with execution times as shown below enter into system** | |
|---|---|
| ***Process*** | ***Execution time in msec*** |
| P1 | 8 |
| P2 | 12 |
| P3 | 6 |
| P4 | 10 |

***4.** What will be the average waiting time if the process enter the system in the order P1, P2, P3, P4?

(*a*) 13 msec (*b*) 13.5 msec

(*c*) 14 msec (*d*) 14.5 msec.

***5.** What will be the average waiting time if the process enters the system in the order P2, P3, P1, P4?

(*a*) 13 msec (*b*) 13.5 msec
(*c*) 14 msec (*d*) 14.5 msec.

***6.** What will be the average waiting time if the process enters the system in the order P3, P2, P4, P1?
(*a*) 13 msec (*b*) 13.5 msec
(*c*) 14 msec (*d*) 14.5 msec.

***7.** What will be the average waiting time if the process enters the system in the order P4, P1, P2, P3?
(*a*) 13 msec (*b*) 13.5 msec
(*c*) 14 msec (*d*) 14.5 msec.

***8.** What will be the average waiting time if the process enters the system in the order P1, P4, P3, P2?
(*a*) 12 msec (*b*) 13 msec
(*c*) 14 msec (*d*) 15 msec.

**9.** Which of the following is not a multi-user operating system?
(*a*) WINDOWS (*b*) DOS
(*c*) UNIX (*d*) Linux.

**10.** Which was the first OS written in High Level Language?
(*a*) DOS (*b*) Multics
(*c*) Linux (*d*) UNIX.

**11.** Tape drives are examples for
(*a*) Random access devices (*b*) Sequential access devices
(*c*) Direct access (*d*) None of the above.

## The Next Three Questions (12–14) are Based on the Following Information and Diagram

**The Diagram Represents a Memory which Shows the Used Block and Free Block With its Available Space**

Assume that a new job with 15 KB requires memory.

| 9Ks | Used | 22K | Used | 19K | Used | 28K | Used | 8K | Used | 34K | Used | 17K |
|---|---|---|---|---|---|---|---|---|---|---|---|---|

***12.** Which free block will be selected according to First-fit algorithm?
(*a*) 19 K (*b*) 22 K
(*c*) 28 K (*d*) 34 K.

***13.** Which free block will be selected according to Best-fit algorithm?
(*a*) 19 K (*b*) 22 K
(*c*) 28 K (*d*) 34 K.

***14.** Which free block will be selected according to worst-fit algorithm?
(*a*) 19 K (*b*) 22 K
(*c*) 28 K (*d*) 34 K.

**15.** Which one is not a direct access storage device?
(*a*) Magnetic Disk (*b*) Magnetic Drum
(*c*) Magnetic Tape (*d*) CD.

**16.** In multiprocessing system several processor share
(*a*) primary storage and single OS
(*b*) primary storage and multiuser OS
(*c*) single OS and not primary storage
(*d*) only multiuser OS.

**17.** DMA stands for
(*a*) Device Memory Adaptor (*b*) Device Memory Allocator
(*c*) Direct Memory Access (*d*) Direct Memory Allocator.

**18.** Set of all addresses available for a program is called
(*a*) available space (*b*) address space
(*c*) allocated space (*d*) assigned space.

**19.** RISC is
(*a*) Reserved Index Set Computing (*b*) Reserved Instruction Set Computer
(*c*) Reduced Index Set Computing (*d*) Reduced Instruction Set Computer.

**20.** IOCS stands for
(*a*) In/Out Condition System (*b*) In/Out Control System
(*c*) Input/Output Condition System (*d*) Input/Output Control System.

**21.** SPOOL is
(*a*) Sequential Peripheral Operation On Line
(*b*) Sequential Peripheral Operation Off Line
(*c*) Simultaneous Peripheral Operations On Line
(*d*) Simultaneous Peripheral Operation Off Line.

**22.** Which of the following is not an IPC mechanism?
(*a*) Socket (*b*) Pipes
(*c*) Shared memory (*d*) Semaphore

## The Next Three Questions (23–25) are Based on the Following Information

**The Following Table Indicates Page, Load Time, Last Reference Time, Dirty Bit and Reference Bit of a System with four Page Frame**

| *Page* | *Load Time* | *Last reference* | *Dirty bit* | *Reference bit* |
|---|---|---|---|---|
| 0 | 177 | 380 | 1 | 1 |
| 1 | 329 | 329 | 0 | 0 |
| 2 | 251 | 301 | 1 | 0 |
| 3 | 155 | 340 | 0 | 1 |

***23.** Which page will be replaced according to FIFO algorithms?
(*a*) Page 0 (*b*) Page 1
(*c*) Page 2 (*d*) Page 3.

***24.** Which page will be replaced according to LRU algorithms?
(*a*) Page 0 (*b*) Page 1
(*c*) Page 2 (*d*) Page 3.

***25.** Which page will be replaced according to NRU algorithms?
(*a*) Page 0 (*b*) Page 1
(*c*) Page 2 (*c*) Page 3.

**26.** Which of the following is not a mechanism for thread process synchronization?
(*a*) Mutex (*b*) Message Queues
(*c*) Semaphore (*d*) Monitors.

**27.** Choose the slowest and cheapest form of memory.
(*a*) Primary memory (*b*) Secondary memory
(*c*) Cache (*d*) Internal processor memory.

**28.** Choose the best answer, when a page size is small
(*a*) minimizes internal fragmentation (*b*) minimizes I/O times
(*c*) minimizes the number of page fault (*d*) page table size will be small.

**29.** Choose the incorrect statement.
(*a*) Process is a program in execution (*b*) Process is an asynchronous activity
(*c*) Process is also known as task (*d*) Process is not a dispatchable unit.

**30.** A process currently holding the CPU is said to be in
(*a*) ready state (*b*) running state
(*c*) blocked state (*d*) suspended state.

**31.** Consider the following task set

| *Task* | *Period* | *Execution Time* |
|---|---|---|
| 1 | 150 | 10 |
| 2 | 100 | 60 |
| 3 | 250 | 20 |
| 4 | 300 | 100 |

What will be the total process utilization?
(*a*) 1.08 (*b*) 2.08
(*c*) 3.08 (*d*) 4.08.

**32.** A process waiting for an event to happen is said to be in
(*a*) ready state (*b*) running state
(*c*) blocked state (*d*) busy state.

## The Next Five Questions (33–37) are Based on the Below Problem

Suppose there are two processes P1 and P2. Both have execution time of 20 msec. Process P1 does an I/O for 5 msec and P2 for 10 msec. The time slice is 5 msec.

**33.** What will be the state of P1 at time instant 0?
(*a*) Ready (*b*) Running
(*c*) Blocked I/O (*d*) None of the above.

**34.** At what time instant P2 is selected for execution?
(*a*) 0 (*b*) 5
(*c*) 10 (*d*) 15.

**35.** At what time instant P1 will be performing I/O operation?
(*a*) 0 (*b*) 5
(*c*) 10 (*d*) 15.

**36.** At what time instant P2 will complete I/O operation?
(*a*) 0 (*b*) 10
(*c*) 30 (*d*) 40.

**37.** At what time instant P2 will exit?
(*a*) 0 (*b*) 10
(*c*) 30 (*d*) 40.

**38.** Process Control Block(PCB) is also known as
(*a*) program control block (*b*) process conditional block
(*c*) process descriptor (*d*) program conditional block.

***39.** Suppose the cache access time is 40 nsec and memory access time is 400 nsec and the hit ratio is 0.9.

What will be the effective access time of the memory?
(*a*) 72 (*b*) 76
(*c*) 78 (*d*) 80.

**40.** The technology used for cache memory is
(*a*) SRAM (*b*) DRAM
(*c*) PROM (*d*) EPROM.

**41.** Which of the following is not relevant to address binding?
(*a*) Compile time (*b*) Load time
(*c*) Access time (*d*) Run time.

**42.** Which of the following comments is not true about PCB
(a) has the current state of the program
(*b*) has a pointer to the process parent
(*c*) does not have pointer to the child process
(*d*) has the unique identification of the process.

**43.** Which of the following operation that cannot be performed on a process
(*a*) create (*b*) destroy
(*c*) resume (*d*) enable.

**44.** An event that alters the sequence in which a processor executes instruction is known as
(*a*) interrupt (*b*) polling
(*c*) blocking (*d*) none of the above.

**45.** Which of the following Inter Process Communication mechanism used for one-way communication of stream of bytes?

(a) Signals (b) Message Queues
(c) Sockets (d) Pipes.

**46.** Choose the incorrect statement
(a) Daemon is short running processes.
(b) Daemon stands for Disk and Execution Monitor
(c) Daemons are background process started immediately after booting the system
(d) Daemons terminate only when the system is shutdown.

## The Next Five Questions (47–51) are Based on the Below Problem and SJF Scheduling Technique.

| Consider the following process with their next execution time | |
|---|---|
| **Process** | **Next execution time in msec** |
| P1 | 8 |
| P2 | 12 |
| P3 | 6 |
| P4 | 10 |

***47.** What will be the order of process entering the system?
(a) P1, P2, P3, P4 (b) P3, P1, P2, P4
(c) P3, P2, P1, P4 (d) P4, P3, P2, P1.

***48.** What will be the waiting time for process P1?
(a) 3 msec (b) 3.5 msec
(c) 4 msec (d) 4.5 msec.

***49.** What will be the waiting time for process P4?
(a) 15 msec (b) 16 msec
(c) 17 msec (d) 18 msec.

***50.** What will be the waiting time for process P3?
(a) 0 msec (b) 8 msec
(c) 12 msec (d) 6 msec.

***51.** What will be the average waiting time?
(a) 4 msec (b) 6 msec
(c) 8 msec (d) 10 msec.

**52.** PSW is
(a) Program Static Word (b) Program Structured Word
(c) Process Static Word (d) Program Status Word.

**53.** When a process is accessing shared modifiable data, the process is said to be
(a) tight corner (b) critical section
(c) in termination (d) none of the above.

**54.** The addresses available in primary storage is called
(*a*) virtual address (*b*) real address
(*c*) cache address (*d*) indirect address.

**55.** Which of the following statement hold good for semaphore?
(*a*) It is programming construct available for IPC.
(*b*) It is programming construct available for process synchronization
(*c*) It is a type of dead lock
(*d*) It is a logical address.

**56.** Counting Semaphore is also called as
(*a*) waiting semaphore (*b*) critical semaphore
(*c*) general semaphore (*d*) special semaphore.

**57.** A process in multiprogramming system is waiting for a particular event that will never happen is said to be in a state of
(*a*) deadlock (*b*) active lock
(*c*) both a and b (*d*) none of the above.

**58.** Which one of the following is not a necessary condition for a deadlock?
(*a*) mutual exclusion (*b*) wait for condition
(*c*) preemption condition (*d*) circular wait.

**59.** Dijstra'a Bankers Algorithm is an algorithm basically for
(*a*) Deadlock prevention (*b*) Deadlock avoidance
(*c*) Deadlock detection (*d*) Deadlock recovery.

## The Next Five Questions (60–64) are Based on the Below Information and SRT Scheduling Technique

| Process arrival and execution times as given below: | | |
|---|---|---|
| **Process** | **Arrival time** | **Execution time in msec** |
| P1 | 0 | 9 |
| P2 | 1 | 3 |
| P3 | 2 | 10 |
| P4 | 3 | 4 |

***60.** What will be the order of process entering the system?
(*a*) P1, P2, P3, P4 (*b*) P3, P1, P2, P4, P3
(*c*) P1, P2, P4, P1, P3 (*d*) P1, P2, P4, P3.

***61.** What will be the waiting time for process P1?
(*a*) 0 msec (*b*) 3 msec
(*c*) 7 msec (*d*) 9 msec.

***62.** What will be the waiting time for process P3?
(*a*) 14 msec (*b*) 16 msec
(*c*) 17 msec (*d*) 18 msec.

***63.** What will be the waiting time for process P4?
(*a*) 0 msec (*b*) 1 msec
(*c*) 3 msec (*d*) 7 msec.

***64.** What will be the average waiting time?
(*a*) 4 msec (*b*) 4.5 msec
(*c*) 5 msec (*d*) 5.5 msec.

**65.** Fixed partition memory management largely face the problem of
(*a*) segmentation (*b*) fragmentation
(*c*) partition (*d*) overlay.

**66.** Collection of free spaces through compaction is called
(*a*) garbage collection (*b*) list collection
(*c*) node collection (*d*) sector collection.

**67.** The software implementation of mutual exclusion was first presented by
(*a*) Dekker (*b*) Dennis Ritche
(*c*) Pascal (*d*) Bill gates.

## The Next Six Questions (68–73) are Based on the Following Information

**A hard disk has 250 cylinder numbered 0 – 249 and currently servicing a request at cylinder 99. Consider a disk queue with request for I/O on cylinder 24, 90, 133, 43, 188.**

***68.** What will be the total head movement for FCFS scheduling?
(*a*) 400 (*b*) 419
(*c*) 440 (*d*) 460.

***69.** What will be the total head movement for SSTF scheduling?
(*a*) 270 (*b*) 271
(*c*) 272 (*d*) 273.

***70.** What will be the total head movement for SCAN scheduling?
(*a*) 260 (*b*) 266
(*c*) 280 (*d*) 287.

***71.** What will be the total head movement for CSCAN scheduling?
(*a*) 315 (*b*) 420
(*c*) 464 (*d*) 460.

***72.** What will be the total head movement for LOOK scheduling?
(*a*) 200 (*b*) 220
(*c*) 239 (*d*) 260.

***73.** What will be the total head movement for C-LOOK scheduling?
(*a*) 280 (*b*) 290
(*c*) 274 (*d*) 294.

***74.** The mechanism of converting virtual address to real address is called
(*a*) dynamic address translator (*b*) dynamic address translation
(*c*) direct address translator (*d*) direct address translation.

**75.** When the memory are divided into equal sizes then it is called
(*a*) pages (*b*) segment
(*c*) frame (*d*) none of the above.

**76.** Which one of the following is not a page replacement strategy?
(*a*) FIFO (*b*) Not-used recently
(*c*) First chance (*d*) Second chance.

**77.** Not bringing the page from secondary memory into primary memory until it is referenced is called
(*a*) request paging (*b*) demand paging
(*c*) page fault (*d*) none of the above.

## The Next Three Questions (78–80) are Based on the Below Problem and Round Robin Scheduling Technique

**Consider the following processes which arrive at time 0, with execution time as shown below**

| Process | Execution time in msec |
|---|---|
| P1 | 25 |
| P2 | 4 |
| P3 | 3 |

Assume that the time slice is 5 msec.

***78.** How will the processes scheduled?
(*a*) P1, P2, P3 (*b*) P1, P3, P1, P1
(*c*) P1, P2, P3, P1, P1 (*d*) P1, P2, P3, P1, P1, P1, P1.

***79.** What will be the waiting time for process P1?
(*a*) 5 msec (*b*) 7 msec
(*c*) 9 msec (*d*) 3 msec.

***80.** What will be the average waiting time?
(*a*) 4 msec (*b*) 6 msec
(*c*) 7 msec (*d*) 10 msec.

**81.** Choose the odd man out
(*a*) Main memory
(*b*) Primary Memory
(*c*) Real memory
(*d*) Secondary memory.

**82.** In contiguous allocation multiprogramming systems, protection is often implemented with several
(*a*) accumulator
(*b*) boundary register
(*c*) instruction register
(*d*) data register.

**83.** In memory management the process of merging adjacent holes to form a single larger hole is called

(*a*) fragmentation (*b*) joining

(*c*) coalescing (*d*) none of the above.

**84.** Which one of the following is not a storage placement strategy?

(*a*) Best-fit (*b*) First-fit

(*c*) Worst-fit (*d*) Last-fit.

**85.** Which memory is fastest and expensive?

(*a*) Cache memory (*b*) Magnetic Tape

(*c*) ROM (*d*) Disk.

**86.** The strategies that are concerned with determining which piece of program or data to displace to make room for the incoming programs is called

(*a*) fetch (*b*) placement

(*c*) replacement (*d*) none of the above.

**87.** Process priority that cannot be changed is called

(*a*) dynamic (*b*) static

(*c*) purchased (*d*) demand.

**88.** The important level of processor scheduling are

(*a*) high-level scheduling

(*b*) intermediate-level scheduling

(*c*) low-level scheduling

(*d*) all the above.

**89.** Which one is not an objective of processor scheduling?

(*a*) Maximize throughput (*b*) Maximize overhead

(*c*) Avoid indefinite postponement (*d*) Enforce priorities.

**90.** Process priority that can be changed is called

(*a*) dynamic (*b*) static

(*c*) purchased (*d*) demand.

**91.** Process priority that is got by paying premium is called

(*a*) dynamic (*b*) static

(*c*) purchased (*d*) demand.

**92.** Which is simple processor scheduling technique?

(*a*) FIFO (*b*) Round Robin

(*c*) Shortest-Job First (*d*) Shortest-Remaining-Time.

**93.** Which of the following statement is not true about thread and process

(*a*) Thread and child process share resources with the parent process

(*b*) Thread and process can change their attributes or can create new resources

(*c*) The process information block is similar to thread information block

(*d*) Threads and process have direct access to the data segment.

## The Next Five Questions (94–98) are Based on the Below Problem and Priority Scheduling Technique

| Consider the following processes which have arrived at time 0 and have execution times and priorities as shown below | | |
|---|---|---|
| **Process** | **Execution time in msec** | **Priority** |
| P1 | 8 | 3 |
| P2 | 2 | 5 |
| P3 | 3 | 4 |
| P4 | 5 | 2 |
| P5 | 7 | 1 |

***94.** How will the processes scheduled?
(*a*) P1, P2, P3, P4, P5
(*b*) P2, P3, P4, P5, P1
(*c*) P2, P3, P1, P4, P5
(*d*) P3, P4, P5, P1, P2.

***95.** What will be the waiting time for process P1?
(*a*) 5 msec
(*b*) 7 msec
(*c*) 9 msec
(*d*) 3 msec.

***96.** What will be the waiting time for process P4?
(*a*) 9 msec
(*b*) 10 msec
(*c*) 12 msec
(*d*) 13 msec.

***97.** What will be the waiting time for process P2?
(*a*) 0 msec
(*b*) 7 msec
(*c*) 9 msec
(*d*) 3 msec.

***98.** What will be the average waiting time?
(*a*) 4.6 msec
(*b*) 6.6 msec
(*c*) 7.6 msec
(*d*) 8.6 msec.

**99.** Which one of the following referred as array processor?
(*a*) SISD
(*b*) SIMD
(*c*) MISD
(*d*) MIMD.

**100.** Connecting two or more independent computer system via a communication link is
(*a*) loosely-coupled multiprocessing
(*b*) loosely-controlled multiprocessing
(*c*) tightly-coupled multiprocessing
(*d*) tightly-controlled multiprocessing.

**101.** Which one of the following is not a processor scheduling technique?
(*a*) Quantum Size
(*b*) Shortest-Job First
(*c*) Biggest-Job First
(*d*) Shortest-Remaining-Time.

**102.** Which one of the following architecture is practically not available?
(*a*) SISD
(*b*) SIMD
(*c*) MISD
(*d*) MIMD.

**103.** Time it takes for data to rotate from current position to position adjacent to read-write is known as

(*a*) seek time (*b*) latency time
(*c*) transmission time (*d*) prime time.

**104.** The time taken to the process of moving the boom to new cylinder is called

(*a*) seek time (*b*) latency time
(*c*) transmission time (*d*) rotation time.

**105.** Desirable characteristics of disk scheduling are

(*a*) throughput (*b*) mean response time
(*c*) variance of response times (*d*) all the above.

**106.** Which is not a seek optimization technique?

(*a*) FCFS (*b*) SSTF
(*c*) S-SCAN (*d*) C-SCAN.

**107.** The expansion of DASD is

(*a*) Direct Access Storage Device
(*b*) Direct Access Storage Directory
(*c*) Direct Accent Storage Device
(*d*) Double Access Storage Device.

**108.** Choose the wrong statement

(*a*) A field is group of characters
(*b*) A record is a group of fields
(*c*) A file is collection of unrelated records
(*d*) A database is collection of file.

**109.** Which one is not a file organization scheme?

(*a*) Sequential (*b*) Direct
(*c*) Indirect (*d*) Indexed Sequential.

**110.** A sequential access file has fixed-size 20 byte records. Assuming the first record is 1, the first byte of record will be at what logical location?

(*a*) 20 (*b*) 80
(*c*) 81 (*d*) 100.

**111.** A file control block is also known as

(*a*) file descriptor (*b*) file divider
(*c*) file controller (*d*) none.

**112.** Microsoft 's PC version of Unix is called

(*a*) Linux (*b*) MS-UNIX
(*c*) XENIX (*d*) MULTICS.

**113.** A system using fixed blocking with 40 byte records and 100 byte. How much space will be wasted in each block?

(*a*) 60 (*b*) 40
(*c*) 20 (*d*) 10.

**114.** Which one is not a database model?

(*a*) Hierarchical database (*b*) Network database
(*c*) Relational database (*d*) Flow database.

**115.** The UNIX system is
(*a*) full duplex (*b*) half-duplex
(*c*) simplex (*d*) none of the above.

**116.** POSIX is
(*a*) Programmable Operating System Interface [for Unix]
(*b*) Progressive Operating System Interface [for Unix]
(*c*) Part Operating System Interface [for Unix]
(*d*) Portable Operating System Interface [for Unix].

**117.** In Unix, the files which contain the rules for managing input-output devices are called
(*a*) ordinary files (*b*) directory files
(*c*) special files (*d*) none of the above.

**118.** Which one of the following comment is not true about UNIX?
(*a*) Multi-user system
(*b*) Multi-tasking
(*c*) Highly programmable
(*d*) Written in JAVA.

**119.** The file system in UNIX is organized in
(*a*) network structure (*b*) hierarchical structure
(*c*) relational structure (*d*) star structure.

**120.** Which one of the following UNIX command lists all files including hidden files?
(*a*) ls –x (*b*) ls –a
(*c*) ls –r (*d*) ls –R.

**121.** Which one of the following is not a shell?
(*a*) MS shell (*b*) Korn shell
(*c*) C shell (*d*) Bourne shell.

**122.** Which of the following network connects different kinds of user in one organization or throughout several organization, providing a variety of resources to these users
(*a*) LAN (*b*) MAN
(*c*) WAN (*d*) Enterprise Network.

**123.** A program that endlessly replicates on same computer or that sends itself to many other computers on a network is called
(*a*) Virus (*b*) Worm
(*c*) Trojan Horse (*d*) Buffer Attack.

**124.** Which of the following is a utility that network users and administrators frequently use to text a network connection?
(*a*) Ping (*b*) Token
(*c*) Ring (*d*) Router.

**125.** Which of the following, the address of the source computer is changed to make a packet appear to come from a different computer?
(*a*) Spoofing (*b*) SPOOLING
(*c*) Polling (*d*) None of the above.

## The Next Six Questions (126–131) are Based on the Following Information

**A Disk System has 16 Data Recording Surfaces With 1024 Tracks Per Surface**

**There are 14 sectors per track, each containing 1024 bytes.**

**The diameter of the inner cylinder is 6 inches and that of the outer cylinder is 10 inches**

***126.** What is the maximum bit density?
(*a*) 6900.78 bits/inch (*b*) 6084.24 bits/inch
(*c*) 7000.78 bits/inch (*d*) 7050.78 bits/inch.

***127.** What is track density?
(*a*) 256 tracks/inch (*b*) 512 tracks/inch
(*c*) 768 tracks/inch (*d*) 1024 tracks/inch.

***128.** What is data transfer rate if rotational speed is 3600 rpm?
(*a*) 700K bytes/sec (*b*) 740K bytes/sec
(*c*) 800K bytes/sec (*d*) 840K bytes/sec.

***129.** What will be the Latency time?
(*a*) 0.1 sec (*b*) 0.008 sec
(*c*) 0.11 sec (*d*) 0.001 sec.

***130.** What is the total capacity of the disk?
(*a*) 220 Mb (*b*) 222 Mb
(*c*) 224 Mb (*d*) 226 Mb.

***131.** A clock interrupt on a computer requires 3 msec per clock tick. The clock runs at 50 Hz. What percent of the CPU time is devoted to the clock?
(*a*) 10 (*b*) 12
(*c*) 15 (*d*) 17.

**132.** Which of the following information is not available in Process Control Block?
(*a*) Process's priority (*b*) Unique identification of the process
(*c*) Process Size (*d*) Current state of the process.

## The Next Five Questions (133–137) are Based on the Following Information

**Consider the disk queue with requests for I/O blocks on cylinders 65, 120, 34, 140, 16, 150. Assume that initially the disk head is at cylinder 55.**

***133.** What will be the order of request according to FCFS disk scheduling?
(*a*) 150, 140, 120, 65, 34, 16 (*b*) 16, 34, 65, 120, 140, 150
(*c*) 65, 120, 34, 140, 16, 150 (*d*) 140, 16, 150, 65, 120, 34.

***134.** What will be the order of request according to SSTF disk scheduling?
(*a*) 65, 34, 16, 120, 140, 150 (*b*) 34, 16, 65, 120, 140, 150
(*c*) 65, 120, 34, 140, 16, 150 (*d*) 140, 16, 150, 65, 120, 34.

*135. What will be the order of request according to SCAN disk scheduling?
(a) 150, 140, 120, 65, 34, 16
(b) 34, 16, 65, 120, 140, 150
(c) 65, 120, 34, 140, 16, 150
(d) 65, 34, 16, 120, 140, 150.

*136. What will be the order of request according to CSCAN disk scheduling?
(a) 150, 140, 120, 65, 34, 16
(b) 16, 34, 65, 120, 140, 150
(c) 65, 120, 34, 140, 16, 150
(d) 65, 120, 140, 150, 16, 34.

*137. What will be the order of request according to FCFS disk scheduling?
(a) 65, 34, 16, 120, 140, 150
(b) 16, 34, 65, 120, 140, 150
(c) 65, 120, 34, 140, 16, 150
(d) 65, 120, 140, 150, 16, 34.

138. Choose an algorithm used for scheduling hard disk input/output
(a) FScan
(b) N-Step-SCAN
(c) Anticipatory scheduling
(d) Completely Fair Queuing.

139. The time interval between the submission of a process and its completion is known as
(a) Response time
(b) Utilization time
(c) Turnaround time
(d) Throughput.

140. The number of process that are completed per unit time is known as
(a) Multitasking
(b) Multiprogramming
(c) Parallel Processing
(d) Throughput.

141. Which of the following scheduler is used to reduce the degree of multiprogramming by swapping out the processes?
(a) Long term scheduler
(b) Medium term scheduler
(c) Short term scheduler
(d) None of the above.

142. The *vi* editor can operate in
(a) input mode only
(b) command mode only
(c) ex mode only
(d) all the above.

143. The command to display the beginning of a file in UNIX is
(a) first
(b) top
(c) head
(d) one.

144. The UNIX command used for search of a simple string, or a group is
(a) grep
(b) fgrep
(c) egrep
(d) none of the above.

145. Choose the best answer
A shell in UNIX can recognize
(a) internal commands
(b) shell scripts
(c) external commands
(d) all the above.

146. Choose the wrong statement
(a) in UNIX every file has one inode
(b) inode can be accessed directly by the user
(c) each inode is accessed by i-number
(d) i-number references the position of the inode in the list.

**147.** Which one of the following is the default shell for UNIX.
(*a*) PDKSH (*b*) BASH
(*c*) TCSH (*d*) Z-shell.

**148.** C shell was developed by
(*a*) William Joy (*b*) David Korn
(*c*) Stephen R Bourne (*d*) Kenneth Almquist.

**149.** The standard type of file for Linux is
(*a*) character file (*b*) text file
(*c*) byte stream file (*d*) binary file.

**150.** In Linux, the directory that stores the data related to the operating system is
(*a*) bin (*b*) dev
(*c*) etc (*d*) lib.

**151.** Which of the following command in UNIX converts plain text files into postscript for printing, and gives you some options for formatting.
(*a*) gzip (*b*) gzcat
(*c*) gunzip (*d*) genscript.

**152.** Choose the command used to change the owner of a file
(*a*) chmod (*b*) chown
(*c*) chgrp (*d*) modify.

**153.** Which of the following is not true for a shell?
(*a*) The shell is both a command interpreter and a programming language
(*b*) As a command interpreter, the shell executes commands you enter in response to its prompt
(*c*) As a programming language, the shell executes commands from files called shell scripts
(*d*) When you start a shell, it typically runs only one startup files.

**154.** The operator is used to execute a command as a background process.
(*a*) @ (*b*) #
(*c*) $ (*d*) &.

**155.** Choose the best answer
In Linux a text editor is a program that enables
(*a*) to create and edit documents (*b*) to create programs and utilities
(*c*) write e-mail message (*d*) all the above.

**156.** The *vi* editor command which enables to move the cursor to the previous character is
(*a*) A (*b*) h
(*c*) L (*d*) j.

**157.** In Linux, which of the following page type can be reclaimed immediately?
(*a*) claimable (*b*) swappable
(*c*) syncable (*d*) discardable.

**158.** Linux identifies processes via
(*a*) process identifier (*b*) program identifier
(*c*) page identifier (*d*) none of the above.

**159.** Which of the following operating system developed recently?
(*a*) Windows 2000 (*b*) Windows 7
(*c*) Windows Vista (*d*) Window XP.

**160.** The expansion of ISR is
(*a*) Interrupt Service Routine (*b*) Instruction Service Routine
(*c*) Input Service Routine (*d*) In Service Routine.

**161.** In Windows Vista once code or data is mapped onto a virtual page, the page is said to be
(*a*) controlled (*b*) committed
(*c*) uncontrollable (*d*) unconditional.

**162.** In Windows vista, the layer which abstracts low-level hardware details is
(*a*) hardware abstraction layer (*b*) user layer
(*c*) kernal layer (*d*) none of the above.

**163.** The process of user updating code in nonvolatile CMOS memory is called
(*a*) flashing (*b*) thrashing
(*c*) paging (*d*) none of the above.

**164.** The object that reduce the time taken to execute ISR in response to an Interrupt from a particular device is
(*a*) Deferred Program Call (*b*) Deferred Procedure Call
(*c*) Dynamic Procedure Call (*d*) Definite Procedure Call.

**165.** In Windows vista each process has user mode system data, called
(*a*) Process Environment Block (*b*) Program Environment Block
(*c*) Procedure Environment Block (*d*) Process Control Block.

**166.** If a page is never modified, it will go onto a special list of free physical pages called
(*a*) free list (*b*) standby list
(*c*) smart list (*d*) none of the above.

**167.** Every Windows Vista user and group is identified by a
(*a*) User ID (*b*) Group ID
(*c*) Security ID (*d*) None of the above.

**168.** Fault that occurs as a result of an error when a process attempts to access a non-resident page is called
(*a*) frame error (*b*) page error
(*c*) segment error (*d*) page fault.

**169.** Computing system that employs more than one processor is called
(*a*) multiprogramming (*b*) multiprocessing
(*c*) timesharing (*d*) batch processing.

**170.** The technique that enables the system to store portions of a process page table in discontiguous locations in main memory and store only those portions that a process is actively using is called
(*a*) Multilevel Paging System (*b*) Single Level Paging System
(*c*) Multiprogramming (*d*) None of the above.

**171.** Average time a system spends waiting for a disk request to be serviced is called
(*a*) Latency Time (*b*) Service Time
(*c*) Mean Response Time (*d*) Transmission Time.

**172.** Operating System components governs communication between processes is
(*a*) Device Manager (*b*) Interprocess Communication Manager
(*c*) Program Manager (*d*) Operating System Manager.

**173.** Virtual memory organization technique that divides an address space into fixed-size blocks of contiguous addresses is called
(*a*) Paging (*b*) Segmentation
(*c*) Both a and b (*d*) None of the above.

**174.** Using multiple independent computer to perform a common task is called
(*a*) centralized computing (*b*) batch processing
(*c*) time sharing (*d*) distributed computing.

**175.** A section of code that performs operations on a share resource is called
(*a*) critical section (*b*) bad sector
(*c*) sharing (*d*) none of the above.

**176.** The ability of Operating System to handle software or hardware errors is called
(*a*) fault tolerance (*b*) error tolerance
(*c*) both a and b (*d*) none of the above.

**177.** A computer program that conducts basic hardware and software communications inside the computer is
(*a*) device drivers (*b*) BIOS
(*c*) macro (*d*) resource manager.

**178.** Choose the operating system which does not support you to configure firewall.
(*a*) Windows XP Professional (*b*) Windows Server 2003
(*c*) DOS (*d*) Red Hat Linum 9.x.

**179.** Which one of the following is not a virus, but a e-mail falsely warning of a virus.
(*a*) Spam (*b*) A reverse worm
(*c*) A virus hoax (*d*) Trojan horse.

**180.** The components of an OS that manage computer memory and use of the CPU are
(*a*) device drivers (*b*) API
(*c*) traffic controller (*d*) resource manager.

**181.** NetBus is an example of
(*a*) worm (*b*) virus
(*c*) Trojan horse (*d*) bug.

**182.** The Melissa virus was sent as an e-mail attachment with the subject header
(*a*) "Important Message From *username*"
(*b*) "Very Important Message From *username*"
(*c*) "You Have an Important Message From *username*"
(*d*) "Important Information From *username*".

**183.** Which of the following type is a virus that appears to run from a file other than the one to which it is actually appended

(*a*) Stealh (*b*) Companion

(*c*) Polymorphic (*d*) Armored.

**184.** A software or hardware placed between two or more networks that selectively allows or denies access is a

(*a*) Spy ware (*b*) Cookie

(*c*) Firewall (*d*) Digital signature.

**185.** The use of a secret code or other means to disguise data that is stored on a computer or transported across a network is called

(*a*) Sniffer (*b*) Encryption

(*c*) Authentication (*d*) Digital Signature.

**186.** The formula (key * 10) / (data / key) is an example of a(an)

(*a*) Random number generator (*b*) Odd number generator

(*c*) Encryption algorithm (*d*) Infinity calculator.

**187.** Which of the following is a form of encryption in which there are two keys, one used to encrypt the data and the other to decrypt it

(*a*) Kerberos (*b*) Symmetric encryption

(*c*) Hashing (*d*) Asymmetric encryption.

**188.** An encryption method in which every bit in a stream of data is encrypted is called

(*a*) Stream cipher (*b*) Sniffer

(*c*) Kerberos (*d*) Hashing.

**189.** The message arrives at the server, the kernel passes it up to a

(*a*) Server stub (*b*) Client stub

(*c*) Server (*d*) Kernel.

**190.** The file system supported by one or more machines called

(*a*) Server (*b*) Client

(*c*) File server (*d*) Name server.

**191.** The remote kernel gives the message to the

(*a*) client stub (*b*) client

(*c*) server stub (*d*) server.

**192.** Inherently distributed system is often called computer supported

(*a*) co-operative work (*b*) co-operative games

(*c*) works (*d*) none.

**193.** To avoid the entire problem in some distributed system ———is used.

(*a*) Dynamic (*b*) Static

(*c*) Dynamic binding (*d*) Static binding.

**194.** Bus based multiprocessors consist of some number of
(*a*) CPU (*b*) Cache
(*c*) Memory (*d*) None.

**195.** The sequence of instructions is executed on every RPC is called
(*a*) Critical path (*b*) Client
(*c*) Serve (*d*) Path.

**196.** The file servers accept requests from user program running on the other machines called ———— to read and write.
(*a*) Server (*b*) Client
(*c*) File server (*d*) Name server.

**197.** A highest synchronization technique is called
(*a*) atomic transaction (*b*) clock synchronization
(*c*) synchronization (*d*) mutual exclusion.

**198.** Different process do not exchange message that event is called as
(*a*) concurrent (*b*) timer
(*c*) clocks new (*d*) none of the above.

**199.** The interval between two consecutive transits of the sun is called
(*a*) mean solar second (*b*) solar day
(*c*) transit of the sun (*d*) solar second.

**200.** System involving multiple processes is often most easily programmed using
(*a*) mutual exclusion (*b*) critical region
(*c*) synchronization (*d*) none of the above.

**201.** The oldest and most widely used concurrency control algorithm is
(*a*) clocking (*b*) rollback
(*c*) two phase locking (*d*) strict phase locking.

**202.** A system in which files can be moved without their names changing is said to have
(*a*) location independence
(*b*) location dependent
(*c*) location transparency
(*d*) location free.

## ANSWERS

| | | | | | | |
|---|---|---|---|---|---|---|
| **1.** (*b*) | **2.** (*b*) | **3.** (*a*) | **4.** (*b*) | **5.** (*c*) | **6.** (*a*) | **7.** (*d*) |
| **8.** (*a*) | **9.** (*b*) | **10.** (*d*) | **11.** (*b*) | **12.** (*b*) | **13.** (*a*) | **14.** (*d*) |
| **15.** (*c*) | **16.** (*a*) | **17.** (*c*) | **18.** (*b*) | **19.** (*d*) | **20.** (*d*) | **21.** (*c*) |
| **22.** (*d*) | **23.** (*d*) | **24.** (*c*) | **25.** (*b*) | **26.** (*b*) | **27.** (*b*) | **28.** (*a*) |
| **29.** (*d*) | **30.** (*b*) | **31.** (*a*) | **32.** (c) | **33.** (*b*) | **34.** (*b*) | **35.** (*c*) |
| **36.** (*c*) | **37.** (*d*) | **38.** (*c*) | **39.** (b) | **40.** (*a*) | **41.** (*c*) | **42.** (*c*) |
| **43.** (*d*) | **44.** (*a*) | **45.** (*d*) | **46.** (*a*) | **47.** (*b*) | **48.** (*c*) | **49.** (*d*) |

**50.** (*a*) **51.** (*c*) **52.** (*d*) **53.** (*b*) **54.** (*b*) **55.** (*b*) **56.** (*c*)
**57.** (*a*) **58.** (*c*) **59.** (*b*) **60.** (*c*) **61.** (*c*) **62.** (*a*) **63.** (*b*)
**64.** (*d*) **65.** (*b*) **66.** (*a*) **67.** (*a*) **68.** (*b*) **69.** (*b*) **70.** (*d*)
**71.** (*c*) **72.** (*c*) **73.** (*d*) **74.** (*b*) **75.** (*a*) **76.** (*c*) **77.** (*b*)
**78.** (*d*) **79.** (*b*) **80.** (*c*) **81.** (*d*) **82.** (*b*) **83.** (*c*) **84.** (*d*)
**85.** (*a*) **86.** (*c*) **87.** (b) **88.** (*d*) **89.** (*b*) **90.** (*a*) **91.** (*c*)
**92.** (*a*) **93.** (*d*) **94.** (*c*) **95.** (*a*) **96.** (*d*) **97.** (*a*) **98.** (*c*)
**99.** (*b*) **100.** (*a*) **101.** (*c*) **102.** (*c*) **103.** (*b*) **104.** (*a*) **105.** (*d*)
**106.** (*c*) **107.** (*a*) **108.** (*c*) **109.** (*c*) **110.** (*c*) **111.** (*a*) **112.** (*c*)
**113.** (*c*) **114.** (*d*) **115.** (*a*) **116.** (*d*) **117.** (*c*) **118.** (*d*) **119.** (*b*)
**120.** (*b*) **121.** (*a*) **122.** (*d*) **123.** (*b*) **124.** (*a*) **125.** (*a*) **126.** (*b*)
**127.** (*b*) **128.** (*d*) **129.** (*b*) **130.** (*c*) **131.** (*c*) **132.** (*c*) **133.** (*c*)
**134.** (*a*) **135.** (*b*) **136.** (*d*) **137.** (*a*) **138.** (*c*) **139.** (*c*) **140.** (*d*)
**141.** (*b*) **142.** (*d*) **143.** (*c*) **144.** (*b*) **145.** (*d*) **146.** (*b*) **147.** (*b*)
**148.** (*a*) **149.** (*b*) **150.** (*c*) **151.** (*d*) **152.** (*b*) **153.** (*d*) **154.** (*d*)
**155.** (*d*) **156.** (*b*) **157.** (*d*) **158.** (*a*) **159.** (*b*) **160.** (*a*) **161.** (*b*)
**162.** (*a*) **163.** (*a*) **164.** (*b*) **165.** (*a*) **166.** (*b*) **167.** (*c*) **168.** (*d*)
**169.** (*b*) **170.** (*a*) **171.** (*c*) **172.** (*b*) **173.** (*a*) **174.** (*d*) **175.** (*a*)
**176.** (*a*) **177.** (*b*) **178.** (*c*) **179.** (c) **180.** (*d*) **181.** (*c*) **182.** (*a*)
**183.** (*b*) **184.** (**c**) **185.** (*b*) **186.** (*c*) **187.** (*d*) **188.** (*a*) **189.** (*a*)
**190.** (*c*) **191.** (*d*) **192.** (*a*) **193.** (*c*) **194.** (*a*) **195.** (*a*) **196.** (*b*)
**197.** (*a*) **198.** (*a*) **199.** (*b*) **200.** (*b*) **201.** (*a*) **202.** (*a*)

## EXPLANATIONS

**4.** The processes will be scheduled for execution in the order given below

| P1 | P2 | P3 | P4 |
|---|---|---|---|

0 8 20 26 36

The waiting time for P1 is 0 msec, for P2 it is 8 msec, for P3 it is 20 msec and P4 it is 26 msec. Therefore, the average waiting time is (0+8+20+26)/4 = 13.5

**5.** If the processes arrive in the order P2, P3, P1 and P4, they will be scheduled as shown below:

| P2 | P3 | P1 | P4 |
|---|---|---|---|

0 12 18 26 36

The average waiting time in this case will be (0+12+18+26)/4 = 14

**6.** If the processes arrive in the order P3, P2, P4 and P1, they will be scheduled as shown below:

| P3 | P2 | P4 | P1 |
|---|---|---|---|

0 12 18 26 36

The average waiting time in this case will be (0+6+18+28)/4= 13

**7.** If the processes arrive in the order P4, P1, P2 and P3, they will be scheduled as shown below:

| P4 | P1 | P2 | P3 |
|---|---|---|---|

0 12 18 26 36

The average waiting time in this case will be (0+10+18+30)/4= 14.5

**8.** If the processes arrive in the order P1, P4, P3 and P2, they will be scheduled as shown below:

| P1 | P4 | P3 | P2 |
|---|---|---|---|

0 12 18 26 36

The average waiting time in this case will be (0+8+18+24)/4= 12.5

**12.** According to FCFS technique, the new job will be placed in the first block which is greater than the new block. Therefore, block with 22K will be selected.

**13.** According to Best Fit technique the free block which is more closely related to the size of the new job will be selected. Therefore, block with 19 K will be selected.

**14.** According to Worst Fit technique the free block which is large in size will be selected. Therefore, block with 34 K will be selected.

**23.** FIFO selects the page loaded first. Page 1 arrived at 155

**24.** LRU selects the page referenced last Page 2 at time 306

**25.** NRU first looks for a clean page that was not recently referenced. Page 1 is the only such page.

**31.** The total process utilization = ( 10/150+60/100+20/250+100/300) = 1.079 33 to 37. The following table shows the state of the process P1 and P2 at different time instant.

| Time Instant | P1 | P2 |
|---|---|---|
| 0 | Running | Ready |
| 5 | Ready | Running |
| 10 | Blocked | Running |
| 15 | Running | Ready |
| 20 | Running | Blocked I/O |
| 25 | Running | Blocked I/O |
| 30 | Exit | Running |
| 35 | | Running |
| 40 | | Exit |

**39.** t=hc+(1-h)Ma Where t= effective access time, h= hit ratio, c= access time, Ma=Memory access time 0.9*40+(1-0.9)*400= 76

**47.** The order of execution will be in the order P3, P1, P2, and P4 since P3 has the shortest processing time followed by P1, P2, P4. The processes will be scheduled for execution in the order given below:

| P3 | P1 | P2 | P4 |
|---|---|---|---|

0 4 10 18 28

**48.** The waiting time for process P1 will be 4 msec

**49.** The waiting time for process P4 will be 18 msec

**50.** The waiting time for process P3 will be 0 msec

**51.** The average waiting time in this case will be (0+4+10+18)/4 = 8

**60.** The processes will be scheduled for execution in the order given below:

| P1 | P2 | P4 | P1 | P3 |
|---|---|---|---|---|

0 1 4 8 16 26

**61.** The waiting time for process P1 will be 8-1 = 7 msec

**62.** The waiting time for process P3 will be 16-2 = 14 msec

**63.** The waiting time for process P4 will be 4-3 = 1 msec

**64.** The average waiting time in this case will be (7+0+14+1)/4 = 5.5 msec

**68.** FCFS – The request will be serviced in the order 24, 90, 133, 43, 188. Therefore, the total head movement will be (99-24)+(90-24)+(133-90)+(133-43)+(188-43) = 419

**69.** SSTF – The request will be serviced in the order 90, 133, 188, 43, 24. Therefore, the total head movement will be (99-90)+(133-90)+(188-133)+(188-43)+(43-24) = 271

**70.** SCAN – Since the head is moving cylinder 0, the request will be serviced in the order 90, 43, 24, 0, 133, 188. Therefore, the total head movement will be (99-90)+(90-43)+(43-24)+(24-0)+(133-0)+(188-133) = 287

**71.** C-SCAN – The request will be serviced in the order 90, 43, 23, 0, 249, 188, 133. Therefore, the total head movement will be (99-90)+(90-43)+(43-24)+(24-0)+(249-0)+(249-188)+(188-133) = 464

**72.** LOOK – The request will be serviced in the order 90, 43, 24, 133, 188. Therefore, the total head movement will be (99-90)+(90-43)+(43-24)+(133-24)+(188-133) = 239

**73.** C-LOOK – The request will be serviced in the order 90, 43, 24, 188, 133. Therefore, the total head movement will be (99-90)+(90-43)+(43-24)+(188-24)+(188-133) = 294

**78.** The processes will be scheduled for execution in the order given below:

| P1 | P2 | P3 | P1 | P1 | P1 | P1 |
|---|---|---|---|---|---|---|

0 5 9 12 17 22 27 32

**79.** The waiting time for process P1 will be 12-5= 7 msec

**80.** The average waiting time in this case will be (7+5+9)/3 = 7 msec

**94.** The processes will be scheduled for execution in the order given below:

| P2 | P3 | P1 | P4 | P5 |
|---|---|---|---|---|

0 2 5 13 18 25

**95.** The waiting time for process P1 will be 5 msec

**96.** The waiting time for process P4 will be 13 msec

**97.** The waiting time for process P2 will be 0 msec

**98.** The average waiting time in this case will be (5+0+2+13+18)/5= 7.6 msec

**110.** Record 5 is preceded by 4 records, each of 20 bytes. The fifth record will start at byte (4×20)+1=81

**113.** Two 40 byte records can be allocated to each block leaving 20 bytes waste.

**126.** The maximum bit density occurs on the innermost track. Therefore, its value is

$$\frac{\text{sectors per track} \times \text{bytes per sector} \times 8}{\text{circumference}} = \frac{14 \times 1024 \times 8}{\pi \times 6} = \frac{114688}{3.142 \times 6} = \frac{114688}{18.85}$$

$$= 6084.24 \text{ bits per inch}$$

**127.** Track density is equal to the number of tracks per surfaces divided by the radial distance between the outermost and the innermost track, Hence its value is

$$\frac{1024}{5-3} = \frac{1024}{2} = 512 \text{ tracks per inch.}$$

**128.** Data transfer rate = sectors per track × bytes per track × rotations per sec. = 14 × 1024 × 60 = 840 KB/sec

**129.** Latency time is the half the time required for one revolution = ½ × 1/60 = 0.008 sec

**130.** Total capacity of the disk = number of recording surfaces × tracks per surfaces × sector per tracks × bytes per sector. i.e. 16 × 1024 × 14 × 1024 = 224 MB

**131.** CPU time devoted to the clock (d. time period = 1/50 sec or 20 msec/percent) = (3/20 *100)=15

**133.** In FCFS (First Come First Serve) scheduling the I/O request are serviced in the order they arrive.

**134.** In SSTF (Shortest Seek Time First) this type of scheduling the I/O request close to the current head position is serviced.

**135.** In SCAN scheduling the disk arm moves at one end of the disk and moves towards the other end, servicing the request as it reaches each cylinder until it reaches the other end of the disk.

**136.** It is similar to SCAN scheduling but the head reaches the end, it comes back to the beginning of the disk without servicing request along the return trip.

**137.** LOOK scheduling the arm moves only as far as the final request in each direction.

CHAPTER 6

# OBJECT-ORIENTED PROGRAMMING IN C++

1. Which of the following is **NOT** true in Object-Oriented Programming approach?
   (*a*) Data is more secured in Object-Oriented Programming compared with Procedure Oriented Programming
   (*b*) Object-Oriented Programming approach follows top-down design concept
   (*c*) In Object-Oriented Programming data and functions are combined together
   (*d*) In Object-Oriented Programming objects exchange messages with each other.
2. In Object-Oriented Programming the data and the function are combined together and this feature is called
   (*a*) encapsulation (*b*) data abstraction
   (*c*) inheritance (*d*) polymorphism.
3. In Object-Oriented Programming when the essential the features are represented without giving the background information is called
   (*a*) encapsulation (*b*) data abstraction
   (*c*) inheritance (*d*) polymorphism.
4. Which of the following is **NOT** true?
   (*a*) OOP requires more memory to process at a greater speed
   (*b*) The traditional languages runs slower than OOP language
   (*c*) The time can be saved in OOP language software development because of the reusability features
   (*d*) OOP languages provide good quality of software and easy to maintain.
5. Which of the following is correct with regard to polymorphism?
   (*a*) An entity to inherit some properties from another class
   (*b*) Combining data and function together
   (*c*) An entity in several form
   (*d*) None of the above.

**6.** The method by which objects of one class get the properties of objects of another class is known as

(*a*) Inheritance (*b*) Encapsulation

(*c*) Abstraction (*d*) Data Hiding.

**7.** Object-Oriented Programming language C++ language was developed by

(*a*) Bjarne Stroustrup (*b*) Dennis Ritche

(*c*) Ken Thompson (*d*) Bill Gates.

**8.** C++ was originally named as

(*a*) C with Classes (*b*) C with Objects

(*c*) C with classes and object (*d*) C with OOP.

**9.** C with classes was developed in the year

(*a*) 1975 (*b*) 1976

(*c*) 1978 (*d*) 1979.

**10.** In which year C with Classes was renamed as C++

(*a*) 1979 (*b*) 1981

(*c*) 1983 (*d*) 1985.

***11.** Which of the following is **NOT** true?

(*a*) Both C and C++ starts with main functions

(*b*) C++ main function returns int value by default

(*c*) C main function returns void value by default

(*d*) C++ allows a maximum of 32 characters in an identifier name.

***12.** What will be the output of the following program?

```
void main()
{
int a=15;
float b=4.1234;
b+=a;
cout<<b-2<<endl;
}
```

(*a*) 15 (*b*) 4.1234

(*c*) 17.1234 (*d*) 0.1234.

**13.** Which of the following is a derived data type?

(*a*) int (*b*) reference

(*c*) class (*d*) union.

***14.** What is the output of the following program?

```
int main()
{
```

```
char buffer[] = "ABCDE";
cout.write(buffer,3);
        return 0;
}
```

(*a*) CDE (*b*) BCD

(*c*) ABC (*d*) DEC.

**15.** Consider the following statement

```
        int a              \\1
        b=float(a)/8;      \\2
```

What will be the data type of 'a' after statement two is executed?

(*a*) 'a' is converted to `float` (*b*) 'a' remains `int` type

(*c*) 'a' is converted to `double` (*d*) none of the above.

***16.** What will be the output of the following program?

```
void main()
{
double a=9876.54321;
int b=int(a);
cout<<b<<endl;
}
```

(*a*) 9876 (*b*) 9876.54321

(*c*) .54321 (*d*) error.

**17.** The octal integer constant begins with

(*a*) leading 8 (eight) (*b*) leading 0 (zero)

(*c*) leading O (Character O) (*d*) leading *x*.

***18.** What is the output of the following statements?

```
int main()
{
const int size = 3;
char buffer[size + 1]="ABC";
buffer[size-1] = '\0';
cout << buffer<<"\n";
return 0;
}
```

(*a*) AB (*b*) BC

(*c*) ABC (*d*) Error.

**19.** Composition of objects in a class is known as

(*a*) delegation (*b*) inheritance

(*c*) polymorphism (*d*) none of the above.

**20.** The existing class can be reused by

(*a*) abstraction (*b*) polymorphism

(*c*) dynamic binding (*d*) inheritance.

## The Next Three Questions (21–23) are Based on the Following Information

**Consider variable 'a' is declared as integer and assigned the value 52**

***21.** What will be the result if `a<<2` is performed?

(*a*) 48 (*b*) 54

(*c*) 52 (*d*) 90.

***22.** What will be the result if `a>>3` is performed?

(*a*) 01 (*b*) 03

(*c*) 09 (*d*) 90.

***23.** What will be the result if `~a` is performed?

(*a*) 0101 0010 (*b*) 1010 0010

(*c*) 1010 1010 (*d*) 1010 1101.

***24.** What will be the outcome when the following statement is executed if the variable 'num' is an `int` data type and assign a value 88.

```
if  (num%2==0)
{
cout<< "I like C++";
}
cout<< "I like C";
}
```

(*a*) 44 (*b*) 88

(*c*) I like C++ (*d*) I like C.

**25.** Choose the statement which is **NOT** true with relevant to switch statement.

(*a*) Switch variable can test only for equal values

(*b*) Switch variable cannot be a float data type

(*c*) Each switch case expression must be a single value

(*d*) Logical operator can be used with switch statement.

***26.** What will be the output when the following statement is executed?

```
for(i=1, j=3; i<10, j<5; i++, j++)
cout<<i<< " "<<j<<endl;
```

(*a*) 1 3
2 2

(*b*) 1 3
2 4

(c) 1 3
1 4

(d) Error.

**27.** The `for` loop is best suited

(a) if the number of iterations are fixed

(b) if we know the test condition

(c) when the number of condition are fixed

(d) if the number of iterations are not fixed.

**28.** Which of the following statement is used to terminate the execution of the program?

(a) `break` statement

(b) `goto` statement

(c) `exit` statement

(d) none of the above.

***29.** Choose the incorrect statement

(a) All statements in C++ are terminated by semicolon

(b) The selection statements are also called conditional statement

(c) In `do-while` loop the body of the loop is executed at least once

(d) Switch statement provides multiple choices for selection.

***30.** What will be the output for the following statements?

```
int main()
{
int i = 0;
++(--(++i));
printf("%d",i);
return 0;
}
```

(a) 1

(b) 2

(c) 4

(d) 7.

**31.** What will be the result of the following program?

```
void main()
{
int a=5, b=1;
do
{
b*=a;
a--;
} while (a>1);
cout<<b<<endl;
}
```

(a) 5

(b) 1

(c) 120

(d) 720.

**32.** The curly braces are not present then the scope of loop is

(*a*) zero statement (*b*) one statement

(*c*) two statement (*d*) multiple statement.

**33.** A function which is called with some parameter and does not return any value is called

(*a*) void function

(*b*) void function with parameter

(*c*) function with parameter and with return type

(*d*) recursion.

**34.** Which of the following statement is true with relevant to inline function?

(*a*) A function which calls itself

(*b*) It is a time consuming process

(*c*) Inline function is good for big function body

(*d*) The inline function is defined by placing the keyword before the function declaration.

**35.** The maximum number of value/values a function can return is

(*a*) zero (*b*) one

(*c*) ten (*d*) infinity.

***36.** What will be the output for the following program?

```
void f(int number=10)
{
printf("%d", number) ;
}
int main()
{
int num = 0 ;
f(num) ;
return 0;
}
```

(*a*) 0 (*b*) 1

(*c*) 2 (*d*) 10.

**37.** The `cin` and `cout` functions require the header file to include

(*a*) `conio.h` (*b*) `stdio.h`

(*c*) `iomanip.h` (*d*) `iostream.h`.

**38.** To fill unused section of the field, the character is set by the function

(*a*) `fill()` (*b*) `width()`

(*c*) `precision()` (*d*) none of the above.

**39.** The manipulator `<<endl` is equivalent to

(*a*) '\n' (*b*) '\t'

(*c*) '\b' (*d*) none of the above.

**40.** Which function accepts the string with blank spaces?

(*a*) `getline()` (*b*) `cin`

(*c*) `scanf()` (*d*) none of the above.

**41.** The stream is a

(*a*) flow of data (*b*) flow of integers

(*c*) flow of statements (*d*) none of the above.

**42.** The buffer is used to move data between

(*a*) input/output devices and computer

(*b*) input and output devices

(*c*) input devices to storage devices

(*d*) none of the above.

**43.** The buffer is a

(*a*) block of memory (*b*) part of ram

(*c*) part of hard disk (*d*) none of the above.

**44.** Choose the storage specifier which initialize the variable to some garbage value.

(*a*) Auto (*b*) Register

(*c*) Extern (*d*) Static.

***45.** What is the output of the following statements?

```
int main(void)
{
char buffer[] = "ABC 1.234 5";
char string[100];
int f;
float n;
sscanf(buffer, "%s%d%f", string, &f, &n);
printf("%d     %f", f,n);
return 0;
}
```

(*a*) 1 0.234000 (*b*) ABC 1

(*c*) ABC 0.234000 (*d*) ABC 1 0.234000.

**46.** In C++, the symbol used for writing comments is

(*a*) // (*b*) //* *//

(*c*) /* */ (*d*) none of the above.

**47.** Which of the following statement is true?

(*a*) Array is collection of different data items

(*b*) The array size must be unsigned integer constant

(*c*) Array elements are stored in different memory locations

(*d*) The index value for the first element is always 1.

**48.** `struct` is

(*a*) an identifier (*b*) user-defined variable

(*c*) constant (*d*) keyword.

***49.** What will be the output for the following program?

```
void main()
{
double a[5]={11.11,12.12,13.13,14.14,15.15};
for(int i=0; i<5;i++)
{
}
cout<<a[i]<<endl;
}
```

(*a*) 13.13 (*b*) 14.14

(*c*) 15.15 (*d*) unknown value.

**50.** The NULL character is represented by

(*a*) /0 (*b*) \0

(*c*) \O (alphabet) (*d*) 0 (zero).

**51.** The ASCII value of NULL character is

(*a*) 0 (*b*) 10

(*c*) 61 (*d*) 100.

***52.** What will be the output of the following program?

```
const int x = 10;
int main(void)
{
int x[x];
int y = sizeof(x) / sizeof(int);
cout<<y;
}
```

(*a*) 5 (*b*) 10

(*c*) 20 (*d*) error.

***53.** What is the output of the following statements, if the input is `"I Like You"`.
`const length = 8;`

```
int main()
{
cin>>ws;
char string[length];
cin.get(string,length);
cout << string;
return 0;
}
```

(*a*) I (*b*) I Like
(*c*) I Like You (*d*) Error.

**54.** The constant function
(*a*) cannot alter values of variable
(*b*) can alter values of a constant variables
(*c*) makes its local variable constant
(*d*) none of the above.

***55.** What will be the output of the following program?

```
void main()
{
int a=99;
int *b=&a;
cout<<--*b*2<<endl;
}
```

(*a*) 0 (*b*) 99
(*c*) 196 (*d*) Error.

**56.** In the prototype `void sum(int &);` arguments are passed by
(*a*) value (*b*) reference
(*c*) address (*d*) none of the above.

**57.** What will be the output of the following program?

```
int main()
{
int sum = 0;
int array[][3] = {{0, 1, 2}, {3, 4, 5}, {6, 7, 8}};
for (int i = 0; i < 3 ; ++i)
{
for (int j = 2; j < 3 ; j++)
{
sum += array[i][j];
```

```
}
}
cout << sum <<endl;
return 0;
}
```

(*a*) 3 (*b*) 14

(*c*) 15 (*d*) 36.

**58.** What will be the output for the following statements?

```
int main()
{
int len;
char s[] = "ABC" ;
len = strlen(s) ;
printf("%s %d", s, len);
return = 0;
}
```

(*a*) ABC 3 (*b*) ABC3

(*c*) "ABC" 3 (*d*) ABC "3".

## The Next Two Questions (59–60) are Based on the Following Program

```
int min =256;                    //1
void main()                      //2
{
int min=156;
cout<<min<<endl;
}
```

**59.** What will be the output of the program?

(*a*) 256 (*b*) 156

(*c*) Compilation error (*d*) Runtime error.

**60.** What will be the output if the statement in line 3 is replaced by `const int min =256;`

(*a*) 256 (*b*) 156

(*c*) Compilation error (*d*) Runtime error.

***61.** What will be the output for the following statements?

```
extern "C"
{
```

```
size_t strlen(const char*);
}
int main()
{
printf("%d\n", strlen("ABC"));
return 0;
}
```

(*a*) 4 (*b*) 2
(*c*) 3 (*d*) 1.

**62.** Choose the incorrect statement
(*a*) Structure can have different data items
(*b*) Memory is allocated when structure is declared
(*c*) Structure has finite number of elements
(*d*) Each structure element has a different name.

**63.** The members in a structure can be accessed by
(*a*) semicolon operator (*b*) dot operator
(*c*) comma operator (*d*) ampersand operator.

**64.** Consider the following code

```
struct hello
{
int a;
float b;
};
```

How much memory will be allocated for the above code?
(*a*) 2 bytes (*b*) 6 bytes
(*c*) 8 bytes (*d*) No allocation.

**65.** The union declared without tag name is called as
(*a*) anonymous union (*b*) nameless union
(*c*) unknown union (*d*) void main.

***66.** Which of the pointer arithmetic equivalent to `ptr=ptr+1` then `*ptr`?
(*a*) `ptr++` (*b*) `ptr--`
(*c*) `* ++ptr` (*d*) `++ *ptr`.

**67.** The members of `struct` are by default
(*a*) public (*b*) private
(*c*) protected (*d*) none of the above.

**68.** The set `precision()` is used to set
(*a*) field width (*b*) number of digits
(*c*) decimal places (*d*) none of the above.

**69.** The use of parenthesis is optional with which of the following statement?

(*a*) return (*b*) main

(*c*) clrscr (*d*) exit.

***70.** What will be the output of the following program?

```
int main()
{
cout << sizeof(int) <<endl;
int x = 10;
x = x << 1;
cout << x << endl;
return 0;
}
```

(*a*) 0 (*b*) 10

(*c*) 20 (*d*) 1.

**71.** What will be the output of the following program?

```
struct set
{
set(int n) : x(n++), y(n++), z(n++) {}
int x;
int y;
int z;
};
int main()
{
set st(3);
cout << "x: " << st.x << endl;
cout << "y: " << st.y << endl;
cout << "z: " << st.z << endl;
rcturn 0;
}
```

(*a*) x = 1, y=2, z= 3 (*b*) x = 2, y=3, z= 4

(*d*) x=3, y=4, z=5 (*d*) x = 4, y=5, z= 6.

**72.** Which one of the following operator cannot be overloaded?

(*a*) dot operator (.) (*b*) plus operator (+)

(*c*) ampersand operator (&) (*d*) decrement operator (—).

**73.** What will be the output of the following program?

```
int& fun(int& a,int& b)
```

```
{
return ( a < b ? a : b);
}
main()
{
int a= 55, b=33;
fun(a,b)=66;
cout<<b<<endl;
}
```

(*a*) 55 (*b*) 33

(c) 66 (*d*) error.

**74.** Which of the following is used to dynamically allocate the memory in C++?

(*a*) new operator (*b*) free operator

(*c*) delete operator (*d*) None of the above.

***75.** Which of the following statement is **NOT** true?

(*a*) A pointer supports dynamic allocation and de-allocation at runtime.

(*b*) Memory can be used efficiently with help of pointer

(*c*) NULL pointer is also called the zero pointers

(*d*) Addition, subtraction and multiplication are possible with pointer variables.

**76.** int A[5]={1,2,3,4,5} and the base address is 2000. What will be the output if the statement `cout<<(A+2)` is executed?

(*a*) 2 (*b*) 3

(*c*) 2002 (*d*) 2004.

**77.** Suppose the array is replaced by `char A[]="Indhu"` in the above question. What will be the output?

(*a*) 2002 (*b*) 2004

(*c*) ndhu (*d*) dhu.

**78.** If char A[ ]= "Anisha" and the base address is 2000. What will be the output if the statement `cout<<*(A+1)` is executed?

(*a*) A (*b*) n

(*c*) An (*d*) garbage value.

**79.** Suppose the `cout` statement in the above question is replaced as `cout<<*A+1`, what will be the output?

(*a*) 65 (*b*) n

(*c*) An (*d*) 66.

**80.** The type of constructor which does not take any parameter is known as

(*a*) default constructor (*b*) dynamic constructor

(*c*) parameterized constructor (*d*) default argument constructor.

**81.** Which one of the following is **NOT** true for a constructor?

(*a*) Constructor does not return any value

(*b*) Constructor are invoked automatically when the objects are created

(*c*) Constructor can be inherited

(*d*) Constructors cannot be virtual.

**82.** Which of the following is true for a destructor?

(*a*) Destructor takes any argument

(*b*) Destructor can be overloaded

(c) Destructor can be virtual

(*d*) Destructor is invoked automatically when object is destroyed.

**83.** Suppose there are three objects A, B and C which are from same class. What will be the sequence of destructor invocation?

(*a*) A B C (*b*) C B A

(*c*) B C A (*d*) none of the above.

**84.** Which one of the following conversions is automatically carried by the compiler?

(*a*) Conversion from basic data type to user-defined data type(class type)

(*b*) Conversion from class type to basic data type

(*c*) Conversion from one class type to another class type

(*d*) none of the above.

**85.** What will be the output of the following program?

```
int add(int x, int y = 10)
{
return x+y+5;
}
int main(void)
{
cout << add(2,1) << endl;
return 0;
}
```

(*a*) 10 (*b*) 12

(*c*) 13 (*d*) 8.

**86.** The destructor is executed when

(*a*) object goes out of scope (*b*) when object is not used

(*c*) when object contain nothing (*d*) none of the above.

**87.** Constructor has the same name as

(*a*) the class they belong to
(*b*) the current program file name
(*c*) class name and preceded by~
(*d*) both (a) and (c).

**88.** The diagram given below represents which type of inheritance?

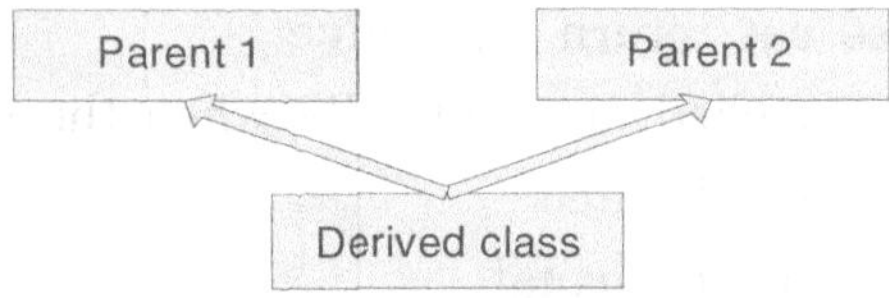


(*a*) Single inheritance
(*b*) Multi-level inheritance
(*c*) Multiple inheritance
(*d*) Hybrid inheritance.

**89.** When many subclasses inherit properties from a single base class, it is called as

(*a*) Single inheritance
(*b*) Multi-level inheritance
(*c*) Multiple inheritance
(*d*) Hierarchical inheritance.

**90.** The diagram given below shows

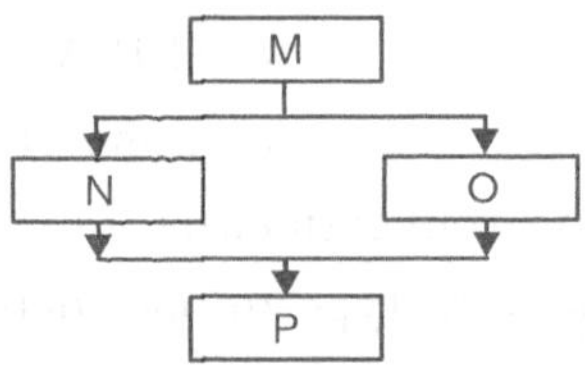


(*a*) Hierarchical inheritance
(*b*) Multi-level inheritance
(*c*) Multiple inheritance
(*d*) Hybrid inheritance.

## The Next Two Questions (91–92) are Based on the Following Information

**class X:class Y, class Z{};**

**91.** What is the type of inheritance?

(*a*) Hierarchical inheritance
(*b*) Multi-level inheritance
(*c*) Multiple inheritance
(*d*) Hybrid inheritance.

**92.** What will be the visibility mode?

(*a*) Private
(*b*) Protected
(*c*) Public
(*d*) both a and b.

**93.** Which of the following is true if a class M is friend of another class N?

(*a*) All member function of class M can use the private members of N
(*b*) All member function of class N can use the private members of M

(*c*) only public member functions of class M can use the private members of class N

(*d*) none of the above.

**94.** Nested is a class that contains

(*a*) object of another class
(*b*) a class within another class
(*c*) a class of another class
(*d*) none of the above.

**95.** In multilevel inheritance, the middle class act as

(*a*) base class as well as derived class
(*b*) only base class
(*c*) only derived class
(*d*) none of the above.

**96.** In postfix overloading of operator (++ or – –), the last argument should have type

(*a*) long
(*b*) void
(*c*) float
(*d*) int.

**97.** Which of the following is a *run time* polymorphism?

(*a*) Function overloading
(*b*) Operator overloading
(*c*) Template
(*d*) virtual function.

**98.** A, B and C are objects of same class. To execute the statement `C=A+B`, which operator need to be overloaded?

(*a*) only '+' operator
(*b*) only '='operator
(*c*) both (*a*) and (*b*)
(*d*) none of the above.

**99.** The operator function returns the value of

(*a*) basic type
(*b*) void type
(*c*) class type
(*d*) all types.

**100.** Choose the operator that cannot be overloaded?

(*a*) ?: (Ternary operator/conditional operator)
(*b*) <<= (Shift left and assign)
(*c*) new (dynamic memory allocation)
(*d*) && (Logical AND).

**101.** Choose the operator that cannot be overloaded using friend function?

(*a*) + (Addition)
(*b*) < (Less than)
(*c*) = (Assignment)
(*d*) ++ (increment).

**102.** The protected keyword allows

(*a*) derived class to access base class member directly
(*b*) prevents direct access to public members
(*c*) allows objects to access private members
(*d*) all of the above.

**103.** The class is declared virtual when

(*a*) two or more classes involved in inheritance have common base class

(*b*) more than one class is derived

(*c*) we want to prevent a base class from inheritance

(*d*) none of the above.

**104.** What will be the output for the following program?

```
int main ()
{
for(int i = 5; i < 7; ++i)
{
static int j = i;
printf("j = %d\n",j);
}
return 0;
}
```

(*a*) j=1;
j=1;

(*b*) j=5
j=5.

(*c*) j=0
j=0

(*d*) j=4
j=4.

**105.** The ambiguity of members normally occurs in

(*a*) single inheritance

(*b*) multilevel inheritance

(*c*) multipath inheritance

(*d*) none of the above.

**106.** Private member variable can be accessed directly using

(*a*) pointer

(*b*) arrays

(*c*) this pointer

(*d*) none of the above.

**107.** The array name itself is a/an

(*a*) pointer

(*b*) reference

(*c*) variable

(*d*) object.

**108.** In C/C++, When function is called, parameters are passed

(*a*) from right to left

(*b*) from left to right

(*c*) from top to bottom

(*d*) from bottom to top.

**109.** When base class is not used for object declaration is called as

(*a*) abstract class

(*b*) container class

(*c*) concrete class

(*d*) derived class.

**110.** The derived class without pure virtual function is called as

(*a*) concrete class

(*b*) abstract class

(*c*) container class

(*d*) derived class.

**111.** When a operator is overloaded then it is not possible to change its

(*a*) syntax (*b*) precedence

(*c*) template (*d*) all the above.

**112.** Consider the statement virtual `void display ()=0`. the display function is

(*a*) pure virtual function (*b*) pure member function

(*c*) normal function (*d*) all the above.

**113.** The do nothing function is nothing but

(*a*) pure virtual function (*b*) pure member function

(*c*) both (a) and (b) (*d*) none of the above.

***114.** What is the output of the following statements?

```
class base
{
public:
void f (int n)
{
printf("n = %d\n", n);
}
};
class derived : public base
{
public:
void f(double n)
{
printf("n = %f\n", n);
}
};
int main()
{
derived d;
d.f(1);
return 0;
}
```

(*a*) 1.1000000 (*b*) 1.111111

(c) 0.111111 (*d*) 1.000000.

**115.** Dynamic binding is done using the keyword

(*a*) void (*b*) inline

(*c*) static (*d*) virtual.

**116.** What is the output of the following statements?

```
void main()
    {
    printf("Hello welcome to C++\n");
    return 0;
}
```

(*a*) Compiler error (*b*) Run time error

(*c*) Hello welcome to C++ (*d*) 0.

**117.** The size of the object is equal to

(*a*) total size of member data variable

(*b*) total size of member function

(*c*) both(*a*) and (*b*)

(*d*) none of the above.

**118.** Which of the following error that is encountered during compilation time?

(*a*) Syntax error (*b*) Falling short of memory

(*c*) Division by zero (*d*) Exceeding the size of the array.

***119.** What is the output of the following statements?

```
int main()
{
char *x="HELLO";
x+=3;
cout<<x;
return 0;
}
```

(*a*) LO (*b*) HE

(*c*) LL (*d*) EL.

**120.** When a program encounters an exception then the control is transferred to some other parts of the program called as

(*a*) try block (*b*) throw block

(*c*) catch block (*d*) none of the above.

**121.** Which of the following requires at least one statement to be followed?

(*a*) default (*b*) continue

(*c*) break (*d*) else.

**122.** To add data at the end of file the file must be opened in

(*a*) read mode (*b*) append mode

(*c*) write mode (*d*) both (*a*) and (*c*).

**123.** Exception is generated in

(*a*) try block (*b*) throw block

(*c*) catch block (*d*) none of the above.

**124.** Template class is also called as

(*a*) generic class (*b*) container class

(*c*) virtual class (*d*) base class.

**125.** What will be the output of the following program?

```
void main()
{
char s[]="";
cout<<strlen(s)<<endl;
}
```

(*a*) 0 (*b*) 1

(*c*) 2 (*d*) error.

**126.** The statement `in.seekg(0,ios::end)` sets the file pointer

(*a*) in the middle of file (*b*) at the beginning of file

(*c*) at the end of file (*d*) none of the above.

**127.** Choose the mode which specifies that the data can be extracted from the file, i.e. the file is open for reading?

(*a*) `ios::in` (*b*) `ios::app`

(*c*) `ios::ate` (*d*) `ios::out`.

**128.** What is the output of the following program?

```
int a= 1;
int f()
{
return 1;
}
int g(int x = f() + a)
{
return x;
}
int main()
{
int a = 2;
int answer = g();
printf("%d\n", answer);
return 0;
}
```

(a) 1 (b) 2
(c) 3 (d) none of the above.

***129.** What will be the output for the following statements?

```
int  main()
{
int  x  =  1;
cout.width(20);
cout  <<  x;
return  0  ;
}
```

(a) 1 (b) 20
(c) 19 blank space followed by 1 (d) Error.

**130.** Function template can accept
(a) only one parameter (b) two parameter
(c) maximum of five parameter (d) any number of parameter.

**131.** In which form of the following `get()` function returns the next character from the stream into the character variable sum.
(a) `sum=inputobj.get()`
(b) `inputobj.get(char & sum)`
(c) `inputobj.get(char *sum, int value, char endmarker)`
(d) None of the above.

**132.** When file is opened in read or write mode the file pointer is set
(a) at the beginning of file (b) at the end of file
(c) in the middle of file (d) anywhere in the file.

**133.** What is the output of the following statements?

```
#  include <iostream.h>
#define  max(x, y)
(((x) > (y))? (x): (y))
int  main  ()
{
cout  <<  max('A'  ,  3L)  <<  endl;
return  0;
}
```

(a) 64 (b) 65
(c) 66 (d) 67.

**134.** Which of the following is used to append in a random access file?
(a) `ios::in` (b) `ios::binary`
(c) `ios::ate` (d) `ios::out`.

**135.** Which of the following function returns true if any invalid file operation has been attempted or there is unrecoverable error?

(*a*) `int bad()` (*b*) `int eof`

(*c*) `int fail` (*d*) `int good()`.

**136.** Choose the function which is used to give the current position of the put operator.

(*a*) `seek()` (*b*) `seekp()`

(*c*) `tellg()` (*d*) `tellp()`.

**137.** The class that supports opening a file in write mode is

(*a*) `ofstream` (*b*) `ifstream`

(*c*) `ostream` (*d*) `istream`.

**138.** We can access string character using

(*a*) at () function (*b*) subscript operator [ ]

(*c*) () operator (*d*) none of the above.

**139.** Select the correct template definition

(*a*) template <class T> (*b*) class <template>

(*c*) template <T> (*d*) temp <T>.

**140.** Normal functions are invoked directly without using object of

(*a*) scope access (*b*) dot operator

(*c*) binary operator (*d*) decrement operator.

**141.** Which function is used to exchange the given string with another string?

(*a*) `assign()` (*b*) `replace()`

(*c*) `swap()` (*d*) `begin()`.

**142.** What will be the output of the following program?

```
int x = 5;
int main()
{
int x = x;
cout<<x++;
}
```

(*a*) 5 (*b*) 6

(*c*) 0 (*d*) unknown.

***143.** What will be the output of the following program?

```
int x = 5;
int main()
{
int x = x;
```

```
cout<<::x++;
}
```

(*a*) 5 (*b*) 6

(*c*) 0 (*d*) unknown.

**144.** Which member function is used to modify the string contents?

(*a*) `insert()` (*b*) `erase()`, `append()`

(*c*) `replace()` (*d*) all the above.

**145.** The string function which is used to compare and exchange the strings

(*a*) `compare()`, `assign()` (*b*) `assign()`, `begin()`

(*c*) `swap()`, `compare()` (*d*) `replace()`, `swap()`.

**146.** Choose the extraction operator?

(*a*) << (*b*) >

(*c*) >> (*d*) <.

***147.** What will be the output of the following program?

```
int main()
{
int a[4] = {4};
cout<<a[0];
return 0;
}
```

(*a*) 2 (*b*) 4

(*c*) 6 (*d*) 0.

**148.** Which conversion is not carried out in parameters of template functions?

(*a*) Explicit (*b*) Type

(*c*) Implicit (*d*) Global.

**149.** Which of the following is **NOT** true for a constructor?

(*a*) Constructor should be declared in the public section

(*b*) Constructor cannot have default arguments

(*c*) An object with a constructor cannot be used as a member of a union

(*d*) Constructors cannot be virtual.

**150.** Choose the vector class member function which gives the number of elements in a vector.

(*a*) `size()` (*b*) `resize()`

(*c*) `capacity()` (*d*) `at()`.

**151.** Choose the operator that can be overloaded

(*a*) Size of operator (*b*) Membership operator

(*c*) Conditional operator (*d*) Arithmetic operator.

**152.** Choose the stream class that acts as a base for filebuf class

(*a*) istream (*b*) ostream

(*c*) iostream (*d*) streambuf.

**153.** What is the task of unsetf ( )?

(*a*) To clear the flags specified

(*b*) To specify the required field size for displaying an output value

(*c*) To specify format flags that can control the form of output display

(*d*) none of the above.

**154.** Choose the manipulator which is equivalent to `ios` function `width()`

(*a*) `setw()` (*b*) `setfill()`

(*c*) `setiosflags()` (*d*) `setprecision()`.

**155.** Which one of the following is the function of `seek()`?

(*a*) moves get pointer to a specified locations

(*b*) moves put pointer to a specified locations

(*c*) gives the current position of the get pointer

(*d*) gives the current position of the put pointer.

**156.** What will be the action of `fout.seekg(o,ios::beg);`

(*a*) Go to the end of the file

(*b*) Go to the start of the file

(*c*) Stay at the current position

(*d*) Go backward by 0 bytes from the end.

**157.** When does the function `good()` returns *true*?

(*a*) if end-of-file is encountered

(*b*) if no error has occurred

(*c*) if an invalid operation is attempted

(*d*) when an input or output operation has failed.

**158.** Which one of the following not an associative container?

(*a*) set (*b*) multiset

(*c*) deque (*d*) map.

**159.** Which one of the following not a derived container?

(*a*) stack (*b*) queue

(*c*) priority queue (*d*) list.

**160.** What is the function of vector class member function `clear()`?

(*a*) Deletes specified elements

(*b*) Deletes all the elements from the vector

(*c*) Deletes the last element

(*d*) Deletes the first element from the vector.

**161.** Which function is used to insert a blank line at the current cursor position and also pushes the subsequent lines down by one line?

(*a*) `delline()` (*b*) `insilne()`

(*c*) `window` (*d*) `cputs()`.

**162.** Choose the function which is used to draw the line from the current cursor position to point `(x,y)`

(*a*) `line()` (*b*) `linerel()`

(*c*) `lineto()` (*d*) none of the above.

## ANSWERS

| | | | | | | |
|---|---|---|---|---|---|---|
| **1.** (*b*) | **2.** (*a*) | **3.** (*b*) | **4.** (*b*) | **5.** (*c*) | **6.** (*a*) | **7.** (*a*) |
| **8.** (*a*) | **9.** (*d*) | **10.** (*d*) | **11.** (*d*) | **12.** (*c*) | **13.** (*b*) | **14.** (*c*) |
| **15.** (*b*) | **16.** (*a*) | **17.** (*b*) | **18.** (*a*) | **19.** (*a*) | **20.** (*d*) | **21.** (*a*) |
| **22.** (*c*) | **23.** (*d*) | **24.** (*c*) | **25.** (*d*) | **26.** (*b*) | **27.** (*a*) | **28.** (*c*) |
| **29.** (*a*) | **30.** (*a*) | **31.** (*c*) | **32.** (b) | **33.** (*b*) | **34.** (*b*) | **35.** (*b*) |
| **36.** (*a*) | **37.** (*d*) | **38.** (*a*) | **39.** (*a*) | **40.** (*a*) | **41.** (*a*) | **42.** (*a*) |
| **43.** (*b*) | **44.** (*a*) | **45.** (*a*) | **46.** (*a*) | **47.** (*b*) | **48.** (*d*) | **49.** (*d*) |
| **50.** (*b*) | **51.** (*a*) | **52.** (*b*) | **53.** (*b*) | **54.** (*a*) | **55.** (*c*) | **56.** (*b*) |
| **57.** (*c*) | **58.** (*a*) | **59.** (*b*) | **60.** (*b*) | **61.** (*c*) | **62.** (*b*) | **63.** (*b*) |
| **64.** (*d*) | **65.** (*a*) | **66.** (*c*) | **67.** (*a*) | **68.** (*c*) | **69.** (*a*) | **70.** (*c*) |
| **71.** (*d*) | **72.** (*a*) | **73.** (*c*) | **74.** (*a*) | **75.** (*d*) | **76.** (*d*) | **77.** (*d*) |
| **78.** (*b*) | **79.** (*d*) | **80.** (*a*) | **81.** (*c*) | **82.** (*c*) | **83.** (*a*) | **84.** (*a*) |
| **85.** (*d*) | **86.** (*a*) | **87.** (*a*) | **88.** (*c*) | **89.** (*d*) | **90.** (*d*) | **91.** (*c*) |
| **92.** (*a*) | **93.** (*a*) | **94.** (*b*) | **95.** (*a*) | **96.** (*d*) | **97.** (*d*) | **98.** (*a*) |
| **99.** (*d*) | **100.** (*a*) | **101.** (*c*) | **102.** (*a*) | **103.** (*a*) | **104.** (*b*) | **105.** (*c*) |
| **106.** (*a*) | **107.** (*a*) | **108.** (*b*) | **109.** (*a*) | **110.** (*a*) | **111.** (*d*) | **112.** (*a*) |
| **113.** (*a*) | **114.** (*d*) | **115.** (*d*) | **116.** (*a*) | **117.** (*a*) | **118.** (*a*) | **119.** (*a*) |
| **120.** (*c*) | **121.** (*d*) | **122.** (*b*) | **123.** (*a*) | **124.** (*a*) | **125.** (*a*) | **126.** (*c*) |
| **127.** (*a*) | **128.** (*b*) | **129.** (*c*) | **130.** (*d*) | **131.** (*a*) | **132.** (*a*) | **133.** (*b*) |
| **134.** (*c*) | **135.** (*a*) | **136.** (*d*) | **137.** (*a*) | **138.** (*a*) | **139.** (*a*) | **140.** (*b*) |
| **141.** (*c*) | **142.** (*d*) | **143.** (*a*) | **144.** (*c*) | **145.** (*c*) | **146.** (*c*) | **147.** (*b*) |
| **148.** (*c*) | **149.** (*b*) | **150.** (*a*) | **151.** (*d*) | **152.** (*d*) | **153.** (*a*) | **154.** (*a*) |
| **155.** (*a*) | **156.** (*b*) | **157.** (*b*) | **158.** (*c*) | **159.** (*d*) | **160.** (*b*) | **161.** (*b*) |
| **162.** (*c*) | | | | | | |

## EXPLANATIONS

**11.** C++ places no limit on identifiers length, whereas the C language allows a maximum of 32 characters in an identifier name.

**12.** Since the expression consists of more than one data type ( a int, b float) , the C++ compiler converts the smaller data type to larger data type element (Automatic or implicit conversion). (15 + 4.1234 – 2 = 17.1234).

**14.** The buffer store ABCDE and the statement cout.write (buffer,3), prints first three character of the array.

**16.** When the statement int b=int (a)is executed the variable 'a' will be converted to integer type and only the integer part (9876) is assigned to the variable 'b'.

**18.** The array will have the value ABC. Since the null character is assigned to locations 2, the value AB will be displayed.

**21.** Performs bitwise left shift operation.

**22.** Performs bitwise right shift operation.

**23.** Performs bitwise negation operation.

**24.** Since 88%2=0, the condition is satisfied, therefore if displays the message "I like C++".

**26.** Multiple conditions can be given in a for loop, only one test condition is considered by the compiler. (In turbo C++ only the right most condition is considered).

**29.** The control statements are not terminated by semicolon.

**30.** The variable 'i' is incremented , decremented and again incremented.

**36.** The default value specified in the function prototype declaration is 10. When the function is called without parameter, the default value is used for the operation. Since the function is called with argument, the argument value will be used for the operation.

**45.** `sscanf` Reads data from *str* and stores them according to the parameter *format* into the locations given by the additional arguments. Locations pointed by each additional argument are filled with their corresponding type of value specified in the *format* string.

**49.** The index variable 'i' becomes 5 after the loop is terminated. Since the location *a(5)* is referenced, which does not exist, the unknown value is displayed.

**52.** The array x is assigned a size of 10.since it is an integer data type, therefore x occupies 10*2=20 bytes. The function sizeof (x) returns 20 and the sizeof(int) returns 2.

**53.** In C++ cin>>ws is used to freely read a keyboard stroke. When 'I Like You' is entered the first seven character will be assigned to the array since array size is 8.

**55.** 'b' is a pointer variable which holds the address of a. The indirection operator *b gives the value of 'a', which is 99. The value 99 is decremented by 1 and multiplied by 2 according to the given expression. Therefore the program returns 196.

**61.** The C++ language provides mechanisms for mixing code that is compiled by compatible C and C++ compilers in the same program. You can experience varying degrees of success as you port such code to different platforms and compilers.

**66.** The ++ operator has higher precedence than * so the statement will increment pointer and then retrieve the content of the new location pointed to by ptr.

**70.** The size of the given array is 10. Since it contains integer data type, the function size of (x) returns 20 and the size (int) returns 2. Therefore 20/2= 10.

**75.** Only addition and subtraction are possible with pointer variables.

**114.** In the program the class variable 'd' is the object derived class. The function call 'd.f (1)' call the derived class version and the value '1' is passed. Since the variable 'n' is double type the value 1.000000 is displayed.

**119.** The pointer variable 'x' is added with 3. Therefore, in the string constant 'HELLO', the character from the 3rd position will be displayed.

**129.** Since the field width is declared as 20, the value '1' is displayed with leading 19 blank spaces.

**133.** The macro max () returns the maximum value of x&y. The ASCII value of 'A ' is 65, the macro returns 65.

**143.** The scope resolution operator in the program access the value of global variable.

**147.** The array a[4] will store the value as {4,0,0,0} and a[0] holds the value 4 which is displayed.

CHAPTER 7

# COMPUTER GRAPHICS AND MULTIMEDIA

1. The maximum number of points that can be displayed without overlap on a CRT is referred as

   (a) resolution (b) persistence

   (c) pixel (d) resistance.

2. Image is measured in terms of

   (a) pixels per inch (b) pixels per sq inch

   (c) pixels per mm (d) pixels per sq cm.

3. Choose the Touch-Sensitive Screen which emits inaudible high-frequency sound waves along two perpendicular edges and reflected back to the emitters by the finger.

   (a) Electrical Touch-Sensitive Screen

   (b) Optical Touch-Sensitive Screen

   (c) Electro-Mechanical Touch-Sensitive Screen

   (d) Acoustic Touch-Sensitive Screen.

4. Which of the following statements is not true?

   (a) Colour monitors have three electron guns

   (b) Colour monitors can be used with image processing as a powerful tool in medical field

   (c) Colour monitors are faster than monochrome monitors

   (d) Colour monitors may not be sharp as monochrome in text processing.

5. A black-and-white system with one bit per pixel, the frame buffer is commonly known as

   (a) bitmap (b) pel

   (c) pixmap (d) none of the above.

6. Consider the following table

| Column A | | Column B | |
|---|---|---|---|
| 1 | MediaWall | A | System with multiple bits per pixel |
| 2 | DVST | B | Used in small systems |
| 3 | LCD | C | Used to grasp a virtual object |
| 4 | Pixmap | D | Multiscreen System |
| 5 | Data glove | E | Stores the picture information as a charge distribution |

Which of the following is the proper match?

(*a*) 1 & B 2 & A 3 & D 4 & C 5 & E
(*b*) 1 & D 2 & A 3 & B 4 & E 5 & C
(*c*) 1 & B 2 & E 3 & A 4 & C 5 & D
(*d*) 1 & D 2 & E 3 & B 4 & A 5 & C.

7. A frame buffer which includes 15 bits per pel of picture memory will be able to display
(*a*) 15 simultaneous colour
(*b*) approximately 32,000 simultaneous colour
(*c*) 225 simultaneous colour
(*d*) approximately 15 million simultaneous colour

8. A system which is specially designed for training applications are called
(*a*) GUI (*b*) simulators
(*c*) video display devices (*d*) calligraphic display.

9. The expansion of PHIGS is
(*a*) Programmer's Help Interactive Graphic Standard
(*b*) Programmer's Hierarchical Interface Graphic Standard
(*c*) Programmer's Hierarchical Interactive Graphic Standard
(*d*) Programmer's Hierarchical Interactive Graphic Station.

10. Consider the following table

| Column A | | Column B | |
|---|---|---|---|
| 1 | Pixel | A | Gas discharge display |
| 2 | Display list | B | Graphics Controller |
| 3 | Plasma Display | C | Pel |
| 4 | Display Processor | D | Vector or Stroke |
| 5 | Calligraphic | E | Refresh buffer |

Which of the following is the proper match?

(*a*) 1 & C 2 & E 3 & A 4 & B 5 & D

(*b*) 1 & D 2 & A 3 & B 4 & E 5 & C

(*c*) 1 & B 2 & E 3 & A 4 & C 5 & D

(*d*) 1 & D 2 & E 3 & B 4 & C 5 & A.

**11.** Which among the following video devices have reduced volume, weight and power?

(*a*) Direct View Storage Tubes (*b*) Flat-panel display

(*c*) Beam Penetrating CRT (*d*) Shadow-Mask CRT.

**12.** Which of the following terms refer to the combination of two dominant characteristics — frequency and purity?

(*a*) Hue (*b*) Luminance

(*c*) Saturation (*d*) Chromacity.

**13.** Which of the following statement is correct for obtaining Tint?

(*a*) Mixing black with pure colour

(*b*) Mixing white with pure colour

(*c*) Mixing red with pure colour

(*d*) Mixing grey with pure colour.

**14.** Which of the following techniques used for Anti-aliasing?

(*a*) Pixel Phasing and Continuous Edge Graphics

(*b*) Symmetric DDA and Simple DDA

(*c*) Cohen-Sutherland method and Sutherland-Hodgman method

(*d*) BSP Tree and Octree method.

**15.** A RGB raster system with 24 bits per pixel and a screen resolution of 1024 by 1024 requires how much memory storage for the frame buffer?

(*a*) 1 MB (*b*) 2 MB

(*c*) 3 MB (*d*) 4 MB.

**16.** Which of the following high level language has no pixel graphics capabilities, but has reverse video and row-location facility in text mode?

(*a*) Fortran (*b*) COBOL

(*c*) C language (*d*) PASCAL.

**17.** In the CMY model, point (1, 1, 1) represents

(*a*) Blue (*b*) Green

(*c*) Black (*d*) White.

**18.** In the RGB model, point (1, 1, 1) represents

(*a*) Blue (*b*) Green

(*c*) Black (*d*) White.

## The Next Three Questions (19–21) are Based on the Following Information

**In a graph and two positions P(x1,y1) and Q(x2,y2) are given where (x1=1,y1=1)&(x2=6,y2=5). A line is drawn between these two points.**

***19.** What would be the value for the slope *m*?

(*a*) 0.5 (*b*) 0.8

(*c*) 0.9 (*d*) 1.0.

***20.** What would be the *y* intercept?

(*a*) 0.2 (*b*) 0.3

(*c*) 0.4 (*d*) 0.5.

***21.** What would be *y* when *x*=5?

(*a*) 8 (*b*) 6

(*c*) 5 (*d*) 4.

**22.** Choose the input device which is commonly used for drawing, painting, or interactively selecting coordinate positions on an object

(*a*) Keyboard (*b*) Image Scanner

(*c*) Data Glove (*d*) Digitizer.

**23.** The path the electron beam takes after refreshing each scan line is known as

(*a*) horizontal retrace (*b*) vertical retrace

(*c*) diagonal retrace (*d*) left to right retrace.

**24.** The value of initial decision parameter in Bresenham's line drawing algorithm for |m|<1 is:

(*a*) $\Delta y - \Delta x$ (*b*) $2\Delta y - \Delta x$

(*c*) $-2\Delta y + \Delta x$ (*d*) $\Delta y - 2\Delta x$.

**25.** Using Bresenham's line drawing algorithm, a line with endpoints (20, 10) and (30, 18) is plotted with the initial point (20, 10). What will be the successive pixel positions along the line path ?

(*a*) (21, 11), (22, 12), (23, 13), (24, 14), (25, 15)...

(*b*) (21, 11), (22, 12), (23, 12), (24, 13), (25, 14)...

(*c*) (20, 11), (21, 12), (22, 13), (23, 14), (24, 15)...

(*d*) (21, 10), (22, 11), (23, 12), (24, 13), (25, 14)...

**26.** The acronym of DDA is

(*a*) Digital Data Analyser (*b*) Differential Data Analyser

(*c*) Digital Differential Analyser (*d*) Data Differential Analyser.

**27.** Which of the following graphics format is a special bitmap image compression format used to reduce the file size after losing some amount of the detail which are not noticeable?

(*a*) GIF format (*b*) JPEG format

(*c*) TIFF format (*d*) PCX format.

***28.** Using Symmetric DDA straight line drawing algorithm, a line with endpoints (10, 16) and (20, 21) is plotted with the initial point (10, 15). What will be the successive pixel positions along the line path?

(*a*) (10, 15), (11, 16), (11, 17), (12, 18), (13, 18)...

(*b*) (10, 15), (11, 15), (11, 16), (12, 17), (13, 18)...

(*c*) (10, 15), (11, 15), (11, 16), (12, 16), (13, 17)...

(*d*) None of the above.

**29.** How many levels of gray pixels are there for a black and white image?

(*a*) 254 (*b*) 255

(*c*) 256 (*d*) 257.

**30.** What is the value of initial decision parameter in mid point circle drawing algorithm? (where $r$ is radius)

(*a*) $3 - 2r$ (*b*) $1 - 2r$

(*c*) $3 - r$ (*d*) $5/4 - r$.

**31.** Which one of the algorithm that identifies the portion of a picture that is either inside or outside a specified region of space?

(*a*) Clipping algorithm (*b*) Viewing algorithm

(*c*) Modeling algorithm (*d*) Transformation algorithm.

**32.** Chose the line clipping algorithm which cannot be applied to three dimensional clipping.

(*a*) Cohen-Sutherland method (*b*) Nicholl-Lee-Nicholl method

(*c*) Liang-Barsky method (*d*) Sutherland-Hodgman method.

**33.** What is the matrix required for translating a two dimensional point $(x, y)$, 6 units in the $x$ direction and 9 units in the $y$ direction?

(*a*) $\begin{pmatrix} 1 & 0 & 6 \\ 0 & 1 & 9 \\ 0 & 0 & 1 \end{pmatrix}$ (*b*) $\begin{pmatrix} 1 & 0 & 6 \\ 9 & 1 & 0 \\ 0 & 0 & 1 \end{pmatrix}$

(*c*) $\begin{pmatrix} 1 & 0 & 6 \\ 0 & 1 & 0 \\ 9 & 0 & 1 \end{pmatrix}$ (*d*) $\begin{pmatrix} 1 & 0 & 0 \\ 6 & 1 & 9 \\ 0 & 0 & 1 \end{pmatrix}$.

**34.** Run-length encoding technique is used for

(*a*) Image smoothening (*b*) Image compression

(*c*) Image coloring (*d*) Image dithering.

**35.** What should be the minimum refresh rate to avoid flickering?

(*a*) 25 frames per second (*b*) 60 frames per second

(*c*) 75 frames per second (*d*) 80 frames per second.

**36.** The transformation that enhances or reduces the size of object is called

(*a*) Translation (*b*) Scaling

(*c*) Shear (*d*) Rotation.

**37.** The transformation that changes the coordinate positions of an object along a circular path is called

(*a*) Translation (*b*) Scaling

(*c*) Rotation (*d*) Reflection.

**38.** The transformation that changes the coordinate position of an object along a straight line path is called

(*a*) translation (*b*) scaling

(*c*) rotation (*d*) reflection.

**39.** The transformation that produces a mirror image of an object is called

(*a*) translation (*b*) scaling

(*c*) rotation (*d*) reflection.

**40.** On a bilevel system moving a block of pixel from one location to another location is called

(*a*) bitBlt (*b*) blkBlt

(*c*) bitBlk (*d*) blkBit.

**41.** Aspect ratio is

(*a*) the ratio of image's width to its height

(*b*) the ratio of window to viewport height

(*c*) the ratio of image's intensity levels

(*d*) the ratio of image's height to its width.

**42.** What is the homogenous matrix for a translation by (20, 30, 40)?

(*a*) $\begin{pmatrix} 1 & 0 & 0 & 20 \\ 0 & 1 & 0 & 30 \\ 0 & 0 & 1 & 40 \\ 0 & 0 & 0 & 1 \end{pmatrix}$ (*b*) $\begin{pmatrix} 0 & 0 & 0 & 20 \\ 0 & 0 & 0 & 30 \\ 0 & 0 & 0 & 40 \\ 0 & 0 & 0 & 1 \end{pmatrix}$

(*c*) $\begin{pmatrix} 1 & 0 & 0 & 20 \\ 0 & 1 & 0 & 30 \\ 0 & 0 & 1 & 40 \\ 0 & 0 & 0 & 0 \end{pmatrix}$ (*d*) $\begin{pmatrix} 20 & 0 & 0 & 1 \\ 0 & 30 & 0 & 1 \\ 0 & 0 & 40 & 1 \\ 0 & 0 & 0 & 1 \end{pmatrix}$.

**43.** When the projection is perpendicular to the view plane, then such type of projection is called

(*a*) Isometric projection (*b*) Axonometric Orthographic projection

(*c*) Orthographic parallel projection (*d*) Oblique parallel projection.

## The Next Seven Questions (44–50) are Based on the Following Information and Related to Move Transformation.

**For the quadrilateral ABCD with vertex coordinates A(10, 8), B(20, 8), C(30, 15) and D(10, 25)**

***44.** Moving the quadrilateral ABCD by 10 length units to right and 5 length units downwards is

(a) $\begin{pmatrix} 20 & 3 & 1 \\ 30 & 3 & 1 \\ 40 & 10 & 1 \\ 20 & 20 & 1 \end{pmatrix}$ (b) $\begin{pmatrix} 10 & 3 & 1 \\ 20 & 3 & 1 \\ 30 & 10 & 1 \\ 10 & 20 & 1 \end{pmatrix}$

(c) $\begin{pmatrix} 20 & 3 & 1 \\ 30 & 3 & 1 \\ 40 & 10 & 1 \\ 20 & 20 & 1 \end{pmatrix}$ (d) $\begin{pmatrix} 20 & 3 & 1 \\ 30 & 3 & 1 \\ 30 & 3 & 1 \\ 30 & 3 & 1 \end{pmatrix}$.

***45.** What will be the transformed coordinates of the quadrilateral ABCD about the *x*-axis?

(a) $\begin{pmatrix} 10 & 8 & 1 \\ 20 & 8 & 1 \\ 30 & 15 & 1 \\ 10 & 25 & 1 \end{pmatrix}$ (b) $\begin{pmatrix} 10 & 3 & 1 \\ 30 & 3 & 1 \\ 30 & 10 & 1 \\ 10 & 20 & 1 \end{pmatrix}$

(c) $\begin{pmatrix} 10 & -8 & 1 \\ 20 & -8 & 1 \\ 30 & -15 & 1 \\ 10 & -25 & 1 \end{pmatrix}$ (d) $\begin{pmatrix} 20 & 1 & 8 \\ 30 & 1 & 8 \\ 40 & 1 & 15 \\ 20 & 1 & 25 \end{pmatrix}$.

***46.** What will be the transformed coordinates of the quadrilateral ABCD about the *y*-axis?

(a) $\begin{pmatrix} 10 & 8 & 1 \\ 20 & 8 & 1 \\ 30 & 15 & 1 \\ 10 & 25 & 1 \end{pmatrix}$ (b) $\begin{pmatrix} 10 & 3 & 1 \\ 20 & 3 & 1 \\ 30 & 10 & 1 \\ 10 & 20 & 1 \end{pmatrix}$

(c) $\begin{pmatrix} 0 & -8 & 1 \\ 20 & -8 & 1 \\ 30 & -15 & 1 \\ 10 & -20 & 1 \end{pmatrix}$ (d) $\begin{pmatrix} -10 & 8 & 1 \\ -20 & 8 & 1 \\ -30 & 15 & 1 \\ -10 & 25 & 1 \end{pmatrix}$.

***47.** What will be the transformed coordinates of the quadrilateral ABCD about the origin?

(a) $\begin{pmatrix} 10 & 8 & 1 \\ 20 & 8 & 1 \\ 30 & 15 & 1 \\ 10 & 15 & 1 \end{pmatrix}$ (b) $\begin{pmatrix} -10 & -8 & 1 \\ -20 & -8 & 1 \\ -30 & -15 & 1 \\ -10 & -25 & 1 \end{pmatrix}$

(c) $\begin{pmatrix} 10 & -8 & 1 \\ 20 & -8 & 1 \\ 30 & -15 & 1 \\ 10 & -25 & 1 \end{pmatrix}$ (d) $\begin{pmatrix} -10 & 8 & 1 \\ -20 & 8 & 1 \\ -30 & 15 & 1 \\ -10 & 25 & 1 \end{pmatrix}$.

***48.** What will be the transformed coordinates of the quadrilateral ABCD sheared by a factor of 0.05 in the $x$ direction and by a factor of –0.1 in the direction of $y$?

(a) $\begin{pmatrix} 10.4 & 8 & 1 \\ 20.4 & 8 & 1 \\ 30.75 & 15 & 1 \\ 11.25 & 25 & 1 \end{pmatrix}$ (b) $\begin{pmatrix} 10.40 & 7 & 1 \\ 20.40 & 6 & 1 \\ 30.75 & 12 & 1 \\ 11.25 & 24 & 1 \end{pmatrix}$

(c) $\begin{pmatrix} -10 & 8 & 1 \\ -20 & 8 & 1 \\ -30 & 15 & 1 \\ -10 & 25 & 1 \end{pmatrix}$ (d) $\begin{pmatrix} -10 & 8 & 1 \\ -20 & 8 & 1 \\ -30 & 15 & 1 \\ -10 & 25 & 1 \end{pmatrix}$.

***49.** What will be the transformed coordinates of the quadrilateral ABCD scaled by a factor of 1.4 in the $x$ direction and by a factor of 0.5 in the direction of $y$?

(a) $\begin{pmatrix} 10.4 & 8 & 1 \\ 20.4 & 8 & 1 \\ 30.75 & 15 & 1 \\ 11.25 & 25 & 1 \end{pmatrix}$ (b) $\begin{pmatrix} 10.40 & 7 & 1 \\ 20.40 & 6 & 1 \\ 30.75 & 12 & 1 \\ 11.25 & 24 & 1 \end{pmatrix}$

(c) $\begin{pmatrix} 14 & 4 & 1 \\ 28 & 4 & 1 \\ 42 & 7.5 & 1 \\ 14 & 7.5 & 1 \end{pmatrix}$ (d) $\begin{pmatrix} -10 & 8 & 1 \\ -20 & 8 & 1 \\ -30 & 15 & 1 \\ -10 & 25 & 1 \end{pmatrix}$.

***50.** What will be the transformed coordinates of the quadrilateral ABCD rotated by a counter-clockwise angle of 60°.

(a) $\begin{pmatrix} 10.4 & 8 & 1 \\ 20.4 & 8 & 1 \\ 30.75 & 15 & 1 \\ 11.25 & 25 & 1 \end{pmatrix}$ (b) $\begin{pmatrix} 10.40 & 7 & 1 \\ 20.40 & 6 & 1 \\ 30.75 & 12 & 1 \\ 11.25 & 24 & 1 \end{pmatrix}$

(c) $\begin{pmatrix} -1.928 & 12.66 & 1 \\ 3.072 & 21.32 & 1 \\ 2.01 & 33.48 & 1 \\ -7.99 & 16.16 & 1 \end{pmatrix}$ (d) $\begin{pmatrix} -1.928 & 8 & 1 \\ 3.072 & 8 & 1 \\ 2.01 & 15 & 1 \\ -7.99 & 25 & 1 \end{pmatrix}$.

**51.** The region against which an object is to clipped is called

(a) Clip Window (b) Clip View-port

(c) Clip Area (d) Clip Region.

**52.** Consider the following information, diagrams and table

The arrows in the picture denote light rays. The dashed lines represent the material type to be considered. The key is in the interaction of the light rays with the material.

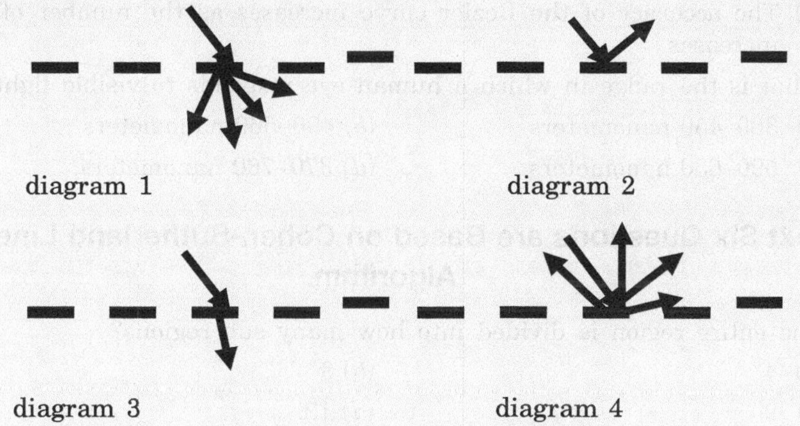


| | Column A | | Column B |
|---|---|---|---|
| 1 | Specular reflection | A | diagram 1 |
| 2 | Translucent | B | diagram 2 |
| 3 | Diffuse reflection | C | diagram 3 |
| 4 | Transparent | D | diagram 4 |

Which of the following is the proper match in the above table?

(a) 1 & C 2 & D 3 & A 4 & B

(b) 1 & B 2 & A 3 & D 4 & C

(c) 1 & B 2 & D 3 & A 4 & C

(d) 1 & D 2 & A 3 & B 4 & C.

**53.** The Phong reflection model simplifies light-matter interactions into (essentially) 4 vectors and a number of constants. Which of the following is **NOT** a vector needed for the Phong reflection model?

(*a*) Surface Normal (*b*) Direction to Viewer
(*c*) Direction to Material Center (*d*) Direction to Light.

**54.** Which of the following statement best describes ambient lighting?
(*a*) The general lighting found everywhere in a scene
(*b*) The shiny highlights of the object
(*c*) It is a technique for wrapping bitmap textures onto model surface
(*d*) Defined solely by the light position relative to the surface.

**55.** Which of the following is true with regard to Bezier curve?
(*a*) It passes through all control points
(*b*) It lies within the convex hull of the control points
(*c*) It is always a collection of cubic polynomials
(*d*) The accuracy of the Bezier curve increases as the number of control points increases.

**56.** What is the range in which a human eye responds to visible light wavelengths?
(*a*) 380–450 nanometers (*b*) 490–560 nanometers
(*c*) 590–630 nanometers (*d*) 370–760 nanometers.

## The Next Six Questions are Based on Cohen-Sutherland Line Clipping Algorithm.

**57.** The entire region is divided into how many sub regions?
(*a*) 4 (*b*) 8
(*c*) 9 (*d*) 12.

**58.** What will be the region code if a point is within the clipping rectangle?
(*a*) 0000 (*b*) 0001
(*c*) 1000 (*d*) 1111.

**59.** How many bits are used for representing each sub region?
(*a*) 1 (*b*) 2
(*c*) 3 (*d*) 4.

**60.** Suppose the codes of the two points P and Q are 0101 and 0110 then the line segment joining the points P and Q will be ________ the clipping window.
(*a*) totally outside (*b*) partially outside
(*c*) totally inside (*d*) partially inside.

**61.** Which of the following statements is more appropriate, when the four bit codes have two ones and two zeros?
(*a*) The regions are in the four corners
(*b*) The regions are on the left side corners
(c) The regions are on the right side corners
(*d*) The regions are on the top corners.

62. Which of the following statement is true when the first bit of four bit code is one (e.g. 1000)

(a) All three regions are on top (b) all the three regions are on bottom

(c) All the regions are on left (d) All the regions are on right.

63. The 3D transformation matrix for $z$-axis shear with parameters 2 and 3 respectively, is given by

(a) $\begin{pmatrix} 1 & 2 & 0 & 0 \\ 0 & 3 & 0 & 0 \\ 0 & 0 & 1 & 0 \\ 0 & 0 & 0 & 1 \end{pmatrix}$ (b) $\begin{pmatrix} 1 & 0 & 0 & 0 \\ 0 & 1 & 0 & 0 \\ 0 & 2 & 1 & 0 \\ 0 & 3 & 0 & 1 \end{pmatrix}$

(c) $\begin{pmatrix} 1 & 0 & 2 & 0 \\ 0 & 1 & 3 & 0 \\ 0 & 0 & 1 & 0 \\ 0 & 0 & 0 & 1 \end{pmatrix}$ (d) $\begin{pmatrix} 1 & 0 & 0 & 2 \\ 0 & 1 & 0 & 3 \\ 0 & 0 & 1 & 1 \\ 0 & 0 & 0 & 1 \end{pmatrix}$.

64. Which of the following primarily intended to help animation applications?

(a) Morphing (b) Double buffer

(c) Diffuse reflection (d) Z-buffer.

65. GKS and PHIGS are

(a) Graphics Controller (b) Graphics Monitors

(c) Graphics software packages (d) Graphics Function.

66. Loseless compression technique achieves a reduction in size in the range of

(a) 1/10 to 1/50 (b) 1/10 to 1/60

(c) 1/15 to 1/20 (d) 1/10 to 1/80.

67. Which one of the following holds good for luminance?

(a) color sensation (b) color intensity

(c) hue (d) brightness.

68. Which of the following statements are correct with regard to the features of nonuniform rational B-splines (NURB)?

(a) NURB surfaces are special form of Bezier surfaces

(b) NURB surfaces have non-uniformity in its knot vectors

(c) NURB surfaces allow accurate modeling of graphics objects

(d) NURB surfaces have uniformity in its knot vectors.

69. In YIQ color model, parameter Y contains

(a) purity (b) brightness

(c) hue (d) luminance.

70. The distance between one set of RGB phosphors and next set is known as

(a) Hot spot (b) dot pitch

(c) dot spot (d) Hot pitch.

**71.** Which of the following projection technique does NOT have the direction of projection perpendicular to the viewing plane.

(*a*) Orthographic Parallel Projection

(*b*) Axonometric Parallel Projection

(c) Oblique Parallel Projection

(*d*) None of the above.

**72.** What is the maximum number of sides which a triangle might have clipped to a rectangular viewport?

(*a*) 3 (*b*) 5

(*c*) 7 (*d*) 9.

**73.** The following shows the general three dimensional transformation pipelines.

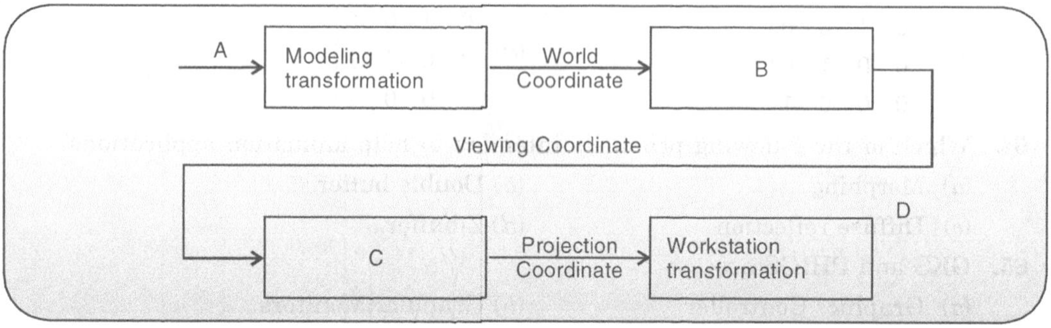


Identify from the following list, the most appropriate terms for A, B, C, D respectively

(*a*) Modeling Coordinate, Projection Transformation, Viewing Transformation, Device Coordinate

(*b*) Device Coordinate, Projection Transformation, Viewing Transformation, Modeling Coordinate

(*c*) Modeling Coordinate, Viewing Transformation, Projection Transformation, Device Coordinate

(*d*) Modeling Coordinate, Viewing Transformation, Projection Transformation, Device Coordinate.

**74.** Which of the following Hidden-line/surface removal method implemented in the world coordinate system?

(*a*) Octree method (*b*) Scan Line method

(*c*) Ray Tracing method (*d*) Back Face Detection method.

**75.** The Cartesian coordinate representation of the equation $x^2 + y^2 + z^2 = r^2$ denotes a

(*a*) Cone (*b*) Cylinder

(*c*) Sphere (*d*) Ellipsoid.

**76.** Which one of the shape of the object can show certain degree of fluidity?

(*a*) Ellipsoidal (*b*) Superellipse

(*c*) Torus (*d*) Blobby.

**77.** The set of coordinate positions that indicate the shape of the Spline curve is called

(*a*) Path points (*b*) Control points

(*c*) Continuity points (*d*) Transition points.

**78.** Master coordinate system is

(*a*) The coordinate system in which the image is defined

(*b*) The coordinate system in which the object is defined

(*c*) The coordinate system in which the surfaces is defined

(*d*) The coordinate system in which the transformation are performed.

**79.** Which of the following color has the low-frequency in the visible band?

(*a*) Violet (*b*) Green

(*c*) Red (*d*) blue.

**80.** Which of the following color has the high frequency in the visible band?

(*a*) Violet (*b*) Green

(*c*) Red (*d*) Blue.

**81.** JPEG refers to

(*a*) Junior Photographic Expert Group

(*b*) Joint Photographic Expert Group

(*c*) Joint Photo Expert Group

(*d*) Joint Photographic Excellent Group.

**82.** The Baseline TIFF bilevel images were called

(*a*) TIFF class A images (*b*) TIFF class B images

(*c*) TIFF class C images (*d*) TIFF class D images.

**83.** Which of the following is true for Sutherland-Hodgman method?

(*a*) The method tests each edge of the polygon for visibility against the window

(*b*) The method tests each edge of the window for visibility against the polygon

(*c*) The method tests each side of the polygon against all four sides of the window

(*d*) This method finds the midpoint of the visible segment of polygon side in a window.

**84.** The file extension for MIDI file is

(*a*) .RMD (*b*) .MID

(*c*) .RMI (*d*) .RIM.

**85.** Music quality requires a normal sampling rate of

(*a*) 4 KHz at 8 bits (*b*) 8 KHz at 16 bits

(*c*) 16 KHz at 32 bits (*d*) 4 KHz at 16 bits.

**86.** Which surface can be described as an extension of a spherical surface?

(*a*) Polygon (*b*) Ellipsoidal

(*c*) Quadric (*d*) Hyperboloids.

*87. Which of the following is not a Blobby object?

(a) Molecular structure (b) Water droplets

(c) Human muscle (d) Human bone.

*88. Identify the incorrect statement with regard to the term spline in computer graphics.

(a) Used to design curves and surface shapes

(b) Used to specify animation paths for an object

(c) The first spline curves developed for graphics application is Kochanek-Bartels splines

(d) Design of automobile bodies is an example of CAD applications for splines.

*89. Which among the following is not modeled with *self-affine fractal* construction method?

(a) Clouds (b) Shrubs

(c) Water (d) Tarrain.

90. From the following table identify the correct match.

| Column A | | Column B | |
|---|---|---|---|
| 1 | Depth-buffer method | A | Depth-sorting method |
| 2 | Lucasfilm | B | Hidden-line detection method |
| 3 | Painters, Algorithm | C | Z-buffer method |
| 4 | Wireframe-visibility method | D | A-buffer method |

(a) 1 & C 2 & D 3 & B 4 & A

(b) 1 & D 2 & A 3 & B 4 & C

(c) 1 & B 2 & D 3 & A 4 & C

(d) 1 & C 2 & D 3 & A 4 & B.

91. Choose the shading technique that computes the most accurate lighting?

(a) Flat Shading (b) Fast Phong Shading

(c) Gouraud Shading (d) Ray Tracing.

92. The Phong reflection model simplifies light-matter interactions into (essentially) 4 vectors and a number of constants. Which piece of the Phong model is responsible for giving spheres their bright white spots?

(a) Ambient (b) Diffuse

(c) Specular (d) None of the above.

93. The following statements are about computer animation.

(i) High Level Languages like C, FORTRAN can be used to program animation functions.

(ii) Key-frame systems are specialized animation language.

(iii) Animation sequences can be constructed using kinematic descriptions.

(*iv*) Animation sequence is designed with storyboard layout, object definitions, Key-frame.

specifications and generation of in-between frames

Which of the above statement is/are true?

(*a*) (*i*) and (*ii*) only (*b*) (*i*) and (*iii*) only

(*c*) (*ii*) and (*iv*) only (*d*) All.

**94.** Which of the following are the primary components of multimedia technology?

(*a*) Computubility, text, graphics, audio, video and animation

(*b*) text, graphics, audio, video, animation and non-interactivity

(*c*) text, graphics, audio, video, animation and interactivity

(*d*) text, graphics, audio, video, computability and interactivity.

**95.** Choose the correct statement.

(*a*) Multimedia technology is interactive and non-linear

(*b*) Multimedia technology is non-interactive and linear

(*c*) Multimedia technology is interactive and linear

(*d*) Multimedia technology is non-interactive and non-linear.

**96.** The term 'sampling' in multimedia technology can be best described as

(*a*) Conversion of analog audio data to digital data

(*b*) Conversion of analog video data to digital data

(*c*) Obtaining discrete signals from an analog input signal

(*d*) none of the above.

**97.** The images that are generated based on some arithmetic calculation using a computer is called

(*a*) Visible image (*b*) Nonvisible image

(*c*) Real image (*d*) Abstract image.

**98.** The file format that allows embedding graphics and other file formats within a document is

(*a*) Palette File Format (PAL) (*b*) Musical Instrument Digital Interface (MIDI)

(*c*) Rich Text Format (RFT) (*d*) Device-Independent Bitmap (DIB).

**99.** Which of the following file format used for digital video animation?

(*a*) Multimedia Movie Format (MMM)

(*b*) Apple's Movie Format

(*c*) Digital Video Command Set (DVCS)

(*d*) Digital Video Media Control Interface (DV-MCI).

**100.** The exact amount of digital data depends on the

(*a*) resolution of scanning (*b*) size of the image

(*c*) colour of the image (*d*) gray shade of the image.

**101.** In multimedia technology compression of data object results in

(*i*) reduction of storage area (*ii*) higher speed of transmission

(*iii*) image quality improvement (*iv*) colour improvement.

In the above statement

(*a*) Only (*i*) and (*ii*) are true (*b*) Only (*i*) and (*iii*) are true

(*c*) Only (*i*) and (*iv*) are true (*d*) All are true.

**102.** Which of the following statement is/are true with regard to data organisation in multimedia system?

(*i*) Users need to know data formats or physical storage structures

(*ii*) Storage design is independent of specific applications

(*iii*) Recovery is independent of the application program

(*iv*) Integrity assurances is independent of application program

(*a*) Only (*i*) (*b*) Only (*i*) and (*iv*)

(*c*) Other than (*i*) (*d*) All.

**103.** The key characteristics that differentiate Hypermedia from Multimedia is

(*a*) Interactivity (*b*) Easy to use

(*c*) Non-linearity (*d*) Modularity.

**104.** On which of the following factor will the quality of digitised audio does not depend?

(*a*) The Sampling Rate (*b*) The Bit Depth

(*c*) The Audio Format (*d*) The Aspect ratio.

**105.** Choose the lossless compression from the following

(*a*) Run-length encoding (*b*) JPEG

(*c*) MPEG (*d*) Fractals.

**106.** The abbreviation of DCT is

(*a*) Digital Cosine Transform (*b*) Direct Cosine Transform

(*c*) Discrete Cosine Transform (*d*) Digital Cosine Transmission.

**107.** Which of the following picture type never used for references?

(*a*) Intrapictures

(*b*) Unidirectionally predicted pictures

(*c*) Bidirectionally predicted pictures

(*d*) none of the above.

**108.** The characteristics on which quality of sampled digital audio depends on

(*a*) The Sampling Rate (*b*) The Bit Depth

(*c*) The Audio Compressor (*d*) Recording format.

**109.** Which of the following components of a Pen collects all pen information and builds pen packets for the recognition context manager?

(*a*) Digitizer (*b*) Pen Driver

(*c*) Recognizer (*d*) Display Driver.

**110.** Which of the following file type is not based on raster graphics format?

(*a*) GIF Format (*b*) Adobe Illustrator

(*c*) TIFF Format (*d*) BMP format.

**111.** Which of the following is a communication standard developed in early 1980s for electronic musical instruments and computers?

(*a*) MIDI (*b*) MIC

(*c*) MP3 (*d*) CCD.

**112.** Which of the following statement regarding graphics file types are correct?

(*a*) TIFF format is used in most digital camera because of their excellent quality?

(*b*) BMP format is widely used due to the small file size with higher image quality?

(*c*) GIF format is widely used web banners

(*d*) TGA format is used to create composite images using alpha channels.

***113.** Which of the following statement is correct with regard to 'TWAIN'?

(*a*) It is a compression technique (*b*) It is an encoding technique

(*c*) It is a file format (*d*) None of the above.

**114.** The following table shows the file type and the filename used for Microsoft Windows Multimedia RIFF file types.

| | File Type | | File Extension |
|---|---|---|---|
| 1 | Waveform Audio File | A | .RMI |
| 2 | Audio Video interleaved File | B | .RDI |
| 3 | MIDI File | C | .WAV |
| 4 | Device Independent Bitmap File | D | .PAL |
| 5 | Palette File | E | .AVI |

Which of the following is the proper match?

(*a*) 1 & C 2 & E 3 & A 4 & B 5 & D

(*b*) 1 & D 2 & A 3 & B 4 & E 5 & C

(*c*) 1 & B 2 & E 3 & A 4 & C 5 & D

(*d*) 1 & D 2 & E 3 & A 4 & C 5 & B.

**115.** Which of the following filter extracts objects from images by highlighting all edges?

(*a*) Low Pass Filter (*b*) High Pass Filter

(*c*) Laplacian Filter (*d*) Edge-detection Filter.

**116.** The following table gives information about wavelength (in nanometre) and frequency (in Hertz) of some colours.

| | Colour | | Wavelength and Frequency | |
|---|---|---|---|---|
| 1 | Blue | A | 490 – 560 | $5.6 \times 10^{14} - 6.1 \times 10^{14}$ |
| 2 | Green | B | 560 – 590 | $5.4 \times 10^{14} - 5.4 \times 10^{14}$ |
| 3 | Yellow | C | 630 – 760 | $3.9 \times 10^{14} - 4.8 \times 10^{14}$ |
| 4 | Orange | D | 450 – 490 | $6.1 \times 10^{14} - 6.6 \times 10^{14}$ |
| 5 | Red | E | 590 – 630 | $4.8 \times 10^{14} - 5.1 \times 10^{14}$ |

Which of the following is the proper match?

(*a*) 1 & C 2 & E 3 & A 4 & B 5 & D

(*b*) 1 & D 2 & A 3 & B 4 & E 5 & C

(*c*) 1 & B 2 & E 3 & B 4 & C 5 & A

(*d*) 1 & D 2 & E 3 & B 4 & C 5 & A.

## The Next Two Questions (117–118) are Based on the Following Information

**A 14 inch monitor has an active display area with a width 9.875 inch, a height of 7.125 inch and a diagonal of 12.25 inch. The resolution is 1024 × 768 pixels.**

***117.** What would be the horizontal dot pitch?

(*a*) 0.18 mm (*b*) 0.24 mm

(*c*) 0.28 mm (*d*) 0.32 mm.

***118.** What would be the vertical dot pitch?

(*a*) 0.18 mm (*b*) 0.24 mm

(*c*) 0.28 mm (*d*) 0.32 mm.

**119.** Choose the vector scan device from the following.

(*a*) Flatbed scanner (*b*) Standard CRT

(*c*) Keyboard (*d*) Plotter.

***120.** What would be the total space required if for a video with a duration of 10 minutes, resolution 320 × 249 with 8-bit colour and 30 frames / sec?

(*a*) 1.50 MB (*b*) 2.23 MB

(*c*) 2.57 MB (*d*) 2.87 MB.

**121.** Which of the following does not belong to the subject typography?

(*a*) Anti-aliasing (*b*) Filtering

(*c*) Fonts (*d*) Typefaces.

**122.** The following table gives information about colours.

| | Colour combined | | Colour obtained |
|---|---|---|---|
| 1 | Black + White | A | Green |
| 2 | Orange + Green | B | Orange |
| 3 | Red + Yellow | C | Violet |
| 4 | Yellow + Blue | D | Cyan |
| 5 | Blue + Green | E | Grey |

Which of the following is the proper match?

(*a*) 1 & C 2 & E 3 & A 4 & B 5 & D

(*b*) 1 & D 2 & A 3 & B 4 & E 5 & C

(*c*) 1 & E 2 & C 3 & B 4 & A 5 & D

(*d*) 1 & D 2 & E 3 & B 4 & C 5 & A.

**123.** Which of the following is a graphics file format created for mobile computing devices such as PDAs etc?

(*a*) JPEG (*b*) MPEG

(*c*) WBMP (*d*) BMP.

**124.** The following table gives information about the six levels of Redundant Array of Inexpensive Disks (RAID) functionality.

| Column A | | Column B | |
|---|---|---|---|
| 1 | Level 0 | A | Block interleaving |
| 2 | Level 1 | B | Byte interleaving |
| 3 | Level 2 | C | Disk stripping |
| 4 | Level 3 | D | Sector interleaving |
| 5 | Level 4 | E | Disk Mirroring |
| 6 | Level 5 | F | Bit interleaving of data |

Which of the following is the proper match?

(*a*) 1 & C 2 & E 3 & F 4 & B 5 & D 6 & A

(*b*) 1 & D 2 & F 3 & B 4 & E 5 & C 6 & A

(*c*) 1 & E 2 & C 3 & F 4 & A 5 & D 6 & B

(*d*) 1 & F 2 & E 3 & B 4 & C 5 & A 6 & D.

**125.** Which of the following is not true about Hypertext?

(*a*) It is used in web pages

(*b*) It is a non-sequential navigation structure for large text data

(*c*) It is a search method for large text data

(*d*) It is essential for reference type applications.

**126.** Which of the following in relation to photography is not correct?

(*a*) The faster the shutter speed (camera) the more blurred is the moving object

(*b*) The depth of field gets deeper or shallower when the aperture of the lens is altered

(*c*) The depth of field gets deeper or shallower when the focal length is altered

(*d*) The shorter the focal length, the wider the view the lens angle covers.

**127.** When a user uses a mouse to define two corners of a rectangle, and copy the selected area in a clipboard is called

(*a*) Panning (*b*) Scaling

(c) Rubber Banding (*d*) Indexing.

## ANSWERS

| | | | | | | |
|---|---|---|---|---|---|---|
| **1.** (*a*) | **2.** (*a*) | **3.** (*d*) | **4.** (*c*) | **5.** (*a*) | **6.** (*d*) | **7.** (*b*) |
| **8.** (*b*) | **9.** (*c*) | **10.** (*a*) | **11.** (*b*) | **12.** (*d*) | **13.** (*b*) | **14.** (*a*) |
| **15.** (*c*) | **16.** (*b*) | **17.** (*c*) | **18.** (*d*) | **19.** (*b*) | **20.** (*a*) | **21.** (*d*) |
| **22.** (*d*) | **23.** (*a*) | **24.** (*a*) | **25.** (*b*) | **26.** (*c*) | **27.** (*b*) | **28.** (*c*) |
| **29.** (*c*) | **30.** (*d*) | **31.** (*a*) | **32.** (b) | **33.** (*a*) | **34.** (*b*) | **35.** (*b*) |
| **36.** (*b*) | **37.** (*c*) | **38.** (*a*) | **39.** (*d*) | **40.** (*a*) | **41.** (*c*) | **42.** (*a*) |
| **43.** (*c*) | **44.** (*a*) | **45.** (*c*) | **46.** (*d*) | **47.** (*b*) | **48.** (*b*) | **49.** (*c*) |
| **50.** (c) | **51.** (*a*) | **52.** (*b*) | **53.** (*c*) | **54.** (*a*) | **55.** (*b*) | **56.** (*d*) |
| **57.** (*c*) | **58.** (*a*) | **59.** (*d*) | **60.** (*a*) | **61.** (*a*) | **62.** (*c*) | **63.** (*c*) |
| **64.** (*a*) | **65.** (*c*) | **66.** (*a*) | **67.** (*d*) | **68.** (*b*) | **69.** (*b*) | **70.** (*b*) |
| **71.** (*c*) | **72.** (c) | **73.** (*c*) | **74.** (*d*) | **75.** (*c*) | **76.** (*d*) | **77.** (*b*) |
| **78.** (*b*) | **79.** (*c*) | **80.** (*a*) | **81.** (*b*) | **82.** (*b*) | **83.** (*b*) | **84.** (*c*) |
| **85.** (*b*) | **86.** (*b*) | **87.** (*d*) | **88.** (*c*) | **89.** (*b*) | **90.** (*d*) | **91.** (*d*) |
| **92.** (*c*) | **93.** (*d*) | **94.** (*c*) | **95.** (*c*) | **96.** (*b*) | **97.** (*d*) | **98.** (*c*) |
| **99.** (*a*) | **100.** (*a*) | **101.** (*a*) | **102.** (*c*) | **103.** (*c*) | **104.** (*d*) | **105.** (*a*) |
| **106.** (*c*) | **107.** (*c*) | **108.** (*d*) | **109.** (*b*) | **110.** (*a*) | **111.** (*a*) | **112.** (*b*) |
| **113.** (*d*) | **114.** (*a*) | **115.** (*c*) | **116.** (*b*) | **117.** (*b*) | **118.** (*b*) | **119.** (*d*) |
| **120.** (*c*) | **121.** (*b*) | **122.** (*c*) | **123.** (*c*) | **124.** (*a*) | **125.** (*c*) | **126.** (*a*) |
| **127.** (*c*) | | | | | | |

## EXPLANATIONS

**19 & 20.** The *Cartesian slope-intercept* equation for a straight line is $y= m. x + b$, where $m$ represents the slope of the line and $b$ as the $y$ intercept. m=y2–y1/x2–x1. So m = (5 – 1)/(6 – 1)= 4/5 = 0.8. b=y1–m.x1. So b = 1 – (0.8)(1) = 1 – 0.8 = 0.2

**21.** So now we have m and b we can get Each occurrence of X! and Y! can be calculated using y = m.x + b. When x = 2, y = 1.8 D 2, x = 3, y = 2.6 D 3, x = 4, y = 3.4 D 3 x = 5, y = 4.2 D 4

**28.** The horizontal and vertical projections of line are given by $D_p = p_2 - p_1$ and $D_q = q_2 - q_1$. i.e. $D_p = 20 - 10 = 10$ and $D_q = 21 - 15 = 6$. The larger value is 10. Therefore, n= log 10 / log 2 = 1/0.30103= 2.322. Taking n = 4, the incremental factor $\varepsilon = 2^{-4} = 0.0625$. Then εp= 0.0625(10) = 0.625 and εq= 0.0625(6)= 0.375.

**44.** The Move Transformation Matrix is represented by $[T_m]$

$$T_m = \begin{pmatrix} 1 & 0 & 0 \\ 0 & 1 & 0 \\ 10 & -5 & 1 \end{pmatrix} \text{ The four points may be transferred as } \begin{pmatrix} 10 & 8 & 1 \\ 20 & 8 & 1 \\ 30 & 15 & 1 \\ 10 & 25 & 1 \end{pmatrix} \begin{pmatrix} 1 & 0 & 0 \\ 0 & 1 & 0 \\ 10 & -5 & 1 \end{pmatrix}$$

$$= \begin{pmatrix} 20 & 3 & 1 \\ 30 & 3 & 1 \\ 40 & 10 & 1 \\ 20 & 20 & 1 \end{pmatrix}$$

**45.** The *x*-Flip Transformation Matrix is represented by $[T_x]$

$$T_x = \begin{pmatrix} 1 & 0 & 0 \\ 0 & -1 & 0 \\ 0 & 0 & 1 \end{pmatrix} \text{ The four points may be transferred as } \begin{pmatrix} 10 & 8 & 1 \\ 20 & 8 & 1 \\ 30 & 15 & 1 \\ 10 & 25 & 1 \end{pmatrix} \begin{pmatrix} 1 & 0 & 0 \\ 0 & -1 & 0 \\ 0 & 0 & 1 \end{pmatrix}$$

$$= \begin{pmatrix} -10 & -8 & 1 \\ -20 & -8 & 1 \\ -30 & -15 & 1 \\ -10 & -25 & 1 \end{pmatrix}$$

**46.** The *y*-Flip Transformation Matrix is represented by $[T_y]$

$$T_y = \begin{pmatrix} -1 & 0 & 0 \\ 0 & 1 & 0 \\ 0 & 0 & 1 \end{pmatrix} \text{ The four points may be transferred as } \begin{pmatrix} 10 & 8 & 1 \\ 20 & 8 & 1 \\ 30 & 15 & 1 \\ 10 & 25 & 1 \end{pmatrix} \begin{pmatrix} -1 & 0 & 0 \\ 0 & 1 & 0 \\ 0 & 0 & 1 \end{pmatrix}$$

$$= \begin{pmatrix} -10 & 8 & 1 \\ -20 & 8 & 1 \\ -30 & 15 & 1 \\ -10 & 25 & 1 \end{pmatrix}$$

**47.** The o-Flip (Origin) Transformation Matrix is represented by $[T_0]$

$$T_0 = \begin{pmatrix} -1 & 0 & 0 \\ 0 & -1 & 0 \\ 0 & 0 & 1 \end{pmatrix} \text{ The four points may be transferred as } \begin{pmatrix} 10 & 8 & 1 \\ 20 & 8 & 1 \\ 30 & 15 & 1 \\ 10 & 25 & 1 \end{pmatrix} \begin{pmatrix} -1 & 0 & 0 \\ 0 & -1 & 0 \\ 0 & 0 & 1 \end{pmatrix}$$

$$= \begin{pmatrix} -10 & -8 & 1 \\ -20 & -8 & 1 \\ -30 & -15 & 1 \\ -10 & -25 & 1 \end{pmatrix}$$

**48.** The twist parameters $t_x$ and $t_y$ are 0.05 and –0.1. We get the twist transformation matrix as

$$T_t = \begin{pmatrix} 1 & -0.1 & 0 \\ 0.05 & 1 & 0 \\ 0 & 0 & 1 \end{pmatrix} \text{ The four points may be transferred as } \begin{pmatrix} 10 & 8 & 1 \\ 20 & 8 & 1 \\ 30 & 15 & 1 \\ 10 & 25 & 1 \end{pmatrix}$$

$$\begin{pmatrix} 1 & -0.1 & 0 \\ 0.05 & 1 & 0 \\ 0 & 0 & 1 \end{pmatrix} = \begin{pmatrix} 10.40 & 7 & 1 \\ 20.40 & 6 & 1 \\ 30.40 & 12 & 1 \\ 10.40 & 24 & 1 \end{pmatrix}$$

**49.** The transformed coordinates of the quadrilateral ABCD scaled by a factor of 1.4 in the $x$ direction and by a factor of 0.5 in the direction of $y$

$$T_s = \begin{pmatrix} 1.4 & 0 & 0 \\ 0 & 0.5 & 0 \\ 0 & 0 & 1 \end{pmatrix} \text{ The four points may be transferred as } \begin{pmatrix} 10 & 8 & 1 \\ 20 & 8 & 1 \\ 30 & 15 & 1 \\ 10 & 25 & 1 \end{pmatrix}$$

$$\begin{pmatrix} 1.4 & 0 & 0 \\ 0 & 0.5 & 0 \\ 0 & 0 & 1 \end{pmatrix} = \begin{pmatrix} 14 & 4 & 1 \\ 28 & 4 & 1 \\ 42 & 7.5 & 1 \\ 14 & 7.5 & 1 \end{pmatrix}$$

**50.** The be the transformed coordinates of the quadrilateral ABCD rotated by a counter-clock-wise angle of 60°.

$$T_r = \begin{pmatrix} 0.566 & 0.866 & 0 \\ -0.866 & 0.500 & 0 \\ 0 & 0 & 1 \end{pmatrix} \text{ Transformed as } \begin{pmatrix} 10 & 8 & 1 \\ 20 & 8 & 1 \\ 30 & 15 & 1 \\ 10 & 25 & 1 \end{pmatrix} \begin{pmatrix} 0.566 & 0.866 & 0 \\ -0.866 & 0.500 & 0 \\ 0 & 0 & 1 \end{pmatrix}$$

$$= \begin{pmatrix} -1.928 & 1266 & 1 \\ 3072 & 2132 & 1 \\ 201 & 3348 & 1 \\ -7.99 & 1616 & 1 \end{pmatrix}$$

**87.** The objects that do not maintain a fixed shape, but change their surface characteristics in certain motions or when proximity to other objects are called blobby object.

**88.** The first spline curves developed for graphics application is Natural Cubic Splines

**89.** *Statistically self-similar fractal* construction method is used to model shrubs

**113.** TWAIN is a working group formed to define open industry standard interface.

**117.** Dot pitch (horizontal) = (width in inches/number of pixels) $x$ 25.5 *i.e.* (9.875/1024) × 25.4=0.24 mm

**118.** Dot pitch (vertical) = (height in inches /number of lines) $x$ 25.5 *i.e.*7.125/768) × 25.4 = 0.24 mm

**120.** Storage space required = (10 × 60 x 320 × 240 × 8 × 30)/8 = 2.57 MB

CHAPTER 8

# MICROPROCESSOR AND INTERFACING DEVICES

**1.** Worlds first microprocessor was

(*a*) Intel 4004 (*b*) Intel 8085

(*c*) Z80 (*d*) MC6800.

**2.** The first 8-bit microprocessor was

(*a*) Z80 (*b*) MC6800

(*c*) Intel 8008 (*d*) Intel 8085.

**3.** The Intel 8085 microprocessor was developed in the year

(*a*) 1977 (*b*) 1980

(*c*) 1985 (*c*) 1990.

**4.** Which one of the microprocessor recently developed?

(*a*) Pentium (*b*) Intel core i7

(*c*) Celeron (*d*) Intel 80486.

**5.** The actual hardware structure of the memory system is

(*a*) logical memory (*b*) virtual memory

(*c*) physical memory (*d*) none of the above.

**6.** Which of the following microprocessor do not have control flags?

(*a*) Intel 8085 (*b*) Intel 80286

(*c*) Intel 80386 (*d*) Intel 80486.

**7.** Which one of the following register holds the temporary result after an arithmetic and logic operation?

(*a*) Program Counter (*b*) Instruction Register

(*c*) SP (*d*) Accumulator.

8. A microprocessor with *n* address bus can address how many memory locations?
   (*a*) $2^n$ address locations (*b*) $n^2$ address locations
   (*c*) n address locations (*d*) 2 address locations.
9. The first 640 KB of the memory in all personal computer is called
   (a) cache memory (*b*) the transient program area
   (*c*) virtual memory (*d*) none of the above.
10. The Intel microprocessors 80286, 80386 are able to address memory above the first 1 MB, and the additional memory is known as
   (*a*) extra memory (*b*) limited memory system
   (*c*) extended memory system (*d*) none of the above.
11. Which of the following bus determines how many bytes are transferred between the microprocessor and the memory at a time
   (*a*) address bus (*b*) data bus
   (*c*) control bus (*d*) transport bus.
12. If the sign flag is set, it indicates the arithmetic sign of the result after addition or subtraction is a
   (*a*) negative (*b*) positive
   (*c*) zero (*d*) none of the above.
13. The register which is always used to address the next instruction executed by the microprocessor is
   (*a*) instruction pointer (*b*) instruction register
   (*c*) stack pointer (*d*) accumulator.
14. Whenever there is borrow (when subtraction is performed), which of the following flag will be set?
   (*a*) Auxiliary Cary Flag (*b*) Sign Flag
   (*c*) Parity Flag (*d*) Carry Flag.
15. The general-purpose register often used to address an array of data in the stack memory is
   (*a*) stack pointer (*b*) base pointer
   (*c*) instruction pointer (*d*) none of the above.
16. Which of the following is a section of memory that holds program and procedures used by programs
   (*a*) code segment (*b*) data segment
   (*c*) stack segment (*d*) extra segment.
17. Choose the Intel microprocessor which can operate either in real or protected mode
   (*a*) 8086 (*b*) 8088
   (*c*) 80186 (*d*) 80486.

18. In protected mode memory addressing allows access to data and programs located above the

(a) First 1 MB of memory (b) First 2 MB of memory

(c) First 3 MB of memory (d) First 4 MB of the memory.

19. The software that translates assembly language into machine language is

(a) compiler (b) interpreter

(c) assembler (d) cross compiler.

20. Various ways of specifying data are called

(a) address mode (d) instruction

(c) program (d) code.

21. Which one of the following is not a microprocessor

(a) 8085 (b) Z80

(c) 8255 (d) MC6800.

22. The addressing mode that takes least time is

(a) direct addressing (b) register addressing

(c) immediate addressing (d) implict addressing.

23. The process of designing more than a thousand gates on a single chip is called

(a) SSI (b) MSI

(c) VLSI (d) none of the above.

24. The timing and control signal provided by

(a) ALU (b) control unit

(c) register (d) none.

25. The expansion of SLSI is

(a) Small_Large_Scale Integration

(b) Super_Large_Scale_ Integration

(c) Scale_Large_Super Integration

(d) None of the above.

## All the Questions, Unless Otherwise Stated, are Relevant to Intel 8085 Microprocessor

26. The voltage applied to Vcc pin of 8085 is

(a) +10v (b) +8v

(c) +6v (d) +5v.

27. The number of pins available in 8085 is

(a) 24 (b) 28

(c) 40 (d) 42.

**28.** How many memory locations does a 8085 microprocessor can address?

(*a*) 65536 (*b*) 65533

(*c*) 65356 (*d*) 65563.

**29.** Which of the following register pair is possible in 8085?

(*a*) AB (*b*) AC

(*c*) DE (*d*) EH.

**30.** The data lines of 8085 are multiplexed with address lines

(*a*) A0–A7 (*b*) A8–A15

(*c*) A4–A11 (*d*) A5–12.

**31.** The instruction that will logically AND the content of register with the content of the Accumulator is

(*a*) ANI 8 bit (*b*) ANA R/M

(*c*) CMA (*d*) none of the above.

**32.** Which of the following instruction will change the program sequence to the location specified by the 16 bit address if the Carry Flag is reset?

(*a*) JZ (*b*) JNZ

(c) JC (*d*) JNC.

**33.** Which of the following instruction will change the program sequence to the location specified by the 16 bit address if the Zero Flag is reset?

(*a*) JZ (*b*) JNZ

(*c*) JC (*d*) JNC.

**34.** Which of the following instruction will change the program sequence to the location specified by the 16 bit address if the Carry Flag is set?

(*a*) JZ (*b*) JNZ

(*c*) JC (*d*) JNC.

**35.** Which of the following instruction will change the program sequence to the location specified by the 16 bit address if the Zero Flag is reset?

(*a*) JZ (*b*) JNZ

(*c*) JC (*d*) JNC.

**36.** Which one of the following is a machine control operation?

(*a*) ADD (*b*) MOV

(*c*) HLT (*d*) JMP.

**37.** Which of the following instruction will alter the content of flag register?

(*a*) CMP (*b*) ORA

(*c*) JMP (*d*) HLT.

**38.** Which one of the following is an example of immediate addressing mode?

(*a*) MVI R, Data (*b*) MOV Rd, Rs

(*c*) IN/OUT (*d*) None of the above.

39. Masking of interrupt means
(*a*) to enable the interrupt
(*b*) to disable the interrupt
(*c*) to reset the microprocessor
(*d*) to enable serial data transfer.

40. Which of the following is not a conditional branch instruction?
(*a*) JNZ
(*b*) JC
(*c*) RET
(*d*) JNC.

*41. Assume that accumulator contains 26H and the previous operation has set the Carry flag. What will be the result when instruction ACI 57H is executed?
(*a*) 7BH
(*b*) 7CH
(*c*) 7DH
(*d*) 7EH.

42. Assume memory location 2051H contains 90H and 2052H contains 09H. Which of the following instruction will transfer the above memory content to register HL.
(*a*) SHLD
(*b*) LHLD
(*c*) LDAX
(*d*) STAX.

*43. What will be the result if the instruction SUI 37H is executed? Assume that accumulator contains 40H.
(*a*) 03H
(*b*) 30H
(*c*) 09H
(*d*) 90H.

*44. Assume that accumulator contains 37H and the Borrow flag is set. What will be the result when instruction SBI 25H is executed?
(*a*) 01H
(*b*) 11H
(*c*) 10H
(*d*) 1AH.

*45. Assume the content of the accumulator is 8FH. What will be the outcome when instruction XRI A2H is executed?
(*a*) 00101101
(*b*) 00111101
(*c*) 01001101
(*d*) 00101001.

## The Next Four Questions (46–49) are Based on the Following Information

**Assume that the content of Accumulator is A7H and carry Flag(CF) is reset**

*46. What will be the result when instruction RLC is executed?
(*a*) 4FH, CF = 0
(*b*) 4FH, CF = 1
(*c*) F4H, CF = 1
(*d*) 4EH, CF = 1.

*47. What will be the result when instruction RRC is executed?
(*a*) 11010011, CF = 0
(*b*) 11010111, CF = 1
(*c*) 11010011, CF = 1
(*d*) 10010011, CF = 0.

*48. What will be the result when instruction RAL is executed?
(*a*) 4FH, CF = 0
(*b*) 4FH, CF = 1
(*c*) 4EH, CF = 1
(*d*) 4EH, CF = 0.

*49. What will be the result when instruction RAR is executed?

(*a*) 11010011, CF = 0 (*b*) 11010111, CF = 1

(*c*) 11010011, CF = 1 (*d*) 01010011, CF = 1.

## The Next Three Questions (50–52) are Based on the Following Information

**Assume that the content of Accumulator is A7H. What will be the state of Carry Flag (CF) and Zero Flag(ZF) when instruction CMP B is executed?**

**50.** If Register B contains 07H.

(*a*) CF = 0, ZF = 1 (*b*) CF = 1, ZF = 0

(*c*) CF = 0, ZF = 0 (*d*) CF = 1, ZF = 1.

**51.** If Register B contains B7H

(*a*) CF = 0, ZF = 1 (*b*) CF = 1, ZF = 0

(**c**) CF = 0, ZF = 0 (*d*) CF = 1, ZF = 1.

**52.** If Register B contains A7H

(*a*) CF = 0, ZF = 1 (*b*) CF = 1, ZF = 0

(*c*) CF = 0, ZF = 0 (*d*) CF = 1, ZF = 1.

**53.** 8085 can manipulate data ranging from

(*a*) 00 to 0F (*b*) 00 to F0

(*c*) 01 to FF (*d*) 00 to FF.

## The Next Three Questions (54–56) are Based on the Following Information

**Assume that the content of Accumulator is AAH. What will be the state of Carry Flag(CF) and Zero Flag(ZF) when instruction CPI is executed and the data is given below**

**54.** If the data is 27H.

(*a*) CF = 0, ZF = 1 (*b*) CF = 1, ZF = 0

(*c*) CF = 0, ZF = 0 (*d*) CF = 1, ZF = 1.

**55.** If the data is AAH

(*a*) CF = 0, ZF = 1 (*b*) CF = 1, ZF = 0

(*c*) CF = 0, ZF = 0 (*d*) CF = 1, ZF = 1.

**56.** If the data is FAH

(*a*) CF = 0, ZF = 1 (*b*) CF = 1, ZF = 0

(*c*) CF = 0, ZF = 0 (*d*) CF = 1, ZF = 1.

***57.** Assume that accumulator contains 99H. What will be content of accumulator after instruction CMA is executed?

(*a*) 55H (*b*) 66H

(*c*) 77H (*d*) 99H.

**58.** The instruction SIM and RIM is related to

(*a*) Parallel I/O (*b*) Serial I/O

(*c*) both a and b (*d*) None of the above.

**59.** The time required to complete the execution of an instruction is called

(*a*) Instruction Cycle (*b*) Machine Cycle

(*c*) T State (*d*) None of the above.

**60.** Transferring data flow from memory locations to the microprocessor bus using control signal MEMR(active low) is called

(*a*) reading from input port (*b*) reading from memory

(*c*) writing to an output port (*d*) writing into a memory.

**61.** Which of the following is not a branch instruction?

(*a*) INR (*b*) ORA

(*c*) JZ (*d*) NOP.

**62.** Which of the following is a machine control instruction?

(*a*) HLT (*b*) JP

(*c*) OR (*d*) DCR.

**63.** What does a microprocessor do to execute an instruction?

(*a*) Places the memory address of the instruction on the address bus

(*b*) Indicates the operation status on the status lines

(*c*) Send the MEMR(active low) signal to enable the memory, fetches the instruction bytes, places it in the instruction decoder and executes

(*d*) Does all the above.

**64.** Which are the four flags are set/reset when a jump instruction is executed?

(*a*) Carry Flag, Zero Flag, Sign Flag & Auxiliary carry Flag

(*b*) Parity Flag, Zero Flag, Sign Flag & Auxiliary carry Flag

(*c*) Carry Flag, Zero Flag, Sign Flag & Parity Flag

(*d*) Carry Flag, Parity Flag & Auxiliary carry Flag.

**65.** Assume that the accumulator content are AAH and CY=0. What will be the accumulator content after the execution of RLC instruction?

(*a*) AAH (*b*) A5H

(*c*) 55H (*d*) 5AH.

**66.** What will be the output of the following statement?

```
MVI A 06H
MVI B 04H
ADD B
HLT
```

(*a*) 10H (*b*) 0AH

(*c*) 02H (*d*) 01H.

**67.** The instruction that transfer the data bytes from the register to stack is

(*a*) POP (*b*) PUSH

(*c*) LXI (*d*) LDA.

**68.** When does the stack pointer register is decremented by two?

(*a*) Only when CALL is executed

(*b*) Only when PUSH is executed

(*c*) Either CALL or PUSH is executed

(*d*) None of the above.

**69.** When does the stack pointer register is incremented by two?

(*a*) Only when RET is executed

(*b*) Only when POP is executed

(*c*) Either RET or POP is executed

(*d*) None of the above.

**70.** Which of the following Interrupt is non-maskable?

(*a*) INTR (*b*) RST 5.5

(*c*) RST 6.5 (*d*) Trap.

**71.** How many pins are dedicated for interrupt in 8085 microprocessor?

(*a*) 4 (*b*) 5

(*c*) 6 (*d*) 7.

**72.** Set Interrupt Mask (SIM) is a 1-byte instruction that can be used for

(*a*) to set RST 5.5, RST 6.5 and RST 7.5 interrupts

(*b*) to reset RST 7.5

(*c*) to implement serial input/output

(*d*) all the above.

## All the Questions, Unless Otherwise Stated, are Relevant to Intel 8086

**73.** Which one of the following is a 16 bit microprocessor?

(*a*) 8008 (*b*) 8085

(*c*) 8086 (*d*) 8088.

**74.** The advantage of using segment register in 8086 microprocessor are

(*a*) allow the memory capacity to be 1 MB

(*b*) allow the instruction data or stack position of a program to be more than 64 K bytes

(*c*) facilitate the use of separate memory area for a program, data and the stack

(*d*) all the above.

**75.** Which one of the following is not a conditional flag?

(*a*) Sign Flag (*b*) Parity Flag

(*c*) Overflow Flag (*d*) Direction Flag.

**76.** If the 16 bit Effective address of the datum is a part of the instruction then it is called

(*a*) Register Addressing Mode (*b*) Implied Address Mode

(*c*) Direct Addressing Mode (*d*) Indexed Addressing Mode.

**77.** To provide flexible base addressing and indexing, a data address may be framed by adding together a combination of the BX or BP register content, S1 or DI the register content and a displacement is called as

(*a*) Absolute Address (*b*) Effective address

(*c*) Real Address (*d*) Physical Address.

**78.** The 20 bit physical address in 8086 is obtained by

(*a*) 16 bit offset + 16 bit segment address

(*b*) 4 bit offset + 16 bit segment address

(*c*) 16 bit offset + 4 bit segment address

(*d*) 10 bit offset + 10 bit segment address.

**79.** The 8086 arithmetic instruction set are classified into

(*a*) Binary & packed BCD (*b*) Binary & unpacked BCD

(*c*) Packed BCD & unpacked BCD (*d*) Binary, packed BCD, unpacked BCD.

**80.** Which one of the following in 8086 microprocessor is an unconditional branch instruction?

(*a*) JZ (*b*) JS

(*c*) JMP (*d*) JNBE.

**81.** Which one of the following flag manipulation instruction that will set Carry Flag?

(*a*) CLC (*b*) CMC

(*c*) STI (*d*) STC.

**82.** 8086 can operate

(*a*) Only in minimum mode

(*b*) Only in maximum mode

(*c*) Either minimum or maximum mode

(*d*) None of the above.

**83.** Which segment is accessed during the current bus cycle when S3 and S4 status pin in 8086 are reset?

(*a*) Stack Segment (*b*) Extra Segment

(*c*) Code Segment (*d*) Data Segment.

***84.** In a 8086 microprocessor, which of the following MOV is not possible

(*a*) MOV S1, 0H (*b*) MOV BX, ES

(*c*) MOV DS, AX (*d*) MOV ES, DS.

**85.** A memory device that contains 1M bytes location requires how many bit address?

(*a*) 12 (*b*) 16

(*c*) 20 (*d*) 24.

## All the Questions, Unless Otherwise Stated, are Relevant to Intel 80186 and Its Successor Microprocessor

**86.** The 80286 microprocessor can address

(a) 1 MB (b) 8 MB

(c) 16 MB (d) 32 MB.

**87.** How much memory is found in the Transient Program Area (TPA) in a computer system?

(a) 64 KB (b) 640 KB

(c) 1 MB (d) 2 MB.

**88.** Choose the register that is used to address source data directly for the use with the string instructions.

(a) Stack Pointer (b) Base Pointer

(c) Source Index (d) Destination Index.

**89.** The segment registers FS and GS are available in which of the following microprocessor?

(a) 8085 (b) 8086 & 8088

(c) 80186 & 80286 (d) 80386 & 80486.

***90.** Consider the Code Segment register contains 15000H and IP/EIP contains 1200H. From which memory location does the microprocessor fetches its next instruction

(a) 15000H (b) 1200H

(c) 16200H (d) none of the above.

**91.** 80186 microprocessor is a

(a) 8 bit microprocessor (b) 16 bit microprocessor

(c) 32 bit microprocessor (d) none of the above.

**92.** 80286 is 16 bit microprocessor which can address

(a) 16 MB of physical memory & 1 GB of virtual memory

(b) 32 MB of physical memory & 1 GB of virtual memory

(c) 16 MB of physical memory & 2 GB of virtual memory

(d) 4 MB of physical memory & 1 GB of virtual memory.

**93.** Intel 80386 is a

(a) 16 bit microprocessor (b) 32 bit microprocessor

(c) 64 bit microprocessor (d) none of the above.

**94.** Intel 80386 microprocessor can address up to

(a) 2 GB Memory (b) 3 GB Memory

(c) 4 GB Memory (d) 5 GB Memory.

**95.** The main disadvantage of interleaved memory system in 80386 is

(a) the speed of the system is improved

(*b*) because of its structure and the cost is more

(*c*) the memory access time can be lengthened without the need for wait states

(*d*) none of the above.

**96.** The series of eight bytes that describe and locate a memory segment in 80286 & 80386 is

(*a*) descriptor (*b*) selector

(*c*) descriptor and Selector (*d*) none of the above.

**97.** In 80386 the information about the location, size and privilege level of the task state segment is available in

(*a*) task state segment descriptor (*b*) task register

(*c*) back-link (*d*) none of the above.

**98.** The page that is addressed with selector and an offset in either real or protected mode in 80386 is called

(*a*) linear memory page (*b*) physical memory page

(*c*) disjoint memory page (*d*) sequential memory page.

**99.** Intel 80486 microprocessor is

(*a*) 16 Bit processor (*b*) 32 bit processor

(*c*) 64 bit processor (*d*) 128 bit processor.

**100.** The data bus width of a Pentium is

(*a*) 16 bit (*b*) 32 bit

(*c*) 54 bit (*d*) 64 bit.

**101.** Which of the following features make Intel 80486 Microprocessor better than the Intel 80386

(*a*) 8 KB unified level 1 cache for code and data was added to the CPU. In later versions of the 80486 the size of level 1 cache was increased to 16 KB.

(*b*) Execution time of instructions was significantly reduced.

(*c*) Featured much faster bus transfers

(*d*) All the above.

## The Next Four Questions are Based on the Interrupt Vectors From 8086 to 80486 Microprocessor.

**102.** Which of the following is Type 0 interrupt?

(*a*) Divide Error (*b*) Nonmaskable Hardware

(*c*) Trap or Single Trap (*d*) One-Byte Interrupt.

**103.** Which of the following is Type 1 interrupt?

(*a*) Divide Error (*b*) Trap or Single Trap

(*c*) Nonmaskable Hardware (*d*) One-Byte Interrupt.

**104.** Which of the following is Type 2 interrupt?

(*a*) Divide Error (*b*) Trap or Single Trap

(*c*) Nonmaskable Hardware (*d*) One-Byte Interrupt.

**105.** Which of the following is Type 3 interrupt?

(*a*) Divide Error (*b*) Trap or Single Trap

(*c*) Nonmaskable Hardware (*d*) One-Byte Interrupt.

**106.** The original Pentium was the first superscalar x86 microprocessor was introduced in the year

(*a*) 1990 (*b*) 1993

(*c*) 2000 (*d*) 2001.

**107.** Which of the following statement is not true for Pentium?

(*a*) The name Pentium was derived from the Greek *pente*, meaning 'five', and the Latin ending *-ium*

(*b*) It is the fourth-generation x86 micro architecture

(*c*) It was a direct extension of the 80486 architecture with dual integer pipelines

(*d*) Vinod Dham is often referred to as the father of the Intel Pentium processor.

**108.** What makes Pentium superior compared to Intel 80486 microprocessor?

(*a*) Superscalar architecture (*b*) 64-bit external data bus width

(*c*) MMX instructions (*d*) All the above.

## The Following Questions, Unless Otherwise Stated, are Relevant to Interfacing Devices.

**109.** Programmable Interrupt Controller (8259 PIC) can manage how many interrupt request?

(*a*) 4 (*b*) 6

(*c*) 8 (*d*) 10.

**110.** 8259 PIC can operate in

(*a*) fully nested mode (*b*) Automatic mode

(*c*) Specific mode (*d*) All the above.

**111.** 8255 PPI can operate in which of the following modes?

(*a*) BSR Mode only (*b*) I/O Mode only

(*c*) Both a & b (*d*) Mode 0 only.

**112.** In BSR mode the 8255 PPI is concerned only with eight bits of

(*a*) Port A (*b*) Port B

(*c*) Port C (*d*) None of the above.

**113.** Which of the Port can be configured as the bi-directional Port in 8255 PPI?

(*a*) Port A (*b*) Port B

(*c*) Port A & Port B (*d*) Port C.

**114.** When the address lines A0 and A1 are reset, which of the following is selected in 8255 PPI?

(*a*) Control Register (*b*) Port A

(*c*) Port B (*d*) Port C.

**115.** Which of the following I/O mode the handshake signals are exchanged between microprocessor and peripherals prior to data transfer?

(*a*) Mode 0 (*b*) Mode 1

(*c*) Mode 2 (*d*) Mode 0 & Mode 2.

**116.** Which one of the following is a Programmable Interval Timer?

(*a*) 8254 (*b*) 8279

(*c*) 8237 (*d*) 8257.

**117.** When does Counter 0 is selected in 8254?

(*a*) When A0 and A1 are reset (*b*) When A0 is set and A1 is reset

(*c*) When A0 is reset and A1 is set (*d*) When A0 and A1 are set.

**118.** Which one of the following is not present in 8254?

(*a*) Counter 0 (*b*) Counter 1

(*c*) Counter 2 (*d*) Counter 3.

## The Next Five (119–122) Questions are Based on the 8254 Programmable Interval Timer and its Mode of Operation of

**119.** Allows the counter to be used as an event counter

(*a*) mode 0 (*b*) mode 1

(*c*) mode 2 (*d*) mode 4.

**120.** Causes the counter to function as retriggerable monostable multivibrator (one-shot)

(*a*) mode 0 (*b*) mode 1

(*c*) mode 2 (*d*) mode 4.

**121.** Allows the counter to generate a series of continuous pulses that are one clock pulse in width.

(*a*) mode 0 (*b*) mode 1

(*c*) mode 2 (*d*) mode 4.

**122.** Generates a continuous square wave at the OUT connection provided the G pin is a logic 1.

(*a*) mode 2 (*b*) mode 3

(*c*) mode 4 (*d*) mode 5.

**123.** Allows the counter to produce a single pulse at the output

(*a*) mode 2 (*b*) mode 3

(*c*) mode 4 (*d*) mode 5.

**124.** Choose the wrong statement

(*a*) The 8237 DMAC is known as a "fly-by" DMA controller

(*b*) The 8237 has two electrical signals for each channel, named DRQ and –DACK

(*c*) The 8237 contains four DMA channels

(*d*) More than one channels may be active at any moment in 8237.

**125.** The 8237 DMAC is capable of DMA transfer at rates up to

(*a*) 1.6 MB per second (*b*) 2 MB per second

(*c*) 2.6 MB per second (*d*) 3 MB per second.

**126.** Which of the following is *true* in the case of N-key rollover in 8279?

(*a*) Prevents two keys from being recognized if pressed simultaneously

(*b*) Will accept two keys pressed simultaneously

(*c*) Will accept all the keys pressed simultaneously, from first to last

(*d*) Will accept all the keys pressed simultaneously, from last to first.

**127.** Which of the statement is not true for 8279 Programmable Keyboard/Display Interface?

(*a*) Scans and encodes up to a 64-key keyboard

(*b*) Controls up to a 16-digit numerical display

(*c*) Keyboard section has a built-in FIFO 16 character buffer

(*d*) The display is controlled from an internal 16x8 RAM that.

**128.** Which of the following transmission data can be transferred both the ways simultaneously?

(*a*) half-duplex (*b*) full duplex

(*c*) simplex (*d*) none of the above.

**129.** In 8251, which of the following accepts parallel data from the microprocessor and converts them into serial data

(*a*) Transmitter section (*b*) Receiver Section

(*c*) Modem control (*d*) Read Write Control Logic.

**130.** In 8251, which of the following accepts serial and converts them into parallel data

(*a*) Transmitter section (*b*) Receiver Section

(*c*) Modem control (*d*) Read Write Control Logic.

**131.** The number of signal changes per second is called?

(*a*) baud rate (*b*) data transfer rate

(*c*) MIPS (*d*) none of the above.

**132.** The 8251 USART is capable of operating at how many Kbaud (Bd-bits per second) in synchronous mode

(*a*) 0 – 32 KBaud (*b*) 0 – 64 KBaud

(*c*) 0 – 128 Kbaud (*d*) 0 – 256 KBaud.

**133.** The 8251 USART is capable of operating at how many Kbaud (Bd-bits per second) in asynchronous mode

(*a*) 0 – 19.2 KBaud (*b*) 0 – 29.2 KBaud

(*c*) 0 – 39.2 Kbaud (*d*) 0 – 49.2 Kbaud.

**134.** Which of the following error cannot be detected by 8251A USART?

(*a*) Parity Error (*b*) Framing Error

(*c*) Overrun Error (*d*) Divide Error.

## ANSWERS

| | | | | | | |
|---|---|---|---|---|---|---|
| **1.** (*a*) | **2.** (*c*) | **3.** (*a*) | **4.** (*b*) | **5.** (*c*) | **6.** (*a*) | **7.** (*d*) |
| **8.** (*a*) | **9.** (*b*) | **10.** (*c*) | **11.** (*b*) | **12.** (*a*) | **13.** (*a*) | **14.** (*d*) |
| **15.** (*b*) | **16.** (*a*) | **17.** (*d*) | **18.** (*a*) | **19.** (*c*) | **20.** (*a*) | **21.** (*c*) |
| **22.** (*c*) | **23.** (*c*) | **24.** (*b*) | **25.** (*b*) | **26.** (*d*) | **27.** (*c*) | **28.** (*a*) |
| **29.** (*c*) | **30.** (*a*) | **31.** (*b*) | **32.** (*d*) | **33.** (*a*) | **34.** (*c*) | **35.** (*b*) |
| **36.** (*c*) | **37.** (*b*) | **38.** (*a*) | **39.** (*b*) | **40.** (*c*) | **41.** (*d*) | **42.** (*b*) |
| **43.** (*c*) | **44.** (*b*) | **45.** (*a*) | **46.** (*b*) | **47.** (*c*) | **48.** (*c*) | **49.** (*d*) |
| **50.** (*c*) | **51.** (*b*) | **52.** (*a*) | **53.** (*d*) | **54.** (*c*) | **55.** (*a*) | **56.** (*b*) |
| **57.** (*b*) | **58.** (*b*) | **59.** (*a*) | **60.** (*b*) | **61.** (*c*) | **62.** (*a*) | **63.** (*d*) |
| **64.** (*c*) | **65.** (*c*) | **66.** (*b*) | **67.** (*b*) | **68.** (*c*) | **69.** (*c*) | **70.** (*d*) |
| **71.** (*c*) | **72.** (*d*) | **73.** (*c*) | **74.** (*d*) | **75.** (*d*) | **76.** (*b*) | **77.** (*b*) |
| **78.** (*a*) | **79.** (*d*) | **80.** (*c*) | **81.** (*d*) | **82.** (*c*) | **83.** (*b*) | **84.** (*d*) |
| **85.** (*c*) | **86.** (*c*) | **87.** (*b*) | **88.** (*c*) | **89.** (*d*) | **90.** (*c*) | **91.** (*b*) |
| **92.** (*a*) | **93.** (*b*) | **94.** (*c*) | **95.** (*b*) | **96.** (*a*) | **97.** (*a*) | **98.** (*a*) |
| **99.** (*b*) | **100.** (*d*) | **101.** (*d*) | **102.** (*a*) | **103.** (*b*) | **104.** (*c*) | **105.** (*d*) |
| **106.** (*b*) | **107.** (*b*) | **108.** (*d*) | **109.** (*c*) | **110.** (*d*) | **111.** (*c*) | **112.** (*a*) |
| **113.** (*a*) | **114.** (*b*) | **115.** (*b*) | **116.** (*a*) | **117.** (*a*) | **118.** (*d*) | **119.** (*a*) |
| **120.** (*b*) | **121.** (*c*) | **122.** (*b*) | **123.** (*c*) | **124.** (*d*) | **125.** (*a*) | **126.** (*c*) |
| **127.** (*c*) | **128.** (*b*) | **129.** (*a*) | **130.** (*b*) | **131.** (*a*) | **132.** (*b*) | **133.** (*a*) |
| **134.** (*d*) | | | | | | |

## EXPLANATIONS

**41.** ACI instruction is used to add the immediate data and the pervious carry with the content of the accumulator. Accumulator: 26H = 00100110, Data: 57H =01010111, Carry =1Therefore 00100110+01010111+00000001= 01111110 = 7EH

**43.** SUI instruction is used to subtract the 8 bit data from the content of the accumulator. Accumulator : 40H = 01000000, Data to be subtracted : 37H = 00110111By adding the content of accumulator with the 2's compliment of 37H, we get the result 01000000+11001001= 00001001=09H

**44.** SBI instruction is used to subtract the 8 bit data from the content of the accumulator along with borrow. Accumulator : 37H =00110111, Data to be subtracted : 25H+01H (Borrow) = 26H. The 2's complement of 26H = 11011010. By adding the content of accumulator with the 2's compliment of 26H, we get the result 00110111+11011010= 1/00010001. By complement carry the result is 0/00010001=11H

**45.** XRI instruction is used to perform Exclusive OR operation. Accumulator: 8FH =10001111, Data : A2H= 10100010. When Exclusive OR operation is performed the result will be 00101101

**46.** The instruction RLC will rotate the content of accumulator to left. Accumulator contents before execution is A7H = 10100111 and the Carry Flag = 0. After the instruction is executed the content of accumulator become 01001111 and Carry Flag = 1. i.e. The content of bit $D_7$ is placed in bit $D_{0.}$

**47.** The instruction RRC will rotate the content of accumulator to right. Accumulator contents before execution is A7H = 10100111 and the Carry Flag = 0. After the instruction is executed the content of accumulator become 11010011 and Carry Flag = 1. i.e. The content of bit $D_0$ is placed in bit $D_7$

**48.** The instruction RAL will rotate the content of accumulator left through Carry. Accumulator content before execution is A7H = 10100111 and the Carry Flag = 0. After the instruction is executed the content of accumulator become 010001110 and Carry Flag = 1.

**49.** The instruction RAL will rotate the content of accumulator right through Carry. Accumulator contents before execution is A7H = 10100111 and the Carry Flag = 0. After the instruction is executed the content of accumulator become 01010011 and Carry Flag = 1

**57.** Instruction CMA is to complement the content of accumulator. Accumulator content before execution was 10011001. After performing compliment operation on 10011001 the result will be 01100110 = 66H.

**84.** In 8086 microprocessor segment-to-segment data transfer is not allowed

**90.** The content of CS and IP/EIP are added to obtain the address of the next instruction to be fetched.

CHAPTER 9

# COMPUTER NETWORKS

**1.** Which is the type of network used within a single building or campus?

(*a*) Local area networks (*b*) Metropolitan area networks

(*c*) Wide Area Networks (*d*) None of the above.

**2.** Point-to-point transmission with one sender and one receiver is called

(*a*) broadcasting (*b*) unicasting

(*c*) multicasting (*d*) telecasting.

**3.** The User Datagram Protocol is found in which layer of the TCP/IP Reference Model

(*a*) Application Layer (*b*) Host-to-Network Layer

(*c*) Internet Layer (*d*) Transport Layer.

**4.** Which layer of the OSI Reference Model is Concerned with the syntax and semantics of the information transmitted

(*a*) Transport layer (b) Physical layer

(*c*) Presentation layer (*d*) Network layer.

**5.** The OSI model has

(*a*) 9 layers (*b*) 10 layers

(*c*) 7 layers (*d*) 5 layers.

## The Next Seven Questions (6–12) are Based OSI Model

**Choose the function which is not performed by the layer mentioned.**

***6.** Physical layer

(*a*) signal encoding (*b*) topology

(*c*) mail services (*d*) bandwidth.

***7.** Data Link layer

(*a*) Addressing (*b*) Flow control

(*c*) Error control (*d*) Interface.

***8.** Network Layer

(*a*) Routing (*b*) World Wide Web

(*c*) Congestion control (*d*) Logical addressing.

***9.** Transport Layer

(*a*) Congestion control (*b*) Connection

(*c*) Segmentation and reassembly (*d*) Host-to-host message delivery.

***10.** Session Layer

(*a*) Synchronization (*b*) Transmission Mode

(*c*) Dialog control (*d*) Session closure.

***11.** Presentation Layer

(*a*) Translation (*b*) Encryption

(*c*) Compression (*d*) Node-to-node delivery.

***12.** Application layer

(*a*) Network abstraction (*b*) File access and transfer

(*c*) Routing (*d*) Remote login.

**13.** The mode of operation where a packet is received and processed by every machine on the network is called

(*a*) unicasting (*b*) multicasting

(*c*) base casting (*d*) broadcasting.

**14.** A collection of interconnected networks is called

(*a*) Internet (*b*) Intranet

(*c*) Ethernet (*d*) Arcnet.

**15.** DQDB is

(*a*) Distributed Queue Dual Bus (*b*) Distributed Queue Digital Bus

(*c*) Data Queue Dual Bus (*d*) Data Queue Digital Bus.

**16.** Transmission lines are also called as

(*a*) Circuits (*b*) Channels

(*c*) Trunks (*d*) all the above.

**17.** The expansion of CDPD

(*a*) Cellular Digital Packet Data (*b*) Cellular Dual Packet Data

(*c*) Cell Device Packet Data (*d*) Cell Dual Packet Data.

**18.** Which one of the following is to connect different and frequently incompatible networks?

(*a*) gateways (*b*) routers

(*c*) bridges (*d*) repeaters.

**19.** The entities comprising the corresponding layers on different machines are called as

(*a*) peers (*b*) levels
(*c*) protocols (*d*) interface.

## The Next Three Questions (20–22) are Based on the Following Information

**An organization has a fully connected mesh network consisting of 10 devices.**

***20.** What will be the total number of cable links needed?

(*a*) 10 (*b*) 25
(*c*) 45 (*d*) 100.

***21.** What will be the number of ports for each device?

(*a*) 9 (*b*) 10
(*c*) 12 (*d*) 15.

***22.** Suppose, the devices are configured as ring instead of mesh, then how many cable links are required.

(*a*) 10 (*b*) 25
(*c*) 45 (*d*) 100.

**23.** Railway track is a good example of

(*a*) Simplex (*b*) Half duplex
(*c*) Full duplex (*d*) None of the above.

**24.** Which of the following layers contains higher level protocols?

(*a*) Network (*b*) Datalink
(*c*) Application (*d*) Session.

***25.** A sine wave has a frequency of 8 Hz. What is its period?

(*a*) 80 microseconds (*b*) 100 microseconds
(*c*) 125 microseconds (*d*) 150 microseconds.

**26.** Attenuation in decibels equals

(*a*) $10\log_{10}$ transmitted power/received power
(*b*) $10\log_{10}$ transmitted power/received speed
(*c*) $10\log_{10}$ transmitted speed/received power
(*d*) $10\log_{10}$ transmitted speed/received speed.

**27.** The sophistication service provided by the data link layer to the network layer is

(*a*) connectionless service (*b*) connection oriented service
(*c*) reliable service (*d*) all the above.

**28.** CSMA stands for

(*a*) Code Sense Multiple Access (*b*) Carrier Sense Multiple Application
(*c*) Carrier Sense Multiple Access (*d*) Code Section Multiple Access.

***29.** A sine wave completes one cycle in 6 seconds. What is its frequency?

(*a*) 20 KHz (*b*) 30 KHz

(*c*) 40 KHz (*d*) 50 KHz.

**30.** In which of the following, a DLE is stuffed into the outgoing stream before DLE in the data?

(*a*) Bit Stuffing (*b*) Character stuffing

(*c*) Word stuffing (*d*) Block stuffing.

**31.** The number of bit positions in which 2 code words differ is called the

(*a*) Error correcting code (*b*) Hamming distance

(*c*) Parity bit (*d*) Error detecting code.

**32.** Polynomial code is also known as

(*a*) CRC code (*b*) hamming code

(*c*) parity code (*d*) none of the above.

**33.** Protocols in which the sender sends one frame and then wait for an acknowledgement before proceeding are called

(*a*) Sliding window (*b*) Stop and Wait

(*c*) Simplex (*d*) Contention.

**34.** Channel allocation uses which of the following.

(*a*) FDM (*b*) TDM

(*c*) WDM (*d*) all the above.

***35.** A sine wave is offset 1/8 of a cycle with respect to time zero. What is its phase?

(*a*) 30 degree (*b*) 45 degree

(*c*) 60 degree (*d*) 75 degree.

**36.** Protocols in which stations listen for a transmission and act accordingly are called

(*a*) Carrier sense protocols (*b*) ALOHA protocols

(*c*) Collision free protocols (*d*) Contention free protocols.

**37.** In which of the following method, each contention period consists of exactly N slots?

(*a*) Binary countdown (*b*) Basic bit mapc

(*c*) Limited contention (*d*) Adaptive tree walk.

**38.** The channel efficiency of binary countdown method is

(*a*) d/(N+ d) (*b*) d/(d+1)

(*c*) $d/(d + \log_2 N)$ (*d*) d/(1 + log N).

***39.** Suppose a periodic signal is decomposed into five sine waves with frequency of 200, 400, 600, 800 and 1000 Hz. What is its bandwidth?

(*a*) 200 Hz (*b*) 400 Hz

(*c*) 600 Hz (*d*) 800 Hz.

**40.** CSMA/CD protocols are

(*a*) Network layer protocols (*b*) WAN protocols

(*c*) Point to point protocols (*d*) MAC sub layer protocols for LAN's.

**41.** Parity bits are used for

(*a*) error detection (*b*) noise reduction

(*c*) error correction (*d*) all the above.

**42.** In which of the following subnet no routes are worked out in advance?

(*a*) Virtual circuit (*b*) Datagram

(*c*) Connection (*d*) All the above.

**43.** If data packets follow the previously established routes, then it is called as

(*a*) Network routing (*b*) Transport routing

(*c*) Datalink routing (*d*) Session routing.

***44.** A digital signal has a bit rate of 2500 bps. What is the duration of each bit?

(*a*) 40 microseconds (*b*) 60 microseconds

(*c*) 80 microseconds (*d*) 90 microseconds.

**45.** Which of the following layer is the heart of the whole protocol hierarchy?

(*a*) Network (*b*) Transport

(*c*) Session (*d*) Data Link.

***46.** Choose the statement which is incorrect for throughput?

(*a*) Network throughput is the average rate of successful message delivery over a communication channel

(*b*) Usually measured in bits per second (bit/s or bps)

(*c*) It is essentially synonymous to digital bandwidth consumption

(*d*) The throughput can be analyzed mathematically by means of probability theory.

***47.** A digital signal has a bit interval of 50 microseconds. What is the bit rate?

(*a*) 15 Kbps (*b*) 20 Kbps

(*c*) 25 Kbps (*d*) 30 Kbps.

**48.** What are the two main protocols of Transport layer?

(*a*) TCP, UDP (*b*) TCP, IP

(*c*) IP, UDP (*d*) DHCP, TCP.

**49.** Expansion of UDP

(*a*) Universal Data Processor (*b*) Unified Digital Protocol

(*c*) User Datagram Protocol (*d*) Universal Datagram Protocol.

**50.** Which of the following method is used for security purpose Data link layer?

(*a*) Link encryption (*b*) Link decryption

(*c*) Layer encryption (*d*) Layer decryption.

**51.** The output of encryption process in cryptography is known as

(*a*) Plain text (*b*) Cipher text

(*c*) Cryptanalysis (*d*) Key.

**52.** Suppose the following string '*HAI bbbbbb COME*' (where *b* represents blank space) has to be transmitted in a network, what would be the compressed message if Null Suppression technique is used?

(*a*) HAI COME (*b*) HAI COME

(*c*) HAI $C_s$ 6COME (*d*) HAI$C_s$b6COME.

## The Next Two Questions (53–54) are Based on Run Length Encoding Technique

**Suppose a Data 983477773499999 to be Transmitted in a Network**

**53.** What would be the compressed data?

(*a*) 9834$C_7$434 $C_9$5 (*b*) 9834$C_4$734 $C_5$9

(*c*) 98344$_7$345$_9$ (*d*) 98347$_4$349$_5$.

***54.** What would be the compression ratio for the above data?

(*a*) 1.00 (*b*) 1.25

(*c*) 0.8 (*d*) 1.50.

**55.** When the original text is encrypted, it is called as

(*a*) plain text (*b*) cipher text

(*c*) decryption (*d*) encryption.

## The Next Three Questions (56–58) are Based on the Following Information

**Suppose we want to transform the plain text *come home today***

***56.** What would be the corresponding Cipher text using Caesar Cipher?

(*a*) frph krph wrgdb (*b*) dpnf ipnf upeba

(*c*) bnld gnld snczx (*d*) eqog jqog vqfca.

***57.** What would be the corresponding Cipher text using Rail Fence technique?

(*a*) oeoeoacmhmtdy (*b*) cmhmtdyoeoeoa

(*c*) cmhoeomtdyeoa (*d*) tdyoeoeoacmhm.

***58.** What would be the corresponding Cipher text using Simple Columnar Transposition technique? (Assume 6 column with the random order 4,6,3,2,5,1)

(*a*) ameootoehdcmy (*b*) toameooehdcmy

(*c*) eooamtoehdcmy (*d*) eootoehdcmyam.

**59.** Which of the following statement is incorrect about RSA algorithm?

(*a*) It is the first major private key cryptography

(*b*) The acronym of RSA is Rivest-Shamir-Aldeman

(*c*) RSA solves the problem of key agreements and distribution

(*d*) RSA was developed in the year 1977.

**60.** Which of the following compression technique uses variable length codes made up of zero's and ones to encode character and other symbols?

(*a*) Morse Code (*b*) Huffman Code

(*c*) Lempet-Ziv Code (*d*) None of the above.

## The Next Two Questions (61–62) are Based on the Following Information

**An analog signal carries 4 bits in each signal element. If 2000 signal elements are sent per seconds**

***61.** What will be the baud rate?

(*a*) 1000 bauds per second (*b*) 2000 bauds per second

(*c*) 3000 bauds per second (*d*) 4000 bauds per second.

***62.** What will be the bit rate?

(*a*) 4000 bps (*b*) 6000 bps

(*c*) 8000 bps (*d*) 10000 bps.

**63.** Which of the Ciphers reorder the letters but do not disguise them?

(*a*) Substitution (*b*) Monoalphabetic

(*c*) Transposition (*d*) One time pad.

**64.** Which cable consists of a stiff copper wire as the core surrounded by an insulating material?

(*a*) Twisted pair cable (*b*) Fibre cable

(*c*) Coaxial cable (*d*) All the above.

**65.** A Situation in which traffic ceases to flow

(*a*) Collision (*b*) Deadlock

(*c*) Degradation (*d*) Distortion.

**66.** Which of the following is a geostationary earth orbit satellite?

(*a*) Iridium (*b*) Telstar

(*c*) Teledesic (*d*) Globalstar.

**67.** In which mobile system the coding theory is used?

(*a*) D-AMPS (*b*) GSM

(*c*) CDMA (*d*) PDC.

***68.** A telephone channel has a bandwidth of 2500 Hz and the signal-to-noise (S/N) is around 3162. What is the maximum data rate of transmission medium (Shannon Capacity)

(*a*) 27.05 Kbps (*b*) 28.05 Kbps

(*c*) 29.05 Kbps (*d*) 30.05 Kbps.

**69.** Which of the following modulation technique is a combination of two technique?
(*a*) Amplitude Shift Keying (ASK) (*b*) Frequency Shift Keying (FSK)
(*c*) Phase Shift Keying (PSK) (*d*) Quadrate Amplitude Modulation (QAM).

**70.** Which of the following is not a method to assign the hardware address to a computer in physical addressing mechanism in a networking technology?
(*a*) Static address (*b*) Configurable address
(*c*) Dynamic address (*d*) Relative address.

**71.** Choose the topology where one central device is connected to all other devices
(*a*) Mesh (*b*) Star
(*c*) Bus (*d*) Ring.

**72.** Fuzz ball is
(*a*) Wireless Technology (*b*) Microcomputer
(*c*) Protocol (*d*) Topology.

**73.** The frequency of electromagnetic waves is measured in
(*a*) ampere (*b*) meter
(*c*) hertz (*d*) none of the above.

**74.** Microwaves travel in
(*a*) curves (*b*) straight lines
(*c*) curves and straight lines (*d*) none of the above.

**75.** A technique for representing analogue speech signal into binary digital form
(*a*) Frequency Division Multiplexing
(*b*) Pulse Code Modulation
(*c*) Encoding
(*d*) Decoding.

**76.** Connectionless networks are sometimes called
(*a*) circuit switched (*b*) packet switched
(*c*) message switching (*d*) message switching or circuit switching.

**77.** A system with fiber for the long-haul runs and coaxial cable to the houses is called
(*a*) ADSL (*b*) HFC
(*c*) DOCSIS (*d*) CMTS.

**78.** The use of one network interface by several processes is
(*a*) encoding (*b*) broadcasting
(*c*) multiplexing (*d*) routing.

**79.** Ethernet was invented at
(*a*) Microsoft Corporation (*b*) IBM
(*c*) Xerox Corporation (*d*) Sun Microsystems.

**80.** The interference between two signals is called
(*a*) collision (*b*) detection
(*c*) transmission (*d*) reaction.

**81.** An Electronic device which connects two LAN segments is

(*a*) router (*b*) bridge

(*c*) firewall (*d*) gateway.

**82.** The network layer is implemented in

(*a*) hosts only (*b*) router only

(*c*) hosts and router (*d*) all network components.

**83.** The Protocol a computer uses to map an IP address in a hardware address

(*a*) file transfer protocol (*b*) address resolution protocol

(*c*) internet protocol (*d*) hypertext transfer protocol.

**84.** Which of the following is true for a bridge?

(*a*) A bridge always broadcasts each incoming frame on all other ports

(*b*) A bridge never broadcasts an incoming frame on all other ports

(*c*) All bridge ports must have unique IP addresses

(*d*) A bridge does not have to be configured.

**85.** A hardware device that plugs into a computer and connects the computer to a network is

(*a*) network terminating interface (*b*) network interface card

(*c*) modem (*d*) splitter.

**86.** A routing protocol is run in a datagram network

(*a*) when a packet arrives at the network and has to be sent to the next hop

(*b*) when a link cost changes

(*c*) non-periodically

(*d*) when the first packet of a new connection arrives at the first router in the network.

**87.** A Computer network developed by the Advanced Research Projects Agency of the US Department of defence

(*a*) Ethernet (*b*) ARPANET

(*c*) ARCNET (*d*) ASTNET.

**88.** Wi-Fi is a

(*a*) type of Computer

(*b*) type of network cable

(*c*) set of popular technologies and standards for wireless computer networking

(*d*) set of computer programs that help people make money on the internet.

**89.** Choose the statement which is incorrect with regard to TCP/IP.

(*a*) TCP/IP suite of protocols forms the basis of the Internet

(*b*) TCP/IP creates an illusion of virtual network when multiple computer network are connected together (*c*) TCP/IP was developed after OSI

(*d*) TCP/IP consists of five layers.

**90.** An IP address is a numeric quantity that identifies

(*a*) the user of a computer

(*b*) the manufacturer of a computer

(*c*) the physical location of a computer

(*d*) none of the above.

**91.** The function of Internal Assigned Number Authority (IANA) is

(*a*) to allocate an IP address prefix to the ISP

(*b*) to allocates IP address to each different customer one by one

(c) to provide security

(*d*) none of the above.

**92.** Which device act as a traffic cop?

(*a*) Router (*b*) Bridge

(*c*) Hub (*d*) Switch.

**93.** Bluetooth technology Supports networking over

(*a*) Wi-Fi standard wireless radio connections

(*b*) its own standard wireless radio connections

(*c*) USB cable connections

(*d*) ethernet cable connections.

## The Next Two Questions (94–95) are Based on the Following Information

**Given a I Mbps Ethernet link, packet size of 10 MB, propagation speed = 2 x 108 m/s and distance between the two end points to be 10 km. Assume there are no routers on the link.**

***94.** What will be the Propagation delay?

(*a*) 30 microsecond (*b*) 40 microsecond

(*c*) 50 microsecond (*d*) 60 microsecond.

***95.** What will be the Transmission delay?

(*a*) 50 sec (*b*) 60 sec

(*c*) 70 sec (*d*) 80 sec.

**96.** The functions of the network layer are

(*a*) guaranteed delivery of a packet from sender host to receiving host

(*b*) determining routes

(*c*) reliable delivery to the next hop in a route

(*d*) flow control between neighboring networks.

**97.** Data transfer between two neighboring routers involves only

(*a*) physical layer

(*b*) physical layer, link layer

(*c*) physical layer, datalink layer, networking layer

(*d*) physical layer, datalink layer, network layer, transport layer.

**98.** ISDN is a

(*a*) digital data network supplied by telephone companies

(*b*) wireless technology

(*c*) networking device

(*d*) private area network.

**99.** An IP address when written in dotted decimal notation, range from

(*a*) 0.0.0.0 to 255.255.255.255
(*b*) 128.0.0.0 to 255.255.255.255

(*c*) 192.0.0.0 to 255.255.255.255
(*d*) 224.0.0.0 to 255.255.255.255.

**100.** Modem is

(*a*) a short for modulator-demodulator

(*b*) a device which converts analog to digital information

(*c*) a device which converts digital to analog information

(*d*) all the above.

**101.** Protection against unauthorized data access refers to

(*a*) data integrity
(*b*) data availability

(*c*) data confidentiality
(*d*) privacy.

**102.** A client is a

(*a*) node which sends information
(*b*) network

(*c*) node which requests information
(*d*) protocol.

**103.** Packets are

(*a*) small chunks of data that can be sent over the network

(*b*) incorporation of data into larger data unit

(*c*) signals transmitted over the network

(*d*) programs transmitted over the network.

**104.** Which feature is not offered by TCP?

(*a*) Reliable, flow control, data may be out of order

(*b*) Congestion control

(*c*) Constant bit rate

(*d*) None of the above.

**105.** Which of the following is a list of TCP services features?

(*a*) Reliable, flow control, data may be out of order

(*b*) Reliable, connection oriented, flow control

(*c*) Congestion control, no hand shaking, flow control

(*d*) Reliable congestion, control, data may be out of order.

**106.** Which of the following are characteristics of packet switching?

(*a*) Bandwidth divided, store and forward, good for bursty data

(*b*) Bandwidth shared, queues at routers, different paths possible

(*c*) Bandwidth shared, low transmission delay, routes may change during transmission

(*d*) Bandwidth divided, translation tables for routing, destination address field in packet.

**107.** The process of converting plain text into cipher text is called

(*a*) decryption (*b*) multiplexing

(*c*) modulation (*d*) encryption.

**108.** Which of the following is a network security technology?

(*a*) Bluetooth (*b*) Pretty Good Privacy

(*c*) GPRS (*d*) GSM.

***109.** Consider your laptop has the following IP configurations: IP address 192.168.1.101, mask 255.255.255.0, default gateway: 192.168.1.1, DNS Server 1: 192.168.1.200, DNS Server 2 : 203.187.192.15. Suppose you telnet to login aaab.ac.in whose IP address is 202.68.145.210. Which of the following scenario is not possible with respect to ARP?

(*a*) ARP query for 192.168.1.1 (*b*) ARP query for 192.168.1.200

(*c*) ARP query for 192.168.1.101 (*d*) No ARP query.

**110.** Data encrypted in such a way that the receiver can verify the identity of the user is

(*a*) firewall (*b*) integrity

(*c*) digital signature (*d*) trojan horse.

**111.** IP version 6 (IPv6) also known as IP Next Generation (IPng) uses

(*a*) 32 bit IP address (*b*) 64 bit IP address

(*c*) 128 bit IP address (*d*) none of the above.

***112.** The Basic Rate Interface (BRI) of ISDN interface rate is

(*a*) 64 Kbps (*b*) 128 Kbps

(*c*) 192 Kbps (*d*) 256 Kbps.

***113.** The Primary Rate Interface (BRI) of ISDN interface is

(*a*) 64 Kbps (*b*) 128 Kbps

(*c*) 192 Kbps (*d*) 256 Kbps.

**114.** A Security mechanism placed at the connection between networks in an organization and networks outside the organization is

(*a*) firewall (*b*) virus

(*c*) encoder (*d*) modem.

**115.** The Art of breaking ciphers is called

(*a*) cryptography (*b*) decoding

(*c*) cryptanalysis (*d*) encoding.

**116.** Virus is a

(*a*) protocol

(*b*) standardized data format to describe web content

(*c*) malicious program

(*d*) mobile technology.

**117.** Sandbox is a

(*a*) type of virus

(*b*) a security mechanism for separating running programs

(*c*) encoder

(*d*) decoder.

**118.** Authentication is the act of

(*a*) protecting data from hackers (*b*) confirming the identity of a user

(*c*) converting text into secret code (*d*) decrypting the data.

**119.** The range of frequencies that can pass over a given circuit is called

(*a*) baud rate (*b*) band width

(*c*) decibel (*d*) hertz.

**120.** Spread spectrum is

(*a*) a transmission path in which the data is transmitted to a satellite

(*b*) a transmissions technique used to avoid interference & achieve higher throughput

(*c*) method for controlling use of a communications channel, employed for some ring networks

(*d*) a situation in which traffic ceases to flow.

**121.** A Private network is

(*a*) used by any subscriber to communicate with other subscriber

(*b*) restricted to the corporate or individual owner

(*c*) oldest packet switching network in the world

(*d*) used by all internet users.

**122.** A packet containing both data and address information is

(*a*) datagram (*b*) data set

(*c*) IP Address (*d*) cluster.

**123.** A logical grouping of connected network devices which are located in close physical proximity to each other on a LAN is called

(*a*) internet (*b*) intranet

(*c*) subnet (*d*) telnet.

**124.** Choose the technology that allows a organization with multiple sites to have a private network and use it as public network as a carrier is

(*a*) ARPANET (b) Integrated digital network

(*c*) Virtual private network (*d*) Public network.

**125.** Congestion is a

(*a*) condition when two or more stations attempt to use the same channel at the same time

(*b*) condition when two signals collide with each other

(*c*) procedure to minimize the band width

(*d*) condition in which each packet sent through a network experiences excessive delay, because the network is overrun with packets.

**126.** Encapsulation is

(*a*) technique IP uses to divide a large datagram into smaller datagram

(*b*) technique in which information to be sent is placed inside the data area of a packet or frame

(*c*) mechanism that provide call setup and termination

(*d*) a term telephone companies used to denote a channel configured to handle a voice telephone circuit.

**127.** A transfer control protocol is

(*a*) connection oriented (*b*) end to end protocol

(*c*) full duplex (*d*) all the above.

**128.** Which of the following is true?

(*a*) TCP & UDP are connection oriented protocols

(*b*) TCP & UDP are connectionless protocols

(*c*) TCP is connectionless & UDP is connection oriented

(*d*) TCP is connection oriented & UDP is connectionless.

**129.** The process of establishing communication parameters such as transmission speed, packet size, buffer size, is called

(*a*) baud rate (*b*) parity

(*c*) handshaking (*d*) none of the above.

**130.** The number of changes in a signal per second is called

(*a*) baud rate (*b*) parity

(*c*) handshaking (*d*) band width.

**131.** Which one of the following is not a network operating system?

(*a*) Windows Millennium Edition (*b*) Windows 2000

(*c*) Windows XP (*d*) Windows Vista.

**132.** A network point that acts as an entrance to another network is called

(*a*) router (*b*) gateway

(*c*) repeater (*d*) bridge.

**133.** In the network operating system Windows NT family, NT stands for

(*a*) network technology (*b*) network topology

(*c*) new technology (*d*) network terminology.

## The Next Two Questions (134–135) are Based on the Following Information

**Consider the below network diagram, where there are 9 networks numbered 1 to 8 connected each other by seven router A to G**

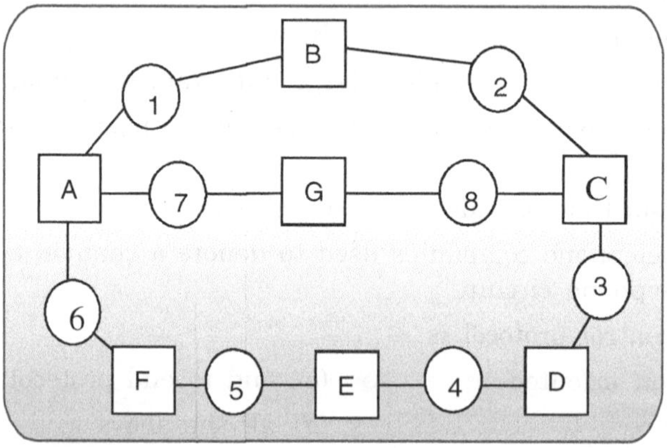


**134.** According to link state routing router G sends information periodically about which of the following node/nodes to other nodes.

(*a*) A and C (*b*) A only

(*c*) C only (*d*) B and E.

**135.** According to vector routing philosophy Router A sends network information periodically to

(*a*) G and F only (*b*) B and F only

(*c*) B, F and G only (*d*) B, F, G and C only.

**136.** The endpoint of a bidirectional communication flow across the internet is called

(*a*) internet protocol (*b*) gateway

(*c*) internet socket (*d*) internet router.

**137.** Which type of connector is used for Ethernet LAN Connection?

(*a*) RJ-11 (*b*) RS-232C

(*c*) RJ-45 (*d*) RJ-36.

**138.** Which one of the following is an IEEE standard for token ring?

(*a*) 802.3 (*b*) 802.5

(*c*) 802.1x (*d*) 802.11b.

**139.** The technical term for gigabit Ethernet is

(*a*) 1000BaseT (*b*) 100BaseT

(*c*) 10BaseT (*d*) 500BaseT.

**140.** A Computer program that accesses and displays information from the World Wide Web is called

(*a*) Virus (*b*) Adware

(*c*) Freeware (*d*) Browser.

**141.** The algorithm used to compute optimal routes is

(*a*) Kruskal algorithm (*b*) Dijkstra's algorithm

(*c*) K-means algorithm (*d*) LDA.

**142.** A form of network attack in which a site is flooded with so many packets that the site cannot respond to legitimate requests is called

(*a*) denial of service (*b*) eavesdropping

(*c*) copyright infringement (*d*) phishing.

**143.** Which of the following type of IP address is permanent on the network?

(*a*) Static IP address (*b*) Dynamic IP address

(*c*) Both (*a*) & (*b*) (*d*) None of the above.

**144.** For which of the following connections a crossover Ethernet cable must be used?

(*a*) A computer to a Hub (*b*) Devices of same type

(*c*) Devices of different types (*d*) For all Ethernet connections.

**145.** An intermediary program that translates requests of different protocols from internal network to the Internet is

(*a*) ping (*b*) compiler

(*c*) gateway (*d*) proxy.

**146.** Ping is

(*a*) packet internet groper

(*b*) a program used to test network connectivity

(*c*) both (*a*) & (*b*)

(*d*) none of the above.

**147.** An extra bit added to a unit of data, usually each character, to verify that the data is transferred without corruption is called

(*a*) Megabit (*b*) Ping

(*c*) Parity (*d*) Proxy.

**148.** The variation in the time between packets arriving caused by network congestion, timing drift, or route changes is called

(a) jitter (b) splitter
(c) baud rate (d) network delay.

**149.** The act of pretending to be an authorized user of a system in order to gain access to it through internet is called
(a) phishing (b) masquerade
(c) denial of service (d) cryptanalysis.

**150.** The scam to steal valuable information from users by sending an official-looking e-mail pretending to be from their bank or retail establishment is called
(a) phishing (b) masquerade
(c) spam (d) denial of service.

**151.** Splitter is
(a) a device which consists of multiple ports
(b) analog device for dividing one input into 2 outputs
(c) a device used to find the shortest route
(d) the endpoint of a bidirectional communication flow across the internet.

**152.** The signal path from the earth to the transponder in the satellite is called
(a) uplink (b) downlink
(c) uploading (d) downloading.

**153.** A device that performs direct digital to digital conversion between two different voice encoding schemes without returning the signal to the analog form is called
(a) transmitter (b) transistor
(c) transcoder (d) transceiver.

**154.** The wireless network technology named after a tenth century Danish king is
(a) Infrared (b) WAP
(c) Wi-Fi (d) Blue tooth.

**155.** A patch cable between two circuits is called
(a) jitter (b) jumper
(c) router (d) hub.

**156.** A protocol which uses strong cryptography so that a client can prove its identity to a server across an insecure network connection is called
(a) transfer control protocol (b) kerberos
(c) user datagram protocol (d) internet protocol.

**157.** Which one of the following is an encryption algorithm?
(a) Kruskal algorithm (b) Dijkstra's algorithm
(c) K-means algorithm (d) RSA algorithm.

**158.** The term for establishing a connection with a forged sender address is called
(a) Phishing (b) Spoofing
(c) Masquerade (d) Intrusion.

**159.** A software entity that appears to do something quite normal but which, in fact, contains a trapdoor or attack program is called

(*a*) Virus (*b*) Worm

(*c*) Trojan Horse (*d*) Intruder.

**160.** Detection of break-ins or break-in attempts by reviewing logs or other information available on a network is called

(*a*) intrusion detection (*b*) copy detection

(*c*) collision detection (*d*) log detection.

**161.** Most packet loss results from

(*a*) hardware failure (*b*) congestion

(*c*) transmission (*d*) switching.

**162.** The syntactic form that IP software uses to express 32 bit binary values when interacting with human is

(*a*) class (*b*) decimal notation

(*c*) dotted decimal notation (*d*) IP address.

**163.** Secure socket layer (SSL) is a

(*a*) system that monitors all packets arriving at a site

(*b*) security standard used with IP datagrams

(*c*) protocol used to provide centralized authentication, authorization and accounting

(*d*) technology that uses encryption to provide authentication and confidentiality.

**164.** A tunnel is

(*a*) any mechanism that encapsulates a packet in a high level protocol for transmission

(*b*) a security standard used with IP datagrams

(*c*) a protocol used to provide centralized authentication, authorization and accounting

(*d*) a technology that uses encryption to provide authentication and confidentiality.

**165.** A syntactic form used to identify a page of information on the World Wide Web is called

(*a*) browser (*b*) navigator

(*c*) uniform resource locator (*d*) IP address.

**166.** A protocol technique in which data is changed by inserting additional bytes to distinguish between data values & packet control values is called

(*a*) circuit switching (*b*) encapsulation

(*c*) byte stuffing (*d*) token passing.

**167.** BOOTP is a

(*a*) protocol that computers used to obtain configuration information

(*b*) protocol used to transfer email from one computer to another across the internet

(*c*) TCP/IP protocol that provides application programs with connectionless communication service

(*d*) protocol that a computer uses when it first starts to obtain information needed to configure the protocol software.

**168.** The protocol used to transfer email from one computer to another across the internet is

(*a*) UDP (*b*) BOOTP

(*c*) SMTP (*d*) RTP.

**169.** A popular application in which the user of a computer sends a memo to one or more recipients is called

(*a*) Cookie (*b*) E-mail

(*c*) Client (*d*) Request.

**170.** A reference to the job of administering, monitoring and controlling network is called

(*a*) Network analyzing (*b*) Network interfacing

(*c*) Network management (*d*) Plug-and-play networking.

**171.** Ethernet uses

(*a*) bus topology (*b*) mesh topology

(*c*) star topology (*d*) ring topology.

***172.** Which of the following does not hold good for ISDN?

(*a*) The fundamental concept of ISDN is the digital bit pipe

(*b*) ISDN offers four separate digital channels

(*c*) BRI and PRI are two interfaces supported by ISDN

(*d*) ISDN aims to integrate voice and non-voice services together in digital form.

**173.** Which of the following reference point in ISDN connection defines the connection between a Network Termination 2 (NT2) and Network Termination 1(NT1)?

(*a*) R (*b*) S

(*c*) T (*d*) U.

***174.** A Frame Relay services needs how many T-lines to connect 8 LANs?

(*a*) 8 (*b*) 16

(*c*) 28 (*d*) 56.

**175.** Which of the following ATM service class is similar to a T-line and useful for customers those who require real-time audio or video services?

(*a*) Variable Bit rate (VBR) (*b*) Constant Bit rate (CBR)

(*c*) Available Bit rate (ABR) (*d*) Unspecified Bit rate (UBR).

**176.** In the context of data transmission, ATM is the acronym for

(*a*) Automatic Transmission Media

(*b*) Automatic Teller Machine

(*c*) Asynchronous Telecommunication Model

(*d*) Asynchronous Transfer Model.

**177.** Which of the following operates at all the seven layers of the OSI model?

(*a*) Repeaters (*b*) Bridges

(*c*) Routers (*d*) Gateways.

***178.** Which of the following does not hold good for a bridge?

(*a*) A bridge does not run application program

(*b*) Bridge divides a big network into smaller sub-networks

(*c*) There are four types of bridge

(*d*) Bridge sends the data frames only to the concerned segment.

**179.** Choose the statement which does not hold good for 'hub'.

(*a*) A hub is a multi-port repeater

(*b*) A hub breaks collision or broadcast domain

(*c*) A hub operates on the Physical layer of the OSI model

(*d*) A hub is also known as concentrators.

**180.** Which of the following are delivered in IP packets and used to report network errors, network congestion, assists trouble shooting and announces timeouts?

(*a*) Internet Control Message Protocol (ICMP)

(*b*) Address Resolution Protocol (ARP)

(*c*) Reverse Address Resolution Protocol(RARP)

(*d*) User Datagram protocol (UDP).

**181.** SNMP is an/a

(*a*) mechanism to map MAC address to IP address

(*b*) network device that could send data in little-endian format

(*c*) network device that could send data in big-endian format

(*d*) application layer protocol that assists the exchange of management information between network devices.

**182.** When the destination IP address specifies that packet should be delivered to specific host in a network is called

(*a*) broadcast (*b*) unicast

(*c*) multicast (*d*) none of the above.

**183.** Choose the default network mask of Class B network.

(*a*) 255.0.0.0 (*b*) 255.255.0.0.

(*c*) 255.255.255.0 (*d*) 255.255.255.255.

## ANSWERS

| | | | | | | |
|---|---|---|---|---|---|---|
| 1. (a) | 2. (b) | 3. (d) | 4. (c) | 5. (c) | 6. (c) | 7. (d) |
| 8. (b) | 9. (a) | 10. (b) | 11. (d) | 12. (c) | 13. (d) | 14. (a) |
| 15. (a) | 16. (d) | 17. (a) | 18. (a) | 19. (a) | 20. (c) | 21. (a) |
| 22. (a) | 23. (b) | 24. (c) | 25. (c) | 26. (a) | 27. (b) | 28. (c) |
| 29. (c) | 30. (b) | 31. (b) | 32. (a) | 33. (b) | 34. (d) | 35. (b) |
| 36. (a) | 37. (b) | 38. (c) | 39. (d) | 40. (d) | 41. (a) | 42. (b) |
| 43. (d) | 44. (a) | 45. (b) | 46. (d) | 47. (b) | 48. (a) | 49. (c) |
| 50. (a) | 51. (b) | 52. (c) | 53. (a) | 54. (b) | 55. (b) | 56. (a) |
| 57. (b) | 58. (c) | 59. (a) | 60. (c) | 61. (b) | 62. (c) | 63. (c) |
| 64. (c) | 65. (b) | 66. (b) | 67. (c) | 68. (c) | 69. (d) | 70. (d) |
| 71. (b) | 72. (b) | 73. (c) | 74. (b) | 75. (b) | 76. (b) | 77. (b) |
| 78. (c) | 79. (c) | 80. (a) | 81. (b) | 82. (c) | 83. (b) | 84. (d) |
| 85. (b) | 86. (b) | 87. (b) | 88. (c) | 89. (c) | 90. (c) | 91. (a) |
| 92. (a) | 93. (b) | 94. (c) | 95. (d) | 96. (b) | 97. (c) | 98. (a) |
| 99. (a) | 100. (d) | 101. (c) | 102. (c) | 103. (a) | 104. (b) | 105. (b) |
| 106. (b) | 107. (d) | 108. (b) | 109. (c) | 110. (a) | 111. (c) | 112. (c) |
| 113. (c) | 114. (a) | 115. (c) | 116. (c) | 117. (b) | 118. (b) | 119. (b) |
| 120. (b) | 121. (b) | 122. (a) | 123. (c) | 124. (c) | 125. (d) | 126. (b) |
| 127. (d) | 128. (d) | 129. (c) | 130. (a) | 131. (a) | 132. (b) | 133. (a) |
| 134. (a) | 135. (c) | 136. (c) | 137. (c) | 138. (b) | 139. (a) | 140. (d) |
| 141. (b) | 142. (a) | 143. (a) | 144. (b) | 145. (d) | 146. (c) | 147. (c) |
| 148. (a) | 149. (b) | 150. (a) | 151. (b) | 152. (a) | 153. (c) | 154. (d) |
| 155. (b) | 156. (b) | 157. (d) | 158. (b) | 159. (c) | 160. (a) | 161. (b) |
| 162. (c) | 163. (d) | 164. (a) | 165. (c) | 166. (c) | 167. (d) | 168. (c) |
| 169. (b) | 170. (c) | 171. (a) | 172. (b) | 173. (c) | 174. (d) | 175. (a) |
| 176. (d) | 177. (d) | 178. (c) | 179. (b) | 180. (a) | 181. (d) | 182. (b) |
| 183. (b) | | | | | | |

## EXPLANATIONS

6. The function performed by physical layer is Signal encoding, Topology, Bandwidth, Medium, Bit Synchronization, Transmission type, Transmission mode, Multiplexeing, Interface, Signal type

7. The function performed by Data Link layer is Addressing, Flow control, Error control, Synchronization, Media Access Control, Node-to-node delivery

**8.** The function performed by Network Layer is Routing, Congestion control, Logical addressing,Address transformation, Accounting and billing, Source to destination error-free delivery

**9.** The function performed by Transport Layer is Connection, Segmentation and reassembly, Host-to-host message delivery, Application-to-application communication

**10.** The function performed by Session Layer is Synchronization, Dialog control, Session closure, Sessions and sub-sessions

**11.** The function performed by Presentation Layer is Translation, Encryption, Compression

**12.** The function performed by Application layer is Network abstraction, File access and transfer, Remote login, Mail services, World Wide Web

**20.** Number of links in a mesh network = $n(n-1)/n$. Where $n$ = the number of devices. Therefore, 10(10–1)/2 = 45

**21.** Number of ports per device = $n$–1, where $n$ = number of devices. Therefore, 10–1 = 9

**22.** To connect $n$ devices in a ring topology, $n$ cable links are needed. Therefore, a 10 device ring needs 10 cable links

**25.** Period = 1 / Frequency. Therefore, 1/8 = 0.125 seconds. 8 KHz = 1/8000 = 0.000125 seconds. i.e. $125 \times 10^{-6}$ = 125 microseconds

**29.** Frequency= 1 / Period. Therefore, 1/6 = 0.17 Hz. In 25 microseconds = $1(25 \times 10^{-6})$ = 40,000 Hz = 40 × 103 Hz = 40 KHz

**35.** One complete cycle is 360 degree. Therefore, 1/8 × 360 = 45 degree

**39.** High frequency = 1000, Low frequency = 200. Therefore, 1000 – 200 = 800 Hz.

**44.** The bit interval is the inverse of the bit rate. Bit interval = 1/bit rate. Therefore, 1/2500 = 0.000400 seconds. i.e., $400 \times 10^{-6}$ = 40 microseconds

**46.** The throughput can be analyzed mathematically by means of queuing theory

**47.** Bit rate is the inverse of the bit interval. Bit rate = 1/bit interval = $1/50 \times 10^{-6}$ = 20,000 bit per second. i.e., $20 \times 10^3$ bits per second = 20 Kbps

**54.** $$\text{Compression ratio} = \frac{\text{Length of uncompressed data}}{\text{Length of compressed data including special code}}$$

**56.** In Caesar Cipher we replace each plain text characters with the corresponding character three places down the line. (*e.g.* c with f, o with r, m with p, e with h etc)

**57.** In a Rail Fence technique the plain text messages are written as a sequence of diagonals and read as sequence of rows.

1st row = cmhmtdy 2nd row = oeoeoa, Therefore the answers is *cmhmtdyoeoeoa*

**58.** In Simple Columnar Transposition Technique write the plain text message row-by-row in a rectangle predefined size and read the message column-by-column in any order order. Therefore, for the original plain text *come home today,* we write the message in rectangle row-by-row as give below:

| Column 1 | Column 2 | Column 3 | Column 4 | Column 5 | Column 6 |
|---|---|---|---|---|---|
| c | o | m | e | h | o |
| m | e | t | o | d | a |
| y | | | | | |

by reading above text in the order of column 4,6,3,2,5,1 we get *eooamtoehdcmy*

**61.** Baud rate = number of signal elements. Therefore, 2000 bauds per second

**62.** Bit rate = Baud rate × number of bits per signal element. i.e. 2000 × 4 = 8000 bps

**68.** Non Capacity = B $\log_2$ (1+S/N), where B= the bandwidth and S/N= signal-to-noise.
Therefore, 2500 $\log_2$ (1+ 3162) = 2500 $\log_2$ (3163) = 2500 × 11. 62 = 29050 bps = 29.05 Kbps

**94.** Propagation delay = $10^4/2$ x $10^8$ = 50 microsecond.

**95.** Transmission delay = L/R = (10mb/1mb) x 8 = 80sec.

**109.** ARP queries will be only be for addresses on the same LAN, Therefore (a) and (b) are possible. Similarly (d) is also possible because all entries could be cached. (c) is not possible because laptop won't make query for itself.

**112.** A BRI specifies a digital bit pipe that contains two B channels and one D channels. A B channel operates at 64 Kbps and D channel at 16 kbps. Therefore, (2B × 64)+91D × 16)+48 overhead = 192 Kbps.

**113.** A BRI specifies a digital bit pipe that contains two B channels and one D channels. A B channel operates at 64 Kbps and D channel at 16 kbps. Therefore, (2B × 64) + 91D × 16) + 48 overhead = 192 Kbps.

**172.** ISDN offers the following three types of channels: Bearer (B) Channel, Data (D) Channels and Hybrid (H) Cannels

**174.** To connect n LANs n × (n-1) T-lines are required.

**178.** Bridge supports three types of bridge, simple, Learning and Multiport

CHAPTER 10

# DATA MINING AND DATA WAREHOUSE

1. Data mining commonly involves
   (*a*) Classification, Clustering and Regression
   (*b*) Classification, Clustering and Association rule learning
   (*c*) Clustering, Regression and Association rule learning
   (*d*) Classification, Clustering, Regression and Association rule learning.
2. A more appropriate name for data mining could be
   (*a*) Web Mining (*b*) Data Warehouse Mining
   (*c*) Knowledge Mining (*d*) Database Mining.
3. Which of the following is a continuous data?
   (*a*) Calorific value of a soft drink
   (*b*) Formatted capacity of a computer disk
   (*c*) Weight of an article
   (*d*) Number of persons visited a website.
4. Which of the following is correct?
   (*a*) Collection of information is called data
   (*b*) Collection of records is called information
   (*c*) Collection of files is called record
   (*d*) Collection of data is called information.
5. Consider the following table:

| | Column A | | Column B |
|---|---|---|---|
| 1 | Hierarchical Database | A | Data are organized using pointers |
| 2 | Network Database | B | Data are stored as multicubes |
| 3 | Relational Database | C | Data are organized as entities |
| 4 | Object oriented Database | D | Data are organized as tables |
| 5 | Multidimensional Database | E | Data are organized as a tree |

Which of the following is the proper match?

(a) 1 & E  2 & A  3 & D  4 & C  5 & A

(b) 1 & D  2 & E  3 & B  4 & C  5 & B

(c) 1 & B  2 & E  3 & A  4 & C  5 & D

(d) 1 & D  2 & E  3 & B  4 & A  5 & C.

**6.** Which of the following statement is not correct?

(a) Non-operational data do not change quite often

(b) Address of a customer is an example for non-operational data

(c) Operational data are used by enterprise in routine business applications

(d) Billing data is an example of non-operational data.

**7.** A Data Warehouse is a good source of data for the downstream data mining applic-ations because it contains

(a) large data

(b) aggregated data

(c) integrated historical data

(d) preprocessed data.

**8.** KDD stands for

(a) Knowledge Discovery in Data warehouse

(b) Knowledge Discovery in Data bases

(c) Knowledge Data Discovery

(d) Knowledge Data Dictionary.

**9.** Choose the right sequence

(a) Data warehouse – OLAP – OLTP – Data Mining

(b) Data Warehouse – OLTP – OLAP – Data Mining

(c) OLTP – Data Warehouse – OLAP – Data Mining

(d) OLAP – Data warehouse –OLTP – Data Mining.

**10.** What makes the business community to accept the application of Data Mining?

(a) Massive data collection

(b) Powerful multiprocessor computers

(c) Data mining algorithms

(d) All the above.

**11.** Which is **NOT** a technique used in data mining?

(a) Artificial neural networks

(b) Decision trees

(c) Flow Chart

(d) Nearest neighbor method.

**12.** The technique that used for extraction of useful if-then rules from data based on statistical significance is

(a) Rule induction

(b) Genetic algorithms

(c) Artificial neural networks

(d) Nearest neighbor method.

**13.** A technique that classifies each record in a dataset based on a combination of the classes of the k record(s) most similar to it in a historical dataset is

(*a*) Artificial neural networks (*b*) Decision trees

(*c*) Genetic algorithms (*d*) Nearest neighbor method.

**14.** The expansion of NOIR is

(*a*) Normal, Ordinary, Important and Repeated

(*b*) Nominal, Ordinal, Interval and Ratio

(*c*) Normal, Ordinal, Interval and Ratio

(*d*) Nominal, Ordinary, Interval and Ratio.

**15.** The process of removing duplicate records is called

(*a*) filtering (*b*) clustering

(*c*) de-duplication (*d*) none of the above.

**16.** Choose the symmetric binary value among the following.

(*a*) Gender = {male, female}

(*b*) House = {rented, owned}

(*c*) Message status = {delivered, lost}

(*d*) Login attempt = {success, failure}.

**17.** Consider the following table which gives various data mining Approaches and techniques.

| | Column A | | Column B |
|---|---|---|---|
| 1 | Association Rule | A | Genetic Algorithm |
| 2 | Clustering | B | ARM Algorithm |
| 3 | Optimisation | C | SVR Technique |
| 4 | Regression | D | Hierarchical Algorithm |

Which of the following is the proper match?

(*a*) 1 & B 2 & A 3 & D 4 & C

(*b*) 1 & D 2 & A 3 & B 4 & C

(*c*) 1 & B 2 & D 3 & A 4 & C

(*d*) 1 & D 2 & C 3 & B 4 & A.

**18.** Which of the following data mining application can be used successfully?

(*a*) A Pharmaceutical Company (*b*) A credit card company

(*c*) A diversified transportation. (*d*) All the above.

**19.** Computers that can generate programs itself, enabling it to carry out new task is called

(*a*) virtual computers (*b*) machine learning computers

(*c*) self learning computers (*d*) none of the above.

20. Expansion of DMQL
(a) Data Mining Query Language
(b) Data Manipulation Query Language
(c) Data Management Query Language
(d) Data Method Query Language.

21. Which of the following is the initial stage of empirical cycle?
(a) Prediction (b) Analysis
(c) Information gathering (d) Observation.

22. Consider the following table which shows different types of data transformation.

| Column A | | | Column B |
|---|---|---|---|
| 1 | Simple transformation | A | Applied to numeric data |
| 2 | Decimal Scaling | B | Applied to decimal data |
| 3 | Smoothing | C | Applied to non-negative numbers |
| 4 | Normaliasation | D | Applied to Attribute level |

Which of the following is the proper match?
(a) 1 & B 2 & A 3 & D 4 & C
(b) 1 & D 2 & A 3 & B 4 & C
(c) 1 & B 2 & D 3 & A 4 & C
(d) 1 & D 2 & C 3 & B 4 & A.

23. Choose the unsupervised data mining model from the following.
(a) Clustering model (b) Regression models
(c) Decision tree (d) Artificial Neural Network.

24. Which of the following is a technique used to break a large heterogeneous population into small number of homogeneous groups?
(a) Classification (b) Clustering
(c) Association rules (d) Regression.

25. Which of the following is a technique used to convert large volumes of raw data into meaningful display images?
(a) Data Integration (b) Data Manipulation
(c) Data Visualisation (d) Data Staging.

26. Which of the following statement is not correct?
(a) Graphics are pictorial representation of data
(b) A segmented bar chart is also known as stacked column chart
(c) The class intervals are usually of fixed size
(d) Contour Plots uses discrete points instead of lines or shades of constant value.

**27.** Which of the following is not true when Datamart is compared with Datawarehouse.

(*a*) Datamart are relatively small

(*b*) Datamart are not secured

(*c*) Datamart is performance optimized

(*d*) Virtual datamart can map to parent datawarehouse.

***28.** Consider the following data A=[5, 7, 11, 13, 17, 20]. What would be the scaling transformation to the range [0, 1]?

(*a*) [0.20, 0.30, 0.50, 0.60, 0.80, 1.0]

(*b*) [0.20, 0.40, 0.60, 0.70, 0.90, 1.0]

(*c*) [0.25, 0.35, 0.55, 0.65, 0.85, 1.0]

(*d*) [0.29, 0.39, 0.59, 0.69, 0.89, 1.0].

**29.** Data Staging is a major pre-processing step in datawarehouse because

(*a*) it involves large amount of data

(*b*) much human intervention is required at various stages

(*c*) data transformation is difficult

(*d*) data are not organized.

**30.** Choose the statement which is **NOT** true with regard to metadata.

(*a*) Metadata is data about data

(*b*) Metadata are associated with a group of entities

(*c*) Metadata can be stored in distributed network

(*d*) Metadata cannot be stored as embedded data.

***31.** What will be the result if smoothing process is applied to the data A=[27.06, 29.67, 35.89,78.45]?

(*a*) [27, 29, 35, 78] (*b*) [0.06, 0.67, 0.89, 0.45]

(*c*) [27, 30, 36, 78] (*d*) [28, 30, 36, 79].

**32.** Choose the incorrect statement

(*a*) ETL tools is a hardware

(*b*) ETL tools are used for data loading

(*c*) ETL tools are developer friendly

(*d*) ETL tools are used in the incremental loading.

**33.** The following table gives information about some popular ETL tools and the company developed. Choose the proper match.

| | Tool Name | | Company Name |
|---|---|---|---|
| 1 | ST/Studio | A | Pervasive Software |
| 2 | DataStage | B | Embarcadero Technologies |
| 3 | Data Junction | C | Oracle Corporation |
| 4 | Oracle Warehouse Builder | D | IBM |

(a) 1 & B 2 & A 3 & D 4 & C (b) 1 & D 2 & A 3 & B 4 & C
(c) 1 & B 2 & D 3 & A 4 & C (d) 1 & D 2 & C 3 & B 4 & A.

**34.** Genetic algorithm is used for
(a) machine learning (b) concept learning
(c) self learning (d) virtual learning.

**35.** The technique used to load the information from the operational database to the data warehouse is called
(a) copying (b) replication
(c) downloading (d) uploading.

**36.** Which of the following describes the structure of the content of the database?
(a) Data marts (b) Data dictionary
(c) Meta data (d) Data flow diagram.

**37.** Data analysis that provides insights into trends, behaviors, or events that have already occurred is
(a) prospective data analysis (b) exploratory data analysis
(c) retrospective data analysis (d) detailed data analysis.

**38.** The following table gives information about the Web-based Data Warehouse software's and their developer.

| | Software | | Developer |
|---|---|---|---|
| 1 | Web Agent | A | Business Objects |
| 2 | Essbase | B | Comshare Commander |
| 3 | Decision Web | C | Arbor software |
| 4 | WebIntelligence | D | Oracle Corporation |

Which of the following is the proper match?
(a) 1 & B 2 & A 3 & D 4 & C
(b) 1 & D 2 & A 3 & B 4 & C
(c) 1 & B 2 & D 3 & A 4 & C
(d) 1 & D 2 & C 3 & B 4 & A.

**39.** The initial stage of KDD process is
(a) Data selection (b) Data acquisition
(c) Data dredging (d) Data snooping.

**40.** Choose the OLAP Schema that splits the dimension table using database normalization.
(a) Star Schema (b) Snowflake Schema
(c) Fact Constellation Schema (d) None of the above.

***41.** Choose the incorrect statement

(*a*) OLAP can work with both data warehouse and data mart

(*b*) OLAP is used in medical sciences

(*c*) The process of mining OLAP data is called OLAM

(*d*) OLAP is a supervised model.

**42.** Which of the following is the correct sequence of data mining integration with other activities?

(*a*) Strategic phase – Training phase – Creation phase – Migration phase

(*b*) Creation phase – Training phase – Strategic phase – Migration phase

(*c*) Creation phase – Strategic phase – Training phase – Migration phase

(*d*) Strategic phase – Training phase – Migration phase – Creation phase.

***43.** Which of the following is an example of Additive fact?

(*a*) Value Added Tax (*b*) Monthly balance

(*c*) Total purchase amount (*d*) Height of the customer.

**44.** Which of the following statement is incorrect with regard to Graph?

(*a*) A graph with loops is called multi-graph

(*b*) A path is a succession of edges between two fixed nodes

(*c*) A fully connected graphs without loop has $n\ (n\text{-}1)/2$ edges

(*d*) The edges of a graph are undirected when the relationship is asymmetric.

**45.** Decision Tree is not good choice in which of the following condition?

(*a*) When some data is missing during data collection

(*b*) When the data set is large

(*c*) When there are redundant attributes

(*d*) When continuous attributes are correlated.

**46.** Among the following statement, which is a valid one to stop growing Decision Tree?

(*a*) If the current node is pure

(*b*) If the number of cases in the current node is below a threshold value

(*c*) If the information gain at a node is insignificant

(*d*) If the tree depth of the current node is above threshold.

**47.** The right term when adding external data in existing database is

(*a*) Appending (*b*) Updating

(*c*) Enrichment (*d*) Copying.

**48.** Removing some irrelevant attributes from data sets is known as

(*a*) Data Pruning (*b*) Normalisation

(*c*) Redundancy elimination (*d*) Attribute subset selection.

**49.** Which of the following measures the 'lack of order' in a system?

(*a*) Gini's Index Measure

(*b*) Shannon's Entropy Measure

(*c*) Minimum Classification Error measure

(*d*) CHAID.

**50.** Consider the following table which gives information about Association Rules:

| | **Column A** | | **Column B** |
|---|---|---|---|
| 1 | Antecedent | A | Item purchased have no priority among themselves |
| 2 | BARM | B | Right side of the Association rule |
| 3 | Association rule mining | C | Left side of the Association rule |
| 4 | Consequent | D | Market-basket analysis |

Which of the following is the proper match?

(*a*) 1 & B 2 & A 3 & D 4 & C

(*b*) 1 & D 2 & A 3 & B 4 & C

(*c*) 1 & C 2 & A 3 & D 4 & B

(*d*) 1 & D 2 & C 3 & B 4 & A.

**51.** The numeric range of Gini Index coefficient is

(*a*) $\varepsilon$ [0,1]

(*b*) $\varepsilon$ $(0, \infty)$

(*c*) $\varepsilon$ [0,2]

(*d*) $\varepsilon$ $(1, \infty)$.

***52.** What will be the *confidence* if 56 out of 160 male in a bakery purchases bun also buys butter.

(*a*) 30%

(*b*) 35%

(*c*) 40%

(*d*) 50%.

**53.** Fraud detection and prevention can be done using

(*a*) Association rules with SVM

(*b*) Clustering

(*c*) Classification

(*d*) Prediction.

**54.** The Association Rule, floopy = (Sony, Puma, Moserbaer, Perfection) is an example of

(*a*) Quantitative AR

(*b*) Multilevel AR

(*c*) Single-Dimensional AR

(*d*) Multidimensional, Multilevel AR.

**55.** Suppose a person purchases some item from a supermarket which sells thousands of other items, then

(*a*) both confidence and support will be high

(*b*) confidence will be high and support will be low

(*c*) support will be high and confidence will be low

(*d*) both confidence and support will be low.

**56.** 'The age levels of employees to be above 40' is an example of

(*a*) knowledge type constraint (*b*) meta-rule constraints

(*c*) content constraint (*d*) dimension level constraint.

## The Next Three Questions (57–59) are Based on the Following Information

**Consider the two vectors $X_1$=(9,5,7) and $X_2$=(3,4,8)**

***57.** What will be the Euclidean distance between the two vectors?

(*a*) 4.241 (*b*) 5.632

(*c*) 6.164 (*d*) 7.245.

***58.** What will be the Manhattan distance between the two vectors?

(*a*) 5 (*b*) 6

(*c*) 7 (*d*) 8.

***59.** What will be the Chebychev distance between the two vectors?

(*a*) 5 (*b*) 6

(*c*) 7 (*d*) 8.

**60.** K-mediods and K-means are

(*a*) Density-based methods (*b*) Hierarchical Agglomerative method

(*c*) Partitioning method (*d*) Hierarchical Divisive method.

**61.** K-harmonic means method for data clustering is

(*a*) similar to K-mediods

(*b*) a variant of K-means for clustering algorithm

(*c*) similar to K-means

(*d*) an efficient version of K-means in terms of convergence.

**62.** Hierarchical divisive methods for clustering

(*a*) Single link (*b*) Complete link

(*c*) Average link (*d*) Minimum spanning tree.

**63.** Choose the linkage method that uses the minimum sum of squared deviations of data items from their respective cluster centroids as the merging criteria.

(*a*) Single linkage (*b*) Complete linkage

(*c*) Average linkage (*d*) Ward's method.

**64.** How is the k-means algorithm terminated?

(*a*) When none of the data items changes cluster during two consecutive iterations

(*b*) When an element assigned to a cluster is reassigned to another cluster

(*c*) When the cluster id hidden

(*d*) When data is scattered throughout the web.

*65. Pick the wrong statement
(a) CHAMELEON is a popular Hierarchical Cluster algorithm
(b) Hierarchical Agglomerative follows a bottom-up approach method
(c) Partitioning algorithm is also called as parametric method
(d) CLARANs is a popular Density-based cluster method.

66. The KDD process consist of stages
(a) 4 (b) 8
(c) 6 (d) 3.

67. Genetic algorithm is suitable for
(a) classification tasks. (b) knowledge engineering tasks
(c) problem solving tasks (d) none of the above.

68. The neurons that connected to each other via
(a) Perceptrons (b) Synapses
(c) Cells (d) none of the above.

69. Which one of the following is a simple optimization technique that modifies a proposed solution by a small amount and then accepts it if it is better than the previous solution
(a) Hill Climbing Search (b) Binary Search
(c) Serial Search (d) Random Search.

70. Choose the neural network often used in clustering, where locality of the nodes learn as local neighborhoods and is important in the training process.
(a) Hebbian Learning (b) Kohonen Networks
(c) Radial Basis Function Networks (d) None of the above.

71. One of the simplest and oldest forms of training a neural network which is based on observations of the human brain is
(a) Hebbian Learning (b) Kohonen Networks
(c) Radial Basis Function Networks (d) None of the above.

72. Bit Map Indexing technique is commonly used in
(a) Hierarchical data base (b) Networked data base
(c) Relational databases (d) Distributed database.

73. Which one of the following is a process to develop the conceptual schema from the external schema
(a) Data normalization (b) Data optimization
(c) Data modeling (d) Data partitioning.

74. Which one of the following is a process that prepares the logical schema from the data view schema
(a) Data normalization (b) Data optimization
(c) Data modeling (d) Data partitioning.

**75.** Web Usage Mining can be used for

(*a*) searching (*b*) site updating

(*c*) target advertising (*d*) personalization.

**76.** Which part of the search engine takes a query as input and retrieves matching web pages as a collection?

(*a*) Query engine (*b*) Crawler

(*c*) An indexer (*d*) User interface component.

**77.** Which of the following cannot be the source for text mining?

(*a*) Online newspapers (*b*) Newsgroup postings

(*c*) Video Clippings (*d*) Patent documents.

**78.** Which of the following is not correct with regard to SVM?

(*a*) It can be used for classification (*b*) It can be used for regression

(*c*) It can be used for clustering (*d*) It can be used for function evaluation.

**79.** The following is a list of statements regarding the advantages of SVM over Neural Network.

(*i*) No backpropagation training (*ii*) No intialisation needed

(*iii*) No hidden layer architecture (*iv*) No activation and output function.

Whch of the above statement is/are correct?

(*a*) Only (*i*) and (*iii*) (*b*) Only (*i*) and (*iv*)

(*c*) Only (*ii*) and (*iii*) (*d*) All.

**80.** Data mining is used to aid in

(*a*) operational Management

(*b*) analyzing past decision made by manages

(*c*) detecting patterns in operational data

(*d*) retrieving archival data.

**81.** Which of the following is a disadvantage of Latent Semantic Indexing?

(*a*) Query execution speed (*b*) Reuses factored matrices

(*c*) Dynamic data updates (*d*) Generalisation capability.

**82.** Data Warehouse can be defined as a

(*a*) subject-oriented, integrated, time variant and volatile collection of data used in strategic decision making

(*b*) subject-oriented, integrated, time variant and non-volatile collection of data used in strategic decision making

(*c*) subject-oriented, integrated, time variant and non-volatile collection of data used in tactical decision making

(*d*) subject-oriented, integrated, time variant and volatile collection of data used in tactical decision making.

**83.** Choose the statement which is more appropriate for data mart.

(*a*) Data marts are a subset of Data mining

(*b*) Data marts are a subset of Data Warehouse

(*c*) Data marts are a subset of Operational Data Store

(*d*) Data marts are a subset of Data bases.

**84.** Which of the following describes the physical structures in the CIF?

(*a*) Administrative meta data (*b*) Business meta data

(*c*) Technical meta data (*d*) None of the above.

**85.** Which of the following data mart is used by researchers?

(*a*) Exploration warehouse (*b*) OLAP data mart

(*c*) Statistical ware house (*d*) None of the above.

**86.** Which of the following is the system component that performs all the operations necessary to support the query management process

(*a*) Query Manager (*b*) Load Manager

(*c*) Data warehouse manager (*d*) DBA.

**87.** Data mining cannot be done if

(*a*) operational data has not been archived

(*b*) earlier management decision are not available

(*c*) the organization is large

(*d*) all processing had been only batch processing.

**88.** Which of the following is a method that ensures the data model meets objectives of accuracy, consistency, simplicity, stability and nonredundancy?

(*a*) Normalization (*b*) Data pruning

(*c*) Data recasting (*d*) Data modeling.

**89.** Transaction data is referred as

(*a*) online data (*b*) referential data

(*c*) fact data (*d*) external data.

**90.** In a decision support data warehouse all queries are based on

(*a*) business meta data (*b*) factual data

(*c*) operational data (*d*) sales data.

**91.** Partitioning the fact table purely on its

(*a*) dimensions (*b*) attributes

(*c*) size (*d*) type.

**92.** The process of testing the entire data warehouse application is called

(*a*) unit testing (*b*) integration testing

(*c*) system testing (*d*) module testing

**93.** Which one of the following technique classifies records in a database by comparing them with similar classified records?

(*a*) Memory-Based Reasoning (*b*) Nominal Categorical Predictor

(*c*) Ordinal Categorical Predictor (*d*) Principle Components Analysis.

**94.** The process of automatically breaking down large chunks of data and metadata based on a client's request for data at a specific data site is called

(*a*) automatic data replication (*b*) automatic data partitioning

(*c*) Automatic data classification (*d*) clustering.

**95.** Choose the hierarchy type where a child may have multiple parents.

(*a*) Ragged tree structure (*b*) Variable depth tree structure

(*c*) Complex tree structure (*d*) Balanced tree structure.

**96.** Data Scrubbing is

(*a*) the process of summarizing primitive evolutional data or derived evolutional data to create more generalized derived evolutional data

(*b*) the process to restructure the source data to the target data during data transformation

(*c*) the process of filtering, merging, decoding, and translating source data to create validated data for the data warehouse

(*d*) none of the above.

**97.** The situation where distributed data need to be continually evaluated and adjusted to meet the business information demand in an optimum manner is called

(*a*) Drill Across (*b*) Static Data Distribution

(*c*) Dynamic Data Distribution (*d*) Drill Down.

**98.** Which of the following statement are not appropriate for Functional Data Warehouse?

(*a*) A warehouse that draws data from nearby operational systems

(*b*) A warehouse that draws data from faraway operational systems

(*c*) Each functional warehouse serves a distinct and separate group, functional area, geographic unit

(*d*) The separate group could be a division.

## ANSWERS

| | | | | | | |
|---|---|---|---|---|---|---|
| **1.** (*d*) | **2.** (*c*) | **3.** (*c*) | **4.** (*d*) | **5.** (*a*) | **6.** (*d*) | **7.** (*c*) |
| **8.** (*b*) | **9.** (*b*) | **10.** (*d*) | **11.** (*c*) | **12.** (*a*) | **13.** (*d*) | **14.** (*b*) |
| **15.** (*c*) | **16.** (*a*) | **17.** (*c*) | **18.** (*d*) | **19.** (*c*) | **20.** (*a*) | **21.** (*d*) |
| **22.** (*b*) | **23.** (*a*) | **24.** (*b*) | **25.** (*c*) | **26.** (*d*) | **27.** (*b*) | **28.** (*c*) |

| | | | | | | |
|---|---|---|---|---|---|---|
| **29.** (*b*) | **30.** (*d*) | **31.** (*c*) | **32.** (*a*) | **33.** (*c*) | **34.** (*a*) | **35.** (*b*) |
| **36.** (*c*) | **37.** (*c*) | **38.** (*d*) | **39.** (*a*) | **40.** (*b*) | **41.** (*d*) | **42.** (*a*) |
| **43.** (*c*) | **44.** (*d*) | **45.** (*d*) | **46.** (*c*) | **47.** (*c*) | **48.** (*a*) | **49.** (*b*) |
| **50.** (*c*) | **51.** (*a*) | **52.** (*b*) | **53.** (*a*) | **54.** (*b*) | **55.** (*b*) | **56.** (*c*) |
| **57.** (*c*) | **58.** (*d*) | **59.** (*b*) | **60.** (*a*) | **61.** (*b*) | **62.** (*a*) | **63.** (*c*) |
| **64.** (*a*) | **65.** (*d*) | **66.** (*c*) | **67.** (*c*) | **68.** (*b*) | **69.** (*a*) | **70.** (*b*) |
| **71.** (*a*) | **72.** (*c*) | **73.** (*a*) | **74.** (*b*) | **75.** (*c*) | **76.** (*b*) | **77.** (*c*) |
| **78.** (*b*) | **79.** (*d*) | **80.** (*c*) | **81.** (*c*) | **82.** (*b*) | **83.** (*b*) | **84.** (*c*) |
| **85.** (*c*) | **86.** (*a*) | **87.** (*a*) | **88.** (*a*) | **89.** (*c*) | **90.** (*c*) | **91.** (*c*) |
| **92.** (*c*) | **93.** (*a*) | **94.** (*b*) | **95.** (*c*) | **96.** (*c*) | **97.** (*c*) | **98.** (*a*) |

## EXPLANATIONS

**28.** In the given list the maximum is 20. Dividing each number by 20, A' = [0.25, 0.35, 0.55, 0.65, 0.85, 1.0]

**31.** Smoothing adjusts the value to the nearest integer or boundary

**41.** OLAP is an analysis tool.

**43.** Additive facts are columns in fact tables that can be added across different dimensions.

**52.** The problem can be expressed as Conf(X,Y)=Supportcount(XUY)/Supportcount (X)=n(XUY)/n(X).Therefore confidence = 56/160=0.35 or 35%

**57.** Euclidean distance = $\sqrt{(9-3)^2+(5-4)^2+(7-8)^2} = \sqrt{(36+1+1)} = \sqrt{38} = 6.164$

**58.** Manhattan distance = |9-3| + |5-4| + |7-8|= 6 + 1 + 1= 6

**59.** Chebychev distance = max(|9-3|, |5-4|, |7-8|) = 6

**65.** CLARANs is a popular K-medoids algorithm

CHAPTER 11

# DIGITAL IMAGE PROCESSING

1. Which of the following is/are true?
   (*i*) Image colour depends on the illumination
   (*ii*) Image colour depends on the device used
   (*iii*) Colour of an image changes with translation
   (*iv*) Colour of an image changes with rotation

   (*a*) only (*i*) and (*ii*) (*b*) only (*ii*) and (*iii*)
   (*c*) only (*iii*) and (*iv*) (*d*) only (*i*) and (*iii*).

2. The abbreviation of CBIR is
   (*a*) Control Based Information Retrieval
   (*b*) Content Based Information Retrieval
   (*c*) Channel Based Information Retrieval
   (*d*) Charge Based Information Retrieval.

3. What is the third step in digital image processing?
   (*a*) Image Enhancement (*b*) Colour Image Processing
   (*c*) Segmentation (*d*) Image Restrotion.

4. Which of the following file formats is an example of lossless compression only?
   (*a*) PNG (*b*) MNG
   (*c*) TIFF (*d*) JPEG.

5. Which of the following file formats is an example of both lossless and lossy compression?
   (*a*) PNG (*b*) GIF
   (*c*) TIFF (*d*) JPEG.

6. Which of the following file formats is an example of lossy compression only?
   (*a*) PNG (*b*) GIF
   (*c*) TIFF (*d*) JPEG.

*7. An image made up of square array of 256 × 256 pixels requires how much storage area?

(*a*) 64 KB (*b*) 128 KB

(*c*) 256 KB (*d*) 512 KB.

**8.** Digitizing the coordinate values of a continuous image is called

(*a*) quantization (*b*) sampling

(*c*) segmentation (*d*) compression.

**9.** The advantages of digital image compression is/are

(*i*) Reduces image storage area

(*ii*) Improves the speed while transmitting the image

(*iii*) The quality of the image is improved

(*iv*) The illumination can be controlled.

(*a*) only (*i*) and (*ii*) (*b*) only (*ii*) and (*iii*)

(*c*) only (*iii*) and (*iv*) (*d*) only (*i*) and (*iii*).

**10.** Which of the following is not a medical application of digital image processing?

(*a*) Nuclear Magnetic Resonance (*b*) CCTV

(*c*) Cineangiograms (*d*) Ultrasonic scanning.

**11.** The technique where the object is scanned by a thin collimated light, which illuminates only a small spot at a time, is called

(*a*) self-scanning (*b*) scan-in method

(*c*) scan-out method (*d*) none of the above.

**12.** The sharpness and accuracy of an image is basically known as

(*a*) Resolution (*b*) Illumination

(*c*) Scaling (*d*) Quantization.

**13.** Image enhancement is

(*a*) to bring out detail that is obscured

(*b*) based on mathematical model of image

(*c*) based on subjective preference

(*d*) based on descriptors.

**14.** Midlevel processing on image involves

(*a*) Quantization (*b*) Acquisition

(*c*) Sampling (*d*) Segmentation.

**15.** The procedure of obtaining images of blood vessels is called

(*a*) angiography (*b*) cryptography

(*c*) biography (*d*) geography.

**16.** The area in which the receptors are absent is called

(*a*) rods (*b*) hot spot

(*c*) blind spot (*d*) fovea.

**17.** Segmentation is

(*a*) partition of an image (*b*) Modification of an image

(*c*) extraction of image components (*d*) Reducing storage.

**18.** Digitizing the amplitude values is called

(*a*) quantization (*b*) sampling

(*c*) uniform sampling (*d*) non-uniform sampling.

**19.** The basic use of smoothing filter is

(*i*) for improving the colour (*ii*) for blurring

(*iii*) for noise reduction (*iv*) to reduce contrast

(*a*) only (*i*) and (*ii*) (*b*) only (*ii*) and (*iii*)

(*c*) only (*iii*) and (*iv*) (*d*) all.

**20.** Which of the following is true with regard to histogram equalization?

(*a*) Image that has equalized illumination

(*b*) Image that has equalized contrast

(*c*) Image that has equalized gray levels

(*d*) Image that has equalized color levels.

**21.** Which of the following is a process in which small gaps and lines are filled?

(*a*) Blurring (*b*) Filtering

(*c*) Transformation (*d*) Scaling.

**22.** Which of the following statement is true with regard to image restoration and enhancement?

(*i*) Image restoration and image enhancement are same

(*ii*) Image enhancement is a subjective analysis whereas image restoration is an objective process

(*iii*) Image restoration involves modeling of degradation in image

(*iv*) Image restoration involves the process to manipulate the image of these.

(*a*) only (*i*) (*b*) only (*ii*)

(*c*) only (*iii*) and (*iv*) (*d*) only (*ii*), (*iii*) and (*iv*).

***23.** Choose the odd man

(*a*) Arithmetic mean filter (*b*) Median filter

(*c*) Max and Min filter (*d*) Alpha-trimmed mean filter.

**24.** The filters producing the average of the pixels contained in the neighbourhood of the filter mark is called

(*a*) low pan filters (*b*) high pan filters

(*c*) band pan filters (*d*) based reject filters.

**25.** A spatial averaging filter in which all co-efficient are equal is sometimes called a

(*a*) box filter (*b*) cube filter

(*c*) cylindevical filter (*d*) adaptive filter.

**26.** The role of high pass filtering
(*a*) Eliminate low frequency components
(*b*) Eliminate high frequency components
(*c*) Eliminate both high & low frequency components
(*d*) Eliminate the contrast & averaging.

**27.** _____________ is the total amount of energy that flows from light source.
(*a*) Luminance (*b*) Brightness
(*c*) Darkness (*d*) Radiance.

**28.** Which of the following is true with regard to chromaticity?
(*a*) Chromaticity = Brightness + Hue
(*b*) Chromaticity = Hue + Saturation
(*c*) Chromaticity = Brightness + Saturation
(*d*) Chromaticity = Contrast + Hue.

**29.** Which of the following is correct with regard to CMY?

(*a*) $CMY = \begin{matrix} R \\ G \\ B \end{matrix} - \begin{matrix} 1 \\ 1 \\ 1 \end{matrix}$ (*b*) $CMY = \begin{matrix} 1 \\ 1 \\ 1 \end{matrix} - \begin{matrix} R \\ G \\ B \end{matrix}$

(*c*) $CMY = \begin{matrix} R \\ G \\ B \end{matrix} + \begin{matrix} 1 \\ 1 \\ 1 \end{matrix}$ (*d*) $CMY = \begin{matrix} 1 \\ 1 \\ 1 \end{matrix} + \begin{matrix} R \\ G \\ B \end{matrix}$.

**30.** Which of the following is a lossy compression technique?
(*a*) Run-length (*b*) Variable length coding
(*c*) LZW coding (*d*) Wavelet coding.

**31.** Choose the correct sequence of encoding using transform coding.
(*a*) Construct *nxn* subimage → Quantizer → DFT → Encoder
(*b*) Construct *nxn* subimage → Encoder → DFT → Quantizer
(*c*) Construct *nxn* subimage → DFT → Quantizer → Encoder
(*d*) Construct *nxn* subimage → Symbol Decoder → Quantizer → Encoder.

**32.** Choose the correct Wavelet coding : Encoder block diagram.

(*a*) 

(*b*) 

(*c*) 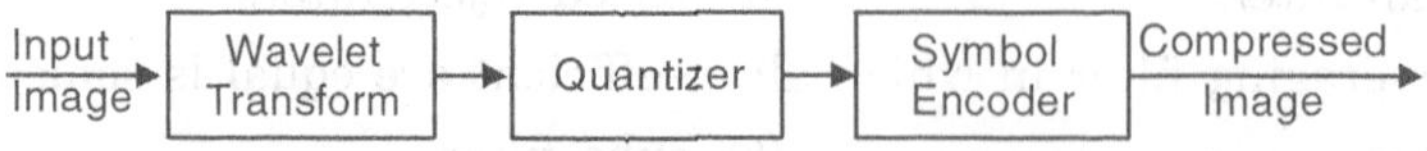


(*d*) 

**33.** Which of the following statement is/are true?

(*i*) Low level features can be extracted directly from image

(*ii*) High level features cannot be extracted directly from image

(*iii*) Segmentation is an approach for feature extraction

(*iv*) Pattern recognition is also an approach for feature extraction of these.

(*a*) only (*i*) and (*ii*) (*b*) only (*iii*) and (*iv*)

(c) only (*ii*), (*iii*) and (*iv*) (*d*) all.

**34.** Bandwidth compression means

(*a*) Digital compression (*b*) Analog Compression

(*c*) Relative compression (*d*) None of the above.

**35.** Lossy compression is useful in

(*a*) Television broad casting (*b*) Medical imaging

(*c*) Space imaging (*d*) Military imaging.

**36.** Some image generation systems having physical artifacts embedded on the imaging sensor itself are called

(*a*) metallic points (*b*) non-metallic points

(*c*) duster (*d*) plots.

**37.** The filters that rejects frequencies in predefined neighbourhoods about center frequency is called

(*a*) notch filter (*b*) band pass filters

(*c*) band reject filter (*d*) adaptive filters.

**38.** The information which has less relative importance then other information in normal visual processing is known as

(*a*) Psychovisually redundant (*b*) Visually non-redundant

(*c*) Visually redundant (*d*) Psychovisually non-redundant.

**39.** Transformations that removes inter pixel redundancy are referred as

(*a*) Mapping (*b*) Relations

(*c*) Filters (*d*) Noise.

**40.** Which of the following is a mask for point detection?

(*a*)

| | | |
|---|---|---|
| 1 | 1 | 1 |
| 1 | 8 | 1 |
| 1 | 1 | 1 |

(*b*)

| | | |
|---|---|---|
| -1 | -1 | -1 |
| 1 | 8 | 1 |
| -1 | -1 | -1 |

(*c*)

| | | |
|---|---|---|
| -1 | 1 | -1 |
| -1 | 8 | -1 |
| -1 | 1 | -1 |

(*d*)

| | | |
|---|---|---|
| -1 | -1 | -1 |
| -1 | 8 | -1 |
| -1 | -1 | -1 |

.

**41.** Which of the following is a mask used for horizontal line detection?

(*a*)

| | | |
|---|---|---|
| -1 | -1 | -1 |
| 2 | 2 | 2 |
| 1 | 1 | 1 |

(*b*)

| | | |
|---|---|---|
| -1 | -1 | 2 |
| -1 | 2 | -1 |
| 2 | -1 | -1 |

(*c*)

| | | |
|---|---|---|
| -1 | 2 | 1 |
| -1 | 2 | 1 |
| -1 | 2 | 1 |

(*d*)

| | | |
|---|---|---|
| 2 | -1 | -1 |
| -1 | -2 | -1 |
| -1 | -1 | -2 |

.

**42.** Which of the following is a mask used for vertical line detection?

(*a*)

| | | |
|---|---|---|
| -1 | -1 | -1 |
| 2 | 2 | 2 |
| 1 | 1 | 1 |

(*b*)

| | | |
|---|---|---|
| -1 | -1 | 2 |
| -1 | 2 | -1 |
| 2 | -1 | -1 |

(*c*)

| | | |
|---|---|---|
| -1 | 2 | 1 |
| -1 | 2 | 1 |
| -1 | 2 | 1 |

(*d*)

| | | |
|---|---|---|
| 2 | -1 | -1 |
| -1 | 2 | -1 |
| -1 | -1 | -2 |

.

**43.** Which of the following is a mask used for +45° line detection?

(*a*)

| | | |
|---|---|---|
| -1 | -1 | -1 |
| 2 | 2 | 2 |
| 1 | 1 | 1 |

(*b*)

| | | |
|---|---|---|
| -1 | -1 | 2 |
| -1 | 2 | -1 |
| 2 | -1 | -1 |

(*c*)

| | | |
|---|---|---|
| -1 | 2 | 1 |
| -1 | 2 | 1 |
| -1 | 2 | 1 |

(*d*)

| | | |
|---|---|---|
| 2 | -1 | -1 |
| -1 | 2 | -1 |
| -1 | 2 | -2 |

.

**44.** Which of the following is a mask used for –45° line detection?

(*a*)

| | | |
|---|---|---|
| -1 | -1 | -1 |
| 2 | 2 | 2 |
| 1 | 1 | 1 |

(*b*)

| | | |
|---|---|---|
| -1 | -1 | 2 |
| -1 | 2 | -1 |
| 2 | -1 | -1 |

(*c*)

| | | |
|---|---|---|
| -1 | 2 | 1 |
| -1 | 2 | 1 |
| -1 | 2 | 1 |

(*d*)

| | | |
|---|---|---|
| 2 | -1 | -1 |
| -1 | 2 | -1 |
| -1 | -1 | -2 |

.

**45.** If the thresholding depends upon only the grey levels of an image is called as

(*a*) adaptive thresholding (*b*) local thresholding

(*c*) global thresholding (*d*) dynamic thresholding.

**46.** Which of the following formulation represents sobel operator (Edge detection)?

(*a*) $G_x = (z_7 + z_8 + z_9) - (z_1 + z_2 + z_3)$ and $G_y = (z_3 + z_6 + z_9) - (z_1 + z_4 + z_7)$

(*b*) $G_x = (z_7 + z_8 + z_9) + (z_1 + z_2 + z_3)$ and $G_y = (z_3 + z_6 + z_9) + (z_1 + z_4 + z_7)$

(*c*) $G_x = (z_7 + 2z_8 + z_9) - (z_1 + 2z_2 + z_3)$ and $G_y = (z_3 + 2z_6 + z_9) - (z_1 + 2z_4 + z_7)$

(*d*) $G_x = (z_7 + 2z_8 + z_9) + (z_1 + 2z_2 + z_3)$ and $G_y = (z_3 + 2z_6 + z_9) + (z_1 + 2z_4 + z_7)$.

**47.** Which of the following formulation represents prewitt operator (Edge detection)?

(*a*) $G_x = (z_7 + z_8 + z_9) - (z_1 + z_2 + z_3)$ and $G_y = (z_3 + z_6 + z_9) - (z_1 + z_4 + z_7)$

(*b*) $G_x = (z_7 + z_8 + z_9) + (z_1 + z_2 + z_3)$ and $G_y = (z_3 + z_6 + z_9) + (z_1 + z_4 + z_7)$

(*c*) $G_x = (z_7 + 2z_8 + z_9) - (z_1 + 2z_2 + z_3)$ and $G_y = (z_3 + 2z_6 + z_9) - (z_1 + 2z_4 + z_7)$

(*d*) $G_x = (z_7 + 2z_8 + z_9) + (z_1 + 2z_2 + z_3)$ and $G_y = (z_3 + 2z_6 + z_9) + (z_1 + 2z_4 + z_7)$.

**48.** Which of the following statement is/are true with regard to Corners Detectors?

(*i*) Robot application is a good example for the applications of Corner Detectors

(*ii*) All true corners should be detected

(*iii*) Corner points should be well localized

(*iv*) Detector should be robust with respect to noise of these.

(*a*) only (*i*)

(*b*) only (*iii*) and (*iv*)

(c) only (*ii*), (*iii*) and (*iv*)

(*d*) all.

***49.** What will be the Euler number if a network has 8 vertices, 12 edges, 2 faces, 1 connected region and 3 holes?

(*a*) 2 (*b*) – 2

(*c*) 3 (*d*) – 3.

**50.** Decision tree and support vector machine is an example of

(*a*) template matching (*b*) statistical classification

(*c*) structural matching (*d*) neural network.

## ANSWERS

| | | | | | | |
|---|---|---|---|---|---|---|
| **1.** (*a*) | **2.** (*b*) | **3.** (*d*) | **4.** (*a*) | **5.** (*c*) | **6.** (*d*) | **7.** (*a*) |
| **8.** (*b*) | **9.** (*a*) | **10.** (*b*) | **11.** (*b*) | **12.** (*a*) | **13.** (*b*) | **14.** (*d*) |
| **15.** (*a*) | **16.** (*c*) | **17.** (*a*) | **18.** (*a*) | **19.** (*b*) | **20.** (*c*) | **21.** (*a*) |
| **22.** (*b*) | **23.** (*a*) | **24.** (*a*) | **25.** (*a*) | **26.** (*a*) | **27.** (*d*) | **28.** (*b*) |

| | | | | | | |
|---|---|---|---|---|---|---|
| **29.** (*b*) | **30.** (*d*) | **31.** (*c*) | **32.** (*c*) | **33.** (*d*) | **34.** (*b*) | **35.** (*a*) |
| **36.** (*a*) | **37.** (*a*) | **38.** (*a*) | **39.** (*a*) | **40.** (*d*) | **41.** (*a*) | **42.** (*c*) |
| **43.** (*b*) | **44.** (*d*) | **45.** (*c*) | **46.** (*c*) | **47.** (*a*) | **48.** (*d*) | **49.** (*b*) |
| **50.** (c) | | | | | | |

## EXPLANATIONS

**7.** 256 × 256 = 65536 bytes = 64 KB.

**23.** Arithmetic filter is a mean filter type whereas the other filters are Order-statistic filter type.

**49.** Euler formula is E = V – Q + F = C – H, where V is vector, Q is edges, F is faces, C is connected and H is holes. Therefore, 8 – 12 + 2 = 1 – 3 = –2.

CHAPTER 12

# J2EE

1. Which of the following is/are true about J2EE?
   (*i*) J2EE Stands for Java 2 Enterprise Edition
   (*ii*) J2EE is an environment for developing and deploying enterprise applications
   (*iii*) J2EE specification is defined by Sun Microsystems Inc
   (*iv*) The J2EE platform is one of the best platform for the development and deployment of enterprise applications.

   (*a*) (*i*) & (*ii*) (*b*) (*i*) & (*iii*)
   (*c*) (*i*), (*ii*) & (*iii*) (*d*) all.

2. Which of the following is a business component in J2EE?
   (*a*) Application clients (*b*) Applets
   (*c*) Java servlet and JSP (Web) (*d*) Enterprise JavaBeans (EJB).

3. Which of the following are J2EE modules?
   (*a*) EJB, Web, Application client and Java servlet
   (*b*) EJB, Web, Application client and Resource adapter
   (*c*) EJB, Web, Application client and Applet
   (*d*) EJB, Web, Applet and Resource adapter.

4. Which of the following statement is true?
   (*a*) J2EE component is a self-contained functional software unit supported by a container.
   (*b*) J2EE applications modules cannot be deployed as stand-alone units
   (*c*) Modules cannot be assembled into J2EE applications
   (*d*) J2EE components are written in the C programming language.

5. Which of the following is not a web-centric component?
   (*a*) Java Server Pages (*b*) Servlets
   (*c*) Applets (*d*) Web Services.

**6.** Which of the following file extension does the EJB modules of the application have?

(*a*) .ear (*b*) .jar

(*c*) .war (*d*) .xml.

***7.** Which of the following J2EE application parts run on the J2EE server?

(*i*) Client-tier components

(*ii*) Web-tier components

(*iii*) Business-tier components

(*iv*) Enterprise information system (EIS).

(*a*) only (*i*) and (*ii*) (*b*) only (*ii*) and (*iii*)

(*c*) only (*iii*) and (*iv*) (d) all.

**8.** Which of the following services provided by a container?

(*i*) Transaction management for the bean

(*ii*) Security for the bean

(*iii*) Lifecycle management of the bean

(*iv*) Database-connection pooling

(*a*) only (*i*) (*b*) only (*ii*) and (*iii*)

(c) only (*iii*) and (*iv*) (d) all.

**9.** Which of the following act as an interface between a component and the low-level platform?

(*a*) Session Bean (*b*) Entity Bean

(*c*) Container (*d*) Applets.

**10.** Which of the following is not a J2EE client?

(*a*) Applets (*b*) Java-Web Start clients

(c) JSP (*d*) Web applications.

**11.** Which of the following statement will compile without warning or error?

(*a*) `float f=1.3;` (*b*) `char c="a";`

(*c*) `byte b=257;` (*d*) `int i=10;`.

***12.** Which technology provides the flexibility to swap between XML processors with no application code changes?

(*a*) JAXP (*b*) SAX

(*c*) XSLT (*d*) JAAS.

**13.** Which of the following is the main drawback of CGI?

(*a*) Resource Intensive (*b*) Scalability

(*c*) Dynamic web pages (*d*) Interfacing with corporate infrastructure.

**14.** Which of the following could be written with little knowledge of java?

(*a*) Java Server Pages (*b*) Java Servelts

(*c*) Common Gateway Interface (*d*) Java Community Program.

***15.** What will happen if you try to compile and run the following code?

```
public class MyClass{
public static void main(String arguments[])
{
amethod(arguments);
}
public void amethod(String[] arguments)
{
System.out.println(arguments);
System.out.println(arguments[1]);
}
}
```

(*a*) Error - can't make static reference to void amethod.

(*b*) Error - method main not correct

(*c*) Error - array must include parameter

(*d*) a method must be declared with string.

**16.** Which of the following will compile without error?

(*a*)
```
import java.awt.*;
package Mypackage;
class Myclass {}
```

(*b*)
```
package MyPackage;
import java.awt.*;
class MyClass{}
```

(*c*)
```
/*This is a comment */
package myPackage;
import java.awt.*;
class MyClass{}
```

(*d*)
```
/*This is a comment */
package mypackage;
import java.awt.*;
class MyClass{}
```

***17.** Which of the following statement is/are true?

(*i*) J2EE application can be written without using any Enterprise JavaBeans

(*ii*) J2EE application cannot be written without using any web components

(*iii*) Session beans do not hold any essential business data

(*iv*) A Message Driven Bean offers an synchronous interface to clients .

(a) only (ii), (iii) and (iv)
(b) only (i), (ii) and (iii)
(c) only (i), (iii) and (iv)
(d) all.

*18. A transactional client receives `TransactionRolledBackException` from a call to a method on an entity bean. What could be the possible reason(s) for this?

(a) The bean method is throwing a checked exception and is configured with a transaction attribute of "Required".

(b) The bean method is throwing an unchecked exception and is configured with a transaction attribute of "Required".

(c) The bean does not throw an exception but is configured with a transaction attribute of "Mandatory".

(d) The bean method is throwing an unchecked exception and is configured with a transaction attribute of "Requires New".

19. Which of the following is correct with regard to Deployment Descriptor?

(a) It is simply an XML(Extensible Markup Language) file with the extension of .xml

(b) It is the first-tier J2EE client component that executes in its own Java virtual machine

(c) It is a Java-based build tool that can be extended using Java classes

(d) It is a qualifier on an XML tag that provides additional information.

20. Which of the following component defines the signature of the business associated with the bean life cycle?

(a) The remote interface
(b) The home interface
(c) The bean itself
(d) The deployment descriptor.

*21. What will be the output if the below code is run with the following command line?

```
java myprog good morning
public class myprog{
public static void main(String argv[])
{
System.out.println(argv[2])
}
}
```

(a) good
(b) morning
(c) good morning
(d) exception raised.

22. Which of the following is not a java reserved word?

(a) if
(b) then
(c) goto
(d) while.

23. Which of the following are not legal identifiers?

(a) 2variable
(b) variable2
(c) _whatavariable
(d) _3_.

**24.** What will be the outcome when the following code is compiled and run?

```
public class MyClass
{
static int i;
public static void main(String argv[])
{
System.out.println(i);
}
}
```

(*a*) 0 (*b*) 1

(*c*) Compilation error (*d*) Runtime error.

**25.** Which of the following is NOT an advantage of using the SessionFacade pattern?

(*a*) Hides model complexity from the client

(*b*) Reduces network traffic

(*c*) Provides a simple interface to the client

(*d*) Enables the client to control transactions.

**26.** Consider the following as the top-level class declarations and not nested class declarations; and suppose all of the declarations are contained in one file named Basics.java. A compile-time error is not generated at which line?

```
public class Basics {}      // 1
public class Basics2 {}     // 2
public class Basics3 {}     // 3
public class Basics4 {}     // 4
```

(*a*) 1 (*b*) 2

(*c*) 3 (*d*) 4.

***27.** Your application supports multiple client types including HTTP clients. Your business layer is implemented using Enterprise Java Beans. Which of the following is best suited for maintaining client state?

(*a*) Stateful session beans (*b*) Entity Beans

(*c*) HttpSession attributes (*d*) Cookies.

**28.** Which one of the following tier in J2EE multi-tier architecture provide internal functionality to J2EE application

(*a*) Presentation Tier (*b*) Enterprise Interface System Tier

(*c*) Web Tier (*d*) Enterprise Java Beans Tier.

***29.** You want to locate an existing bean object but do not want to create a new instance, if an existing instance is not available. Which of the following bean attributes will you use in the `jsp:useBean action?`

(*a*) class (*b*) type

(*c*) beanName (*d*) class and type.

**30.** Which one of the following that controls communication between tiers in J2EE multi-tiers architecture

(*a*) RMI (*b*) ACL

(*c*) JDBC (*d*) API.

**31.** What will be the output when the following code is executed?

```
public class Q
{
public static void main(String argv[])
{
int anar[]=new int[5];
System.out.println(anar[0]);
}
}
```

(*a*) 0

(*b*) 1

(*c*) 5

(*d*) Error: anar is referenced before it is initialized.

**32.** Which enterprise bean type is defined without any client view interfaces?

(*a*) BMP Entity bean (*b*) Stateful Session bean

(*c*) Stateless Session bean (*d*) Message Driven Bean.

***33.** Which of the following is not a feature of Message-Driven Bean?

(*a*) It has no client visibility

(*b*) The container cannot pool instances

(*c*) It does not have a local or remote interface

(*d*) It is invoked asynchronously by the container.

**34.** What will be the maximum size for a cookie?

(*a*) 1 KB (*b*) 2 KB

(*c*) 4 KB (*d*) 10 KB.

**35.** Which of the following statement is/are true about cookies?

(*i*) Cookies are not secure

(*ii*) Cookies can be viewed by other users of the same workstation

(*iii*) Can allow user to impersonate another user

(*iv*) Cookies are not available when the user changes workstation or browser

(*a*) only (*i*) and (*ii*) (*b*) only (*ii*) and (*iii*)

(*c*) only (*iii*) and (*iv*) (*d*) all.

**36.** Which of the following should NOT be used to share data between servlets in a distributed web application?

(*a*) Attributes of ServletContext (*b*) Enterprise Java Beans

(*c*) Attributes of HttpSession (*d*) Database.

**37.** Which of the following is a challenge in a J2EE?

(*a*) Fault-tolerance (*b*) Scalability

(*c*) Reliability (*d*) Durability.

***38.** You want to use URL rewriting to support client browsers, which do not use cookies. Which method will you use to attach the session id to a URL that is to be used for the `sendRedirect()` method of the HttpServletResponse?

(*a*) encodeURL (*b*) encodeRedirectURL

(*c*) encodeSessionURL (*d*) encodeSessionRedirectURL.

**39.** The following statements are about Java Bean and Enterprise Java Bean.

(*i*) EJB are used for building distributed applications

(*ii*) EJB is used for server side programming

(*iii*) Java Bean is used for client side programming

(*iv*) Examples of EJB are Session Bean, Entity Bean and Message Driven Bean

Which of the above statements is/are true?

(*a*) (*i*), (*ii*) and (*iii*) only (*b*) (*i*) and (*iv*) only

(c) (*ii*), (*iii*) and (*iv*) only (*d*) all.

**40.** A JMS message producer is created by a

(*a*) session (*b*) connection

(*c*) destination (*d*) industry.

**41.** What will be the output of the following statements?

```
int i=1;
switch (i)
{
case 0:
     System.out.println("zero");
     break;
case 1:
     System.out.println("one");
case 2:
     System.out.println("two");
     default:
     System.out.println("default");
     }
```

(*a*) one (*b*) one, default

(*c*) one, two, default (*d*) default.

**42.** From the below list which is/are the statement that differentiates Message-Driven Bean (MDB) from Session Bean and Entity Bean.

(*i*) MDB has a bean class and XML deployment descriptor

(*ii*) MDB can encapsulate business logic

(*iii*) MDB cannot be called directly by the client

(*iv*) MDB does not have passive state

(*a*) (*i*) and (*iii*) only (*b*) (*ii*) and (*iii*) only

(*c*) (*iii*) and (*iv*) only (*d*) all.

***43.** A servlet needs to acquire a data source through a JNDI naming lookup. Which of the following is the best place to do this?

(*a*) constructor (*b*) init method

(*c*) service method (*d*) doGet method.

**44.** JMS Publish/Subscribe Messaging Domain is an

(*a*) one-to-one relationship between sender and receiver

(*b*) one-to-many relationship between sender and receiver

(*c*) many- to- one relationship between sender and receiver

(*d*) many- to- many relationship between sender and receiver.

**45.** Which of the following is not true in JMS point-to-point message domain?

(*a*) There is only one receiver

(*b*) The receiver can request a message

(*c*) The receiver must acknowledge the receipt of the message

(*d*) The receiver does not need to exist when the message is produced.

**46.** Consider the following statements. Which of the following statements will compile without error?

```
(i)    int i=0;
       if(i)
       {
        System.out.println("Hello");
       }
(ii)  boolean b=true;
       boolean b2=true;
       if(b==b2)
       {
        System.out.println('So true");
       }
(iii)  int i=1;
       int j=2;
```

```
        if(i==1  ||  j==2)
        System.out.println("OK");
(iv)  int  i=1;
        int  j=2;
        if(i==1  &|  j==2)
        System.out.println("OK");
```

(*a*) (*i*) (*b*) (*ii*)

(*c*) (*iii*) (*d*) (*iv*).

**47.** The following table provides an overview of the most commonly used email protocols.

| | **Protocol** | | **Purpose** |
|---|---|---|---|
| 1 | SMTP | A | for supporting email attachments |
| 2 | POP3 | B | for reading and storing email |
| 3 | IMAP | C | for reading email |
| 4 | MIME | D | for sending email |

Which of the following is the proper match?

(*a*) 1 & D  2 & C  3 & B  4 & A

(*b*) 1 & D  2 & A  3 & B  4 & C

(*c*) 1 & B  2 & D  3 & A  4 & C

(*d*) 1 & C  2 & D  3 & A  4 & B.

***48.** In JAAS, which of the following uses a CallbackHandler object?

(*a*) LoginModule (*b*) Credential

(*c*) AuthPermission (*d*) Policy.

**49.** Consider the following statements

```
class  GFC215
{
static  String  m(float  i)  {return  "float";}
static  String  m(double  i)  {return  "double";}
public  static  void  main  (String[]  args)  {
int  a1  =  1;  long  b1  =  2;  System.out.print(m(a1)+","+ m(b1));
}
}
```

What will the output when above statements are executed?

(*a*) Prints: float, float (*b*) Prints: float, double

(*c*) Prints: double, float (*d*) Prints: double, double.

*50. A web application is located in a directory named 'college'. Its deployment descriptor will be located in which of the following?
(a) college (b) college/WEB-INF
(c) college/META-INF (d) none of these.

51. Which of the following modifiers can not be applied to a method?
(a) abstract (b) private
(c) protected (d) public.

52. Which of the following is a file that describes the style of elements that appear on the webpage?
(a) cascading style sheet (b) controlling style sheet
(c) cascading strong sheet (d) none of the above.

53. Designing as enterprise application using interface provides built in flexibility is known as
(a) Ripple effect (b) Pluggability
(c) Model view controller (d) Cascading style sheet.

54. An EJB is required to perform debit card verification. All necessary information such as card number and amount will be supplied as parameters to a single business method invocation that processes the verification. Assuming that performance is critical, which bean type BEST suits the requirement?
(a) Stateful Session Bean (b) Stateless Session Bean
(c) Message Driven Bean (d) Entity Bean.

55. Choose the objective of the distributor pattern
(a) Manages communication between components used by one or more applications
(b) To convert a message written in one style to another style of message
(c) To create a handle or forward model infrastructure
(d) To receive and distribute message.

*56. A Container Managed Persistence (CMP) entity bean A has a one-to-many unidirectional relationship (CMR) to another Container Managed Persistence (CMP) entity bean B. Which interface can expose the methods related to this relationship?
(a) Only local interface of bean A
(b) Local interfaces of both beans A and B
(c) Only local home interface of bean A
(d) Local home interfaces of both beans A and B.

*57. Which of the following statements is NOT true about the Common Client Interface of JCA?
(a) CCI cannot connect to non-relational systems
(b) CCI defines a set of interfaces and classes whose methods allow a client to perform typical data access operations
(c) A resource adapter is not required to provide support for the CCI
(d) CCI can connect to relational database systems.

**58.** Which of the following statements will produce an output 4.0?

(*i*) `System.out.println(Math.floor(-4.7));`

(*ii*) `System.out.println(Math.round(-4.7));`

(*iii*) `System.out.println(Math.ceil(-4.7));`

(*iv*) `System.out.println(Math.Min(-4.7));`

(*a*) (*i*)
(*b*) (*ii*)
(*c*) (*iii*)
(*d*) (*iv*).

**59.** Which of the following modifiers can be applied to a constructor?

(*a*) private
(*b*) abstract
(*c*) final
(*d*) volatile.

**60.** What will happen if you attempt to compile and run the following code?

```
Integer ten=new Integer(10);
Long nine=new Long (9);
System.out.println(ten + nine);
int i=1;
System.out.println(i + ten);
```

(*a*) The output will be: 19 followed by 20
(*b*) The output will be: 19 followed by 11
(*c*) Error: Can't convert java lang Integer
(*d*) The output will be: 10 followed by 1.

**61.** Which one of the following is the advantage of the status flag pattern?

(*a*) Easy to maintain and coordinate by using one component
(*b*) Facilitate a common link between independent components
(*c*) Simplification the data gathering process
(*d*) None of these.

**62.** Which is the first step that must be performed to create a data base schema?

(*a*) Define data
(*b*) Create primary & foreign key
(*c*) Identify information used in the exiting system
(*d*) Decompose the information into data.

**63.** What will be the output if you run the following code?

```
String s=new String("Bicycle");
int iBegin=1;
char iEnd=3;
System.out.println(s.substring(iBegin,iEnd));
```

(*a*) bic
(*b*) ic
(*c*) icy
(*d*) error: no method matching substring(int,char).

**64.** Which one of the following is not characteristic of attribute?
(*a*) Attribute name (*b*) Attribute type
(*c*) Attribute source (*d*) Attribute destination.

**65.** Given the following declarations
```
String s1=new String("Hello");
String s2=new String("there");
String s3=new String();
```
Which of the following is legal operation?
(*a*) `s3=s1+s2;` (*b*) `s3=s1-s2;`
(*c*) `s3=s1&s2;` (*d*) `s3=s1&&s2;`.

***66.** Which of the following is equivalent to the give EJB QL expression?
```
p.age BETWEEN 20 AND 30
```
(*a*) p.age >= 20 AND p.age <= 30 (*b*) p.age > 20 AND p.age < 30
(*c*) p.age > 20 AND p.age <=30 (*d*) p.age >= 20 AND p.age < 30.

**67.** What will be the output of the following statement?
```
System.out.println(4 | 3);
```
(*a*) 4 (*b*) 3
(*c*) 0 (*d*) 7.

**68.** Consider the following statements
```
public class MyClass1
{
public static void main(String argv[])
{ }
/*Modifier at XX */ class MyInner {}
}
```
What modifiers would be legal at XX in the above code?
(*a*) Public (*b*) Private
(*c*) Static (*d*) all the above.

***69.** Which method cannot be called by a stateful session bean using bean-managed transactions?
(*a*) getUserTransaction() (*b*) getRollbackOnly()
(*c*) getStatus() (*d*) none of the above.

**70.** What will be the result when the following statements are executed?
```
public class Conv{
public static void main(String argv[])
```

```
    {
    Conv c=new Conv();
    String s=new String("ello");
    c.amethod(s);
    }
    public void amethod(String s){
    char c='H';
    c+=s;
    System.out.println(c);
    }
}
```

(*a*) "Hello" (*b*) "ello"

(*c*) elloH (*d*) Compile time error.

**71.** Choose an index key whose value represents data contained is multiple column of the corresponding table

(*a*) Derived key (*b*) Clustered key

(*c*) Foreign key (*d*) Primary key.

**72.** Which JDBC driver type is also referred as the java protocol?

(*a*) type 1 JDBC to ODBC protocol (*b*) type 2 java 1 native code driver

(*c*) type 3 JDBC driver (*d*) type 4 JDBC driver.

***73.** Which of the following statements are true about the given method declaration?

`MyEJBObject createWithName(String name) throws CreateException, Remote Exception`

(*a*) It is declared in the local home interface of a stateful session bean

(*b*) It is declared in the local home interface of a stateless session bean

(*c*) It is declared in the remote home interface of a stateful session bean

(*d*) It is declared in the remote home interface of a stateless session bean.

**74.** Which of the following statement is/are true?

(*a*) An interface declaration can be a member of an interface

(*b*) A method declared within an interface must have a body represented by empty curly braces

(*c*) An interface can implement another interface

(*d*) An abstract class that implements an interface must implement all abstract methods declared within the interface.

**75.** JDBC driver is loaded by calling which of the following methods

(*a*) `Call()method` (*b*) `Class.forName() methods`

(c) `Close()method` (*d*) `Connect()methods.`

**76.** Which of the following is not a kind of exception that is thrown by JBDC method?

(*a*) SQLException (*b*) SQLWarning

(*c*) DataRounding (*d*) DataTruncation.

**77.** Given the following code, what test would you need to put in place of the comment line?

```
//place test here to result in an output of Equal
public class EqTest{
public static void main(String argv[]){
EqTest e=new EqTest();
}
EqTest(){
String s="Java";
String s2="java";
//place test here {
System.out.println("Equal");
}else
  {
System.out.println("Not equal");
}
 }
}
```

(*a*) `if(s==s2)` (*b*) `if(s.equals(s2)`

(*c*) `if(s.equalsIgnoreCase(s2))` (*d*) `if(s.noCaseMatch(s2))`.

**78.** Choose the modifier that is used to define a set of values by the DBMS to matchvalues is a specified Column.

(*a*) IN Modifier (*b*) Distinct Modifier

(*c*) NOT IN Modifier (*d*) None of the above.

**79.** Consider the following statements

```
class MCZ11{
public static void main (String[] args)
{
char a = '\c';   // 1
char b = '\r';   // 2
char c = '\"';   // 3
char d = '\b';   // 4
char e = '\'';   // 5
 }
}
```

A compile-time error is generated at which line?

(*a*) 1 (*b*) 2

(*c*) 4 (*d*) 4.

**80.** Which of the following line complier error will occur in the following statements?

```
class MCZ31
{
public static void main (String[] args)
{
char a = '\t';    // 1
char b = '\\';    // 2
char c = '\"';    // 3
char d = '\'';    // 4
char e = '\?';    // 5
}
}
```

(*a*) 1 (*b*) 2

(*c*) 3 (*d*) 5.

**81.** What will be the outcome when the following statements are executed?

```
private class Base
{
Base()
{
int i = 100;
System.out.println(i);
}
}
public class Pri extends Base
{
static int i = 200;
public static void main(String argv[])
{
Pri p = new Pri();
System.out.println(i);
}
}
```

(*a*) 200 (*b*) 100 followed by 200

(*c*) 100 (*d*) Compilation Error.

82. What will the output of the following code?

```
public class Oct
{
public static void main(String argv[])
{
Oct o = new Oct();
o.amethod();
}
public void amethod()
{
int oi= 012;
System.out.println(oi);
}
}
```

(*a*) 12 (*b*) 012
(*c*) 10 (*d*) 10.0.

83. Which of the following statements are true?

(*a*) A constructor can invoke another constructor of the same class using the alternate constructor invocation, "this(argumentListopt);"

(*b*) A constructor can invoke itself using the alternate constructor invocation, "this(argumentListopt);"

(*c*) The alternate constructor invocation, "this(argumentListopt);", can legally appear anywhere in the constructor body

(*d*) A constructor is not permitted to throw an exception.

84. Consider the following statements?

```
class Black {
public static void main(String[] args)
{
short s1 = 1;            //1
char c1 = 1;             //2
byte b1 = s1;            //3
byte b2 = c1;            //4
final short s2 = 1;      //5
final char c2 = 1;       //6
yte b3 = s2;             //7
byte b4 = c2;            //8
}
}
```

In which lines the compile-time errors will be generated?

(*a*) 1 & 2 (*b*) 3 & 4

(*c*) 5 & 6 (*d*) 7 & 8.

**85.** Choose the operator that is used to define a large of values that is to be used as the value of the selection expression

(*a*) LIKE (*b*) BETWEEN

(*c*) IS NULL operator (*d*) none of the above.

**86.** What will be the output of the following statements?

```
class A {void m1(A a) {System.out.print("A");}}
class B extends A {void m1(B b) {System.out.print("B");}}
class C extends B {void m1(C c) {System.out.print("C");}}
class D extends C
{
void m1(D d) {System.out.print("D");}
public static void main(String[] args)
{
A a1 = new A(); B b1 = new
B(); C c1 = new C(); D d1 = new D();
d1.m1(a1); d1.m1(b1); d1.m1(c1);
}
}
```

(*a*) AAA (*b*) ABC

(*c*) DDD (*d*) ABCD.

**87.** What will be the output of the following statements?

```
class A {void m1(A a){System.out.print("A");}}
class B extends A {void m1(B b){System.out.print("B");}}
class C extends B {void m1(C c){System.out.print("C");}}
class D {public static void main(String[] args)
{
A a1 = new A(); B b1 = new B(); C c1 = new C();
C c2 = new A();
c2.m1(a1); c2.m1(b1); c2.m1(c1);
}
}
```

(*a*) Prints: AAA (*b*) Prints: ABC

(*c*) Prints: CCC (*d*) Compile-time error.

**88.** Which one of the following statement justifies the difference between inner and outer join

(*a*) inner join excludes rows of either table that don't have a matching value

(*b*) inner join excludes rows of either table that have a matching value

(*c*) inner join includes rows of either table that don't have a matching value

(*d*) inner join includes rows of either table that have a matching value.

**89.** Which one of the following is not a kind of outer join?

(*a*) Left outer join (*b*) Center outer join

(*c*) Right outer join (*d*) Full outer join.

**90.** Which of the following are not methods of the `java.lang.String class`?

(*a*) append (*b*) concat

(*c*) replace (*d*) substring.

**91.** What will be the output of the following statements?

```
public class Test
{
public static void main(String str[])
{
System.out.print(5+5+"s"+6+6);
}
}
```

(*a*) prints "10s66" (*b*) prints "10s12"

(*c*) prints " 55s66 " (*d*) compiles, runs and does not print anything.

**92.** What will be the output of the following statements?

```
public class Test
{
static private String st;
public static void main(String str[])
{
System.out.print(st+"yes");
}
}
```

(*a*) compiles, runs and prints "yes"

(*b*) error

(*c*) compiles, runs and prints "nullyes"

(*d*) compiles, runs and prints " null+yes ".

**93.** What will be the output of the following statements?

```
public class Test
```

```
{
public static void main(String st[])
{
Boolean b1 = new Boolean("true");
Boolean b2 = new Boolean(false);
System.out.println(b1);
System.out.println(b2);
}
}
```

(*a*) true false
(*b*) true
(*c*) runtime error
(*d*) Compiles, runs and does not print anything.

**94.** What will be the output of the following statements?

```
public class Test
{
public static void main(String st[])
{
String s1 = "java";
String s2 = "java";
String s3 = "JAVA";
s2.toUpperCase();
s3.toUpperCase();
boolean b1 = s1==s2;
boolean b2 = s1==s3;
System.out.print(b1);
System.out.print("  "+b2);
}
}
```

(*a*) compiles, runs and prints "true false"
(*b*) compiles, runs and prints "true true"
(*c*) compiles, runs and prints "false false"
(*d*) compiles, runs and prints "false true".

**95.** Which implementation of the List interface produces the slowest access to an element in the middle of the list by means of an index?

(*a*) Vector (*b*) ArrayList
(*c*) LinkedList (*d*) None of the above.

**96.** What will be the output of the following statements?

```
class A
{
public static void main (String[] args)
```

```
{
Error error = new Error();
Exception exception = new Exception();
System.out.print((exception instanceof Throwable) + ",");
System.out.print(error instanceof Throwable);
}
}
```

(*a*) Prints: false,false & Prints: true,true

(*b*) Prints: false, true

(*c*) Prints: true, false

(*d*) Run-time error.

**97.** What will be the output if the following statements are executed?

```
class SRC102
{
public static void main (String[] args)
{
int i1 = Math.round(0.5f);
int i2 = Math.round(1.5d);
System.out.print(i1 + "," + i2);
}
}
```

(*a*) Prints: 0,1 (*b*) Prints: 0,2

(*c*) Prints: 1,1 (*d*) Compile-time error.

**98.** Which of the following is not a standard method called as part of the JSP life cycle?

(*a*) `jspInit()` (*b*) `jspService()`

(*c*) `jspservice()` (*d*) `jspDestroy()`.

**99.** Choose the conditional test of a sub query determines if a value in the current row of the table used by the query also exists in the temporary table.

(*a*) Existence test (*b*) Set membership test

(*c*) Qualified test (*d*) Comparison test.

**100.** If you want to override a JSP file's initialization method, within what type of tags should you declare the method?

(*a*) <@ @> (*b*) <%@ %>

(*c*) <% %> (*d*) <%! %>.

**101.** What is the key difference between using a `<jsp:forward>` and `HttpServelet Response.sendRedirect()`?

(*a*) Forward executes on the client while sendRedirect() executes on the server

(*b*) Forward executes on the server while sendRedirect() executes on the client (*c*) The two methods perform identically.

(*d*) None of the above.

**102.** Consider the following four valid comment styles that are used within JSP pages. Which of the following the end user can see?

(*a*)
```
<%–
My comments
<% out.println("Hello World"); %>
–%>
```

(*b*)
```
<!– (c)2000 jGuru.com –>
```

(*c*)
```
<% // For Loop
for (int i=1; i<=4; i++) {
%>
<H<%=i%>>Hello</H<%=i%>>
<% } %>
```

(*d*)
```
<% /** yet another comment */
JavaDoc Rules
%>
```

**103.** How can a servlet call a JSP error page?

(*a*) This capability is not supported

(*b*) When the servlet throws the exception, it will automatically be caught by the calling JSP page

(*c*) The servlet needs to forward the request to the specific error page URL. The exception is passed along as an attribute named `"javax.servlet.jsp.jspException"`

(*d*) The servlet needs to redirect the response to the specific error page, saving the exception off in a cookie.

**104.** Choose the statement that best describes the relationship between JSP and servlets:

(*a*) Servlets are built on JSP semantics and all servlets are compiled to JSP pages for runtime usage

(*b*) JSP and servlets are unrelated technologies

(*c*) Servlets and JSP are competing technologies for handling web requests. Servlets are being superseded by JSP, which is preferred. The two technologies are not useful in combination

(*d*) JSPs are built on servlet semantics and all JSPs are compiled to servlets for runtime usage.

**105.** Which of the following represents the XML equivalent of the statement <%@ include file="a.jsp"%>.

(*a*) `<jsp:include file="a.jsp"/>`

(*b*) `<jsp:include page="a.jsp"/>`

(*c*) `<jsp:directive.include file="a.jsp"/>`

(*d*) There is no XML equivalent of include directive.

## ANSWERS

| | | | | | | |
|---|---|---|---|---|---|---|
| **1.** (*d*) | **2.** (*d*) | **3.** (*b*) | **4.** (*a*) | **5.** (*c*) | **6.** (*c*) | **7.** (*b*) |
| **8.** (*d*) | **9.** (*c*) | **10.** (*c*) | **11.** (*d*) | **12.** (*a*) | **13.** (*b*) | **14.** (*a*) |
| **15.** (*a*) | **16.** (*b*) | **17.** (*c*) | **18.** (*b*) | **19.** (*a*) | **20.** (*b*) | **21.** (*d*) |
| **22.** (*b*) | **23.** (*a*) | **24.** (*a*) | **25.** (*d*) | **26.** (*a*) | **27.** (*a*) | **28.** (*c*) |
| **29.** (*b*) | **30.** (*b*) | **31.** (*a*) | **32.** (*d*) | **33.** (*b*) | **34.** (*c*) | **35.** (*d*) |
| **36.** (*a*) | **37.** (*c*) | **38.** (*b*) | **39.** (*d*) | **40.** (*a*) | **41.** (*a*) | **42.** (*c*) |
| **43.** (*b*) | **44.** (*b*) | **45.** (*b*) | **46.** (*c*) | **47.** (*a*) | **48.** (*a*) | **49.** (*a*) |
| **50.** (*c*) | **51.** (*a*) | **52.** (*a*) | **53.** (*b*) | **54.** (*b*) | **55.** (*a*) | **56.** (*a*) |
| **57.** (*a*) | **58.** (*c*) | **59.** (*a*) | **60.** (*c*) | **61.** (*b*) | **62.** (*c*) | **63.** (*b*) |
| **64.** (*d*) | **65.** (*a*) | **66.** (*a*) | **67.** (*d*) | **68.** (*d*) | **69.** (*b*) | **70.** (*d*) |
| **71.** (*b*) | **72.** (*c*) | **73.** (*c*) | **74.** (*a*) | **75.** (*b*) | **76.** (*c*) | **77.** (*c*) |
| **78.** (*a*) | **79.** (*a*) | **80.** (*d*) | **81.** (*d*) | **82.** (*c*) | **83.** (*a*) | **84.** (*b*) |
| **85.** (*b*) | **86.** (*d*) | **87.** (*a*) | **88.** (*b*) | **89.** (*a*) | **90.** (*a*) | **91.** (*c*) |
| **92.** (*a*) | **93.** (*a*) | **94.** (*a*) | **95.** (*c*) | **96.** (*a*) | **97.** (*d*) | **98.** (*c*) |
| **99.** (*a*) | **100.** (*d*) | **101.** (*b*) | **102.** (*b*) | **103.** (*c*) | **104.** (*d*) | **105.** (*c*) |

## EXPLANATIONS

**7.** Client-tier components run on the client machine and Enterprise information system (EIS)-tier software runs on the EIS servers.

**12.** Java API for XML Processing (JAXP) technology enables applications to parse and transform XML documents independent of a particular XML processing implementation. It supports the processing of XML documents using DOM, SAX, and XSLT.

**15.** Error - can't make static reference to void *amethod.*

**17.** J2EE application cannot be written without using any web components.

**18.** If the client started the transaction and propagated to the bean, and if there is a system exception then the transaction is rolled back and `javax.transaction.TransactionRolledbackException` is thrown to the client by the container. In the case of transaction attributes—'Required', 'Mandatory' and 'Supports', the client transaction is propagated to the bean.

**21.** Exception raised : "java.lang.ArrayIndexOutOfBoundsException: 2"

**27.** In applications using enterprise beans, it is best to maintain session state with stateful session beans in the EJB tier. Web-tier components can access the session state through the stateful session bean's component interface and store just the reference as a session attribute.

29. If we use the type attribute without the class or beanName attributes, it attempts to locate an existing bean object of the given type, but does not create a new instance even if an existing instance is not available.

33. The container can pool instances

36. Context attributes are stored in ServletContext and are shared by all servlets in a Web application. But context attributes are specific to the JVM instance in which they were created. Context attributes do not replicate between Web containers in different JVM instances.

38. The `encodeRedirectURL()` method of HttpServletResponse encodes the specified URL for use in the sendRedirect method or, if encoding is not needed, returns the URL unchanged. All URLs sent to the

    `HttpServletResponse.sendRedirect` method should be run through this method. Otherwise, URL rewriting cannot be used with browsers which do not support cookies.

43. A `javax.sql.DataSource` is obtained through a JNDI naming lookup. Servlets should acquire the `javax.sql.DataSource` in the `init()` method of the servlet and maintain it in a common location for reuse.

48. A LoginModule uses the CallbackHandler both to gather input from users (such as a password or smart card pin number) and to supply information to users (such as status information). By allowing the application to specify the CallbackHandler, underlying LoginModules can remain independent of the different ways applications interact with users.

50. The deployment descriptor of a web application is named web.xml and is located in the WEB-INF folder within the root directory of the application.

56. Abstract accessor methods are used to define relationships between beans. In unidirectional relationships, which can be navigated only one way, only one of the beans define these abstract accessor methods. So, in the relationship from bean A to bean B, so bean A maintains references to many beans of bean B.

57. CCI is a programming interface that application developers and client programs can use to connect and access back-end systems.

66. The BETWEEN clause is an inclusive operator specifying a range of values. The syntax for the use of the comparison operator [NOT] BETWEEN in a conditional expression is as follows: arithmetic_expression [NOT] BETWEEN arithmetic-expression AND arithmetic-expression

69. The `getRollbackOnly` method belongs to the SessionContext interface. The transactional methods of this interface must not be called by session beans using bean-managed transactions (BMT).

73. This method is declared in the remote home interface of a stateful session bean. A stateless session bean has only a no-argument `create()` method because its `create()` method is not delegated to the `ejbCreate()` method of the bean. Its `create()` method only associates the EJB Object with the bean. So, this method is defined in the home of a stateful bean itself. Since it is declaring

    RemoteException in its throws clause, it is a remote home.

# GLOSSARY

**A* algorithm** an algorithm for heuristic search using an admissible heuristic function f (n) = g(n) + h (n), where g(n) is the known cost to reach node n from the start, and h (n) is the estimated cast from node n to a goal.

**active value** in a frame system, a means of associating procedures will be called when the data is accessed.

**adjective** a word that modifies a noun, e.g., big or red.

**admissible** describes a heuristic function that does not over-estimate the cost of reaching a goal from a given state.

**AFSTN** augmented finite state transition network.

**agent** a program that acts independently, perhaps on a different computer, to attempt to accomplish a goal.

**alpha/beta search** a kind of game tree search that uses alpha and beta cutoffs to avoid unnecessary search.

**ambiguity** in understanding natural language, images or other inputs, the superficial possibility of interpreting an input in more than one way.

**AND/OR graph** a graph or tree structure describing the decomposition of a goal in terms of alternative sub-goals (OR nodes) or combinations of sub-goals that must all be satisfied (AND nodes).

**antecedent** the left-hand side of an implication or rule; e.g., in the rule P → Q, is the antecedent.

**antecedent method** if added method.

**antecedent reasoning** forward chaining.

**AO* algorithm** an algorithm similar to A* for heuristic search of an AND/OR graph.

**assert** to add a fact to the database of currently believed facts; like forward chaining.

**assertion** a logical expression in the database of true or currently believed facts.

**association list** in lisp, a list composed of pairs of a symbolic name and associated value used to represent variable bindings and data sets.

**ATN** augmented transition network a formalism of describing parsers, especially for natural language.

**automated reasoning** the derivation of conclusions from observed or given data, often by a proof procedure operating on the data and a set of axioms.

**auxiliary verb** an extra verb that modifies a main verb eg, will, have, been.

**axiom** in theorem producing, an initially given fact, rule or theorem.

**back propagation** the adjustment of the weights of connections in a neural network, using reward and punishment based on training data for which the desired out come is known.

**back prop** back propagation.

**backward chaining** a proof that starts with the conclusion and searches for rules or facts that support the conclusion.

**best first search** a search in which the next fringe node to be expanded is the node that is estimated to be the best according to an evaluation function.

**bidirectional search** a search that is done both from the start toward the goal and from the goal back toward the start, until the fringes of the two searches intersect.

**bigram** a sequence of two words.

**blind search** a search in which no heuristic information is available to distinguish one search path from another.

**bottom up** a form of parsing in which structure is built from the bottom up to phrases and sentences.

**bounded depth-first search** a depth-firth search in which a bound is placed on the number of operator applications that can be considered, any sequence of operations that exceeds the depth bound is considered a failure.

**breadth first** a search strategy in which all nodes at a given depth are examined before any deeper nodes are examined.

**break** in lisp, the halting of execution due to occurrence of an error.

**canonical form** a convention for representing a symbolic expression that allows easier manipulation of such expressions.

**car** in lisp, the function that extracts the first half of a cons cell, usually containing a value that is an element of a list.

**case frame** in NLP, a lexical entry that specifies a single sense meaning of a verb, togethor with information about related phrases such as case relation slots.

**cdr** in lisp, the function that extracts the second half of a cons cell, usually pointing to the reminder of a list following the first element.

**CF** certainty factor a numeric measure of the degree of belief in a proposition. In EMYCIN, the CF ranges from –1 to 1.

**character macro** in lisp, a macro that is invoked by a single character in the source code.

**Chomsky hierarchy** a hierarchy of language types defined by chomsky-Type 0 (no restriction) is the highest class, containing Type 1 (context sensitive), Type 2 (context free) and Type 3 (regular).

**clause** in resolution theorem poring, a logical formula consisting of a disjunction of literals that is treated as a unit.

**CNF** conjunctive normal form.

**common lisp** a large, standardized dialect of lisp.

**complied knowledge** knowledge, of humans or machines, that is analogous to a compiled procedure.

**context sensitive** a grammar in which the left hand side of each production rule has a length that is less than or equal to the length of the right hand side.

**data-driven search** a search in which arrival of data causes conclusions to be drawn, which cause further conclusions and so forward chaining.

**declarative representation** a form of knowledge should be represented declaratively (e.g., as axioms or rules) rather than procedurally.

**dendral** an early AI program that determined molecular structure of organic compounds given mass spectrometer data.

**depth bound** a maximum depth that is permitted in a bounded depth-first search.

**disjunction** a compound logical statement using OR operator.

**Disjunctive Normal Form (DNF)** a canonical form of writing predicate calculus formulae as a disjuncts of conjuncts.

**explanation** a justification of a conclusion is terms of the facts and rules that led to it.

**extension** that actual object denoted by a description, or the enumeration of the members of a set.

**factor** to break a problem into relatively independent subproblems.

**finite automation** an automation that is organized as a transition network, where transitions between nodes are labeled by input symbols.

**FOL** First Order Logic

**FOPC** First Order Predicate Calculus.

**forward chaining** a process or reasoning in which known facts and rules are used to deduce additional facts.

**frame** a representation of an object, with slots that represent properties of the object or connections to other frames.

**Free variable** 1. in a logical formula an occurrence of a variable that is not within the scope of a quantifier. 2. In lisp, a variable that is not bound within a function in which it appears.

**garbage** memory space that has become unused because there are no pointers to it.

**generation** the production of a statement in a language given a grammar of the language and a representation of the meaning.

**goal** something to be achieved by a program.

**goal state** a state of a search that represents the goal.

**GPS** General Problem slower, an early program for state space search.

**heuristic function** a function that estimates the value of a state.

**hill climbing** a form of search in which the path of steepest ascent towards the goal is taken at each step.

**hough transform** an algorithm for identifying desired objects in image data by mapping each input point.

**induction** inference of a rule that explains a body of data.

**inference rule** a rule that allows derivation of additional true statements from a given set of true statements.

**knowledge acquisition** the process of collecting the knowledge for an expert system from a human domain expert and formalizing it.

**knowledge base** the collection of knowledge of an expert system.

**lexical** in NLP, referring to information contained in the lexicon.

**lexicon** in NLP, a table of words with their parts of speech, root words etc.

**lisp** programming language known as list processing.

**List** in lisp, a linked list structure, composed of cons cells.

**machine learning** study of ways by which a program can automatically modify its knowledge and procedures to improve its performance.

**means-ends analysis** in GPS, the connection of goals with operates that might accomplish those goals.

**modus pouens** a rule of logical inference if P is true and $P \rightarrow Q$, concludes Q.

**natural language** a human language, such as English German, Hindi.

**natural language processing** computer processing of speech or machine readable text in natural language.

**neural network** a computational network, of ten for pattern recognition, composed of mathematically defined elements that are though to approximate the working of neurons.

**parse tree** a tree structure describing the derivation of a sentence in a language according to the rules of a context-free grammar.

**quantifier** in predicate calculus formula, a universal or existential quantification of a variable.

**script** a frame like structure that describes a sequence of actions.

**semantics** the study of how statements in a language denote meanings.

**setq** in lisp, the function that assigns a value to a variable.

**stolen function** in mathematical logic, a constant introduced as a substitute for an existentially quantified variable.

**start state** the initial state of a state space search.

**steepest ascent** in hill climbing search, taking the moves that give the largest improvement in the evaluation function.

**taxonomy** in a knowledge representation system, the tree structure formed by the class superclass relations.

**uncertain reasoning** see reasoning under uncertainty.

**unification** an algorithm for finding a substitution of terms for variables in a set of predicate calculus.

**well-formed formula (wff)** a formula composed of symbols that are arranged in a way that is allowed under the rules of the language.

